THIS PLACE OF PROSE AND POETRY

THIS PLACE OF PROSE AND POETRY

Lucian Krukowski

WIPF & STOCK · Eugene, Oregon

THIS PLACE OF PROSE AND POETRY

Wipf & Stock
An Imprint of Wipf and Stock Publishers
199 W. 8th Ave., Suite 3
Eugene, OR 97401

www.wipfandstock.com

ISBN 13: 978-1-4982-3078-0

Manufactured in the U.S.A. 10/13/2015

CONTENTS

PRELUDE

It was an older building on the campus of an affluent mid-western university. Inside, a group of students stood around a bulletin board on which was written:

Schedule Change
Phil. 369
HARD AND SOFT PHILOSOPHY
Prof. Krukowski
MWF, 11—12

A man walked slowly down the hall and stopped before the group. "Good morning to you all. I am the Dean and I want to ask you a question: Why are you taking this course?"

There was silence, then a student said:
"I want to find out who I am, and I want to know what I should do."

The man who calls himself the Dean kicked off his loafers,
placed his hands flat on the floor and pressed into a handstand.
He held the position for a moment, then lowered his feet back to the floor.
Lightly flushed but beaming, he intoned:
"Beneath this pelt of hair and blemish, there is a living spirit.
Long before your time, I was totally—like you—with it."

There was silence, then another student said:
"You need to cut your toe-nails."

MY PLACE

What place, Place, do you have in art?
Do random visits create clutter in your spaces?
In my house, tidy sweepers safeguard clarity
and promote friendship between the lookers-on and runners-in-place.
When die Reine, die Feine, die Eine, comes knocking, I let her in.
She knows I am as one with her despite our many names.

Truth, Goodness, Beauty, need no subordination.
They are engorged—enough already—with their parochial instances.
They should not—cannot—be further reduced to just one.
But their progeny: The purely factual, wholly universal, and
indisputably tasteful—although too hard, too soft, and too just right —
can be made friends.

For this, they need a nice cold shower in the all-together
which would merge their separate quivers into one big shaking.
Otherwise, the long contention between inherited forms
begins to smell of sediment and a stale crotch quaking.

Red-spot-here-now, you are not invited to my place.
For you are prone, with your cowboy hat and downtown spurs,
to cutting my continuum into separated pieces.
In a different light and other times, you appear as
four-square, large and somewhere there.
But your now is mostly past and yet not here.
You do not care, alas, that each true piece of reference,
when bereft of out-of-date compliants,
becomes more overtly nasty than the last.
Why don't you then, failed reference, abandon
the Church of Truth that preens as context-free —
avoid out-of-date states of the Good and Beautiful —
and join the flow of beer and bragadoccio
that woos and cools us on a summer's day?

This is my place—the best I know
where I can be free of you—
you nit-pickers for the knowable.
But now the day is done.
I have to let the sweepers go
in order to let all the Reine, Feine—
and, yes, Meine—stay.

PLACES IN MIND

Mind, when considered in its purity, does not show us something in a place. Rather, it shows us that there is nothing in experience which can construct a something that denies the attraction of other times and places. Particular minds that are appalled by the notion of a something-become-something-else, will always want an inviolable place—like a brain—to which we can trace everything we think and do. Some such minds may want more—perhaps a Heaven, or a Hell—which conquers time and change, and gives us ways to approach before-beginnings and after-ends. But such wanting requires making a nothing beyond existence into a something which has value as pure and boundless being—and also is the source of our becoming us. God is like that, but may not—however often it is said—want us to believe in something so arcane. But most believers do not want a cherished something to come from nothing, nor do they either want that something to end in nothing. For them, existence stretches infinitely in both ways, as it mounts a challenge to the nothing that others, mostly non-believers, believe lurks darkly on either side of beginnings and ends.

Those who have Faustian souls say we may begin at birth, but do not end in death—as we are a mirror of the world that begins at its own inception and, like us, will only end when it is finished—which is not so much death as a pause (for no worldly reason) in all that has been happening since the start. But pauses, as they are part of time, can herald a world that begins after we and ours are gone.

There are some (austere and nasty ones) who would rather have no commerce with either mind or soul—the brain is quite enough. For them, birth and death is all there is. Speculation to the contrary, they say, is just so much poetry. So much—(a great deal, actually)—for poetry.

Although many may reject theological solutions to the question of beginnings and ends, there remain the difficulties that have to do with the relationship of mind to body—a comparable tension—and a recapitulation in modern dress of the fugue that has provided historical continuity for both art and philosophy. Mind that has no place, and a brain that is empty of mind, are both unsettling notions—perhaps unthinkable. Nevertheless,

attempts to resolve this have successively championed one or the other as the only feasible view of reality. But there is this:
Either we create the world (we know) through our perceptions, or accept an unperceived world that is beyond the one we know and live in. Then there is this:

Will God (if we go that way) still exist after all intelligible life in the universe has ended—or does (will) He (continue to) exist in a context that is no longer teleological—one that (for us) has no point or purpose?

After life and progress have ended—after all that—what else can God have in mind?

Those not entranced by the myth of divine creation, might believe that we do not, anymore than do tadpoles, create the world through our perceptions. The world is antecedent to the unexamined solipsism of tadpoles—and it also precedes the fretful solipsism of our own existence. Whether the world will continue beyond us, is a matter of extrapolation from the evidence—itself a matter of belief—that it was there before us.

WALKING

I went walking down the street one day.
T'was not the merry month of May.
It was rather on a rainy morning in October
when, last I looked, I found myself to be
deeply underneath the weather.

The rain came down; the news was bad.
My girlfriend, just turned sixty, had reverted,
rightly so, to her younger dear old dad.
My future had never been so poorly laid.
On reflecting, I could only see a crooked path.

The facts are clear—nothing could be clearer
than that I am alive—although barely, as she said.
But "barely" takes the prize for being better
in every way (I say) than being "not-alive."

My building will eventually crumble. Weary
It has been of late—and largely empty, too.
But now the rubble shows a face—much like
Papa Fraga's "Miss O'Murphy" smirking at me
from her couch. I should-a, would-a, jumped her then,
before she could exhale and denigrate my little lust
by laughing with her big and raucous mouth.

But I was proud—yes, proud enough to just
stand still and watch her divine—behind contract —
as the smoke of lust came out in puffs and gusts.
Penelope then showed up—she was tall and bony —
but surely very smart. We left shortly, P and I,
to find a sunrise of the kind that would enhance
our chance to prematurely find that pot of gold
which usually waits for darkness to appear.

But it's now dark enough—she said.
Sunrise is too late for us to wait.
I know. But I'll be dead by light of day,
and you will have just passed sixty-eight —
still young enough to do your own cavorting.
I said to her—I need a different now.
I need a woman who will zip me up.
I could use a bitch to knock me down —
not merely nibble at my toes—one that runs
upstairs, will do the dishes and wash the clothes.

Then, on command, she'll fetch the Holy Grail
from which we'll drink our fill until such time
when full and weeping,
I set sail to find a whiter whale.
I cannot wait for the crease to cross her dimples,
or hair to sprout from-out my inner ear, or feet
that wander and don't come back on call.

Did you call just now?
I thought I heard a bell.
No—not the one that tolls.
Write—please do—when
you again are well.

A DEAD HORSE IN BROOKLYN

When I was young, my mother and I lived for extended periods in my aunt's house, one of many red-brick two-family buildings on east fifth street in Brooklyn, which my uncle had bought with money he made running a saloon—free lunch and a nickle a beer—during the great depression.
The reasons for our frequent stays were always the same—battles between my mother and father. But intrusive as these reasons are on the memories I have of that time, the story I want to tell is not about them—rather, it is about a dead horse.

The year was 1934; I was five, and the streets were filled with push-carts and horse-drawn wagons moving up and down the streets, selling ice and coal, fruit and vegetables. A little truck whose backside was loaded with ice and dead fish, would come once a week—announced by the cry of "fishi-up." The fish were mostly flounder, and the little Italian fish-monger (in a Slavic-Jewish neighborhood) protected himself from criticism by his inordinate skill at filleting: "Why, you can see daylight through the bones."

There were also some who came to buy what little we had—their voices punctuating our young shouts with the stentorian cry, "Buy-cash-clothes." And then there were the street musicians, transient but festive decorations on the shapes of poverty.

I particularly remember one such group whose leader had diseased eyes—I could tell; they were red and crusted and didn't move. But he walked slowly down the center of the street, playing most marvelously on the violin (much better than my father, I thought) while an accordion and a singer accompanied him on either side. A young boy, my age—perhaps his son—scurried to pick up the pennies, wrapped in newspaper, that the women would throw down from their windows.

The only motor vehicles I remember were the huge black truck that delivered ice in summer and coal in winter, and the small electric truck (a technological miracle) that whirred along the avenue bringing Stuhmer's Pumpernickle to the corner grocery.

Each brought along it's own fantasy: The coal truck had sliding chutes on its sides under which thick dirty men would position barrels and fill them, making clouds of dust. The barrels were then wheeled up the alleys between the houses and emptied into coal bins like the one in my uncle's basement—three barrels of large soft coal to one barrel of the small hard stuff—the mix for burning depended on how cold the weather was. Although I knew that the house belonged to my aunt, the basement with its stove, coal-bin and shovels, belonged to my uncle.

The bread truck was the opposing principle to the coal trick in the contest for the future of our young souls. This truck was small, spotless, and rectilinear, and it was painted a golden brown, the same color as its bread and the uniform of the driver.

I found out later that the truck was an early experiment in electric vehicles. It made a soft whirring sound as it moved slowly down the street, and it seemed to us to float above the turning of its wheels. The driver was also small, a somewhat bony man; he sat very straight on a backless stool, steering with a bar and two large pedals; and he seemed so immersed in the good fortune of his job and his responsibility as emissary of the Stuhmer Company, that he never looked at us when he drove past. Nevertheless, he was the wind-gust that contested with the coal-lump for our allegiance.

The women of the neighborhood would often talk about the relative virtues of the coal-man and the bread-man, and their concerns seemed centered on the relative size of body and hands, and the cleanliness of each, especially the fingernails. The women thought their conversation to be quite beyond our understanding and they sometimes expanded it to other matters that led them to laugh in ways I had not heard before.

I laughed with them—even when they frowned and tried to shoo me away. But, of all the children on the block, I especially hung around to listen, for it seemed to me important to know which men the women preferred—although they often changed their minds about the one when the other truck would reappear.

The other vehicles that came down the street were not as magical. They were situated somewhere between the borders of our lives, between the extremes of coal, ice, and eating, and so were more familiar yet less instructive—less emblematic of our needs.

But the ordinary vehicle this story is about was once transformed in an extra-ordinary way—and it took on a magic far beyond the others. It was actually not a truck, this one, but a wagon, pulled by a slow horse and driven by a heavy man with a thick face who was deaf. The wagon carried a load of watermelons, and it only came by in summer. As the deaf-man drove the wagon down the street, he would shout out "warramerroo"—not a word, of course, but a signifier we all understood.

One very hot summer's day, I was standing on my aunt's stoop when I heard shouts and saw people running. I ran after them, and in the middle of the street, just down the block, I saw the watermelon horse, still in harness, sprawled flat on the hot street in front of the wagon—quite dead, as it turned out.

The women came quickly from their houses with pots of water that they poured upon the horse—it was midday, you see, so the men were working; and those who had no work would stay hidden indoors until after dark. When the water did no good—did not revive the horse—the women turned upon the driver and berated him for not taking better care of his animal—for many of the women had come from farms in eastern Europe and knew about such things. The old man, hearing nothing, but surrounded by flushed gesticulating women, waved his arms—at the horse, the melons, the heavens—and uttered loud croaking sounds which punctuated the spittle and the sweat running down his face.

Eventually, a wagon from the Sanitation Department came along, also pulled by horses—which to my amazement took no notice of their species-mate—and the dead one was cranked up and taken away. But the city wagon was quite long in coming, so we all (half the neighborhood was there by now) had a good while to gape, recapitulate, and explicate—to offer competing versions of how this natural disaster came to be, and how it would fit into our lives. To me, the horse seemed much larger dead than living. Before, he was just an ordinary wagon-horse, about which mothers would say: "Don't get too close or he'll step on your feet or kick you." Now, dead, the horse was not only monumental, but also unique, for he was my first dead horse—my first dead animal—although I had already seen dead people in their open-for-view perfumed coffins.

But this horse was lying dead without a ceremony or a wake. I looked carefully at the twisted neck still dangling in its harness, and the head with its opaque eye, the tongue spilled out onto the pavement, and I watched the green flies as they settled down to feed upon the moisture of its sweat. But my greatest interest was in the view from behind—following the crease between the haunches that travel from the opening beneath the tail, and culminating—my first portent of natural sublimity—in a huge black penis, quite stiff and longer than my arm. The swollen balls that supported it seemed as big as the watermelons they once swayed in front of—only darker.

Although the women said that such a thing is not for us to see, they also were interested, and they seemed not to mind, after they shooed us off a bit, that we snuck back and looked some more. I was much moved by the spectacle—indeed, entranced—beyond the point I would ever reach in front of human nakedness—but I was also puzzled. How could this most powerful pecker, this super-model of my early morning tugs and dreams, this exemplary priapus, be on something that is dead—how could an erection come into being just when its body dies?

Peeing, as I realized later, is the enemy of erections; it imparts a dual function to something which should be autonomous, free of the mundane task of waste-disposal. My pecker always seemed restless when I peed, as if it were over-qualified for the job. But when it was free, not working at peeing, it became the least physical thing about me, for it provided a clear contrast between the ecstasy at its tip and the grunge of ordinary life. Is the pecker—despite what the tight-ones say—an instrument of the higher things? Do they (those wet mysterious emanations) become clearer—more doctrinal—each time it (the pecker) gets bigger? Could it be, then, that the pecker in its final erection is the launching-pad of the soul—the sturdy sign that shows us the straightest way to Heaven?

In the dead horse lying on the street in the summer's heat in Brooklyn, I had found a bridge between my earlier and later life, and for the first time I realized that I was a traveler on that bridge as well; and I thought that dying wouldn't be so bad if one had a cock and balls that big to show.

THE TIMES OF LIFE

For you and me, it's time to pee—
but after you my dear, my second me—
or done by us in tandem, holding hands.
Then we'll fly, both you and I,
across the waning summer's sky.

To that other shore we'll go,
although it lies too far for us
to appreciate its flowers and trees—
because our purpose (really) is to contemplate
the doings just before the pearly gate.

But we'll try—the door to excess is ajar:
Apfel Strudel. Wiener Schnitzel.
Cunnilingus by the Sea.
Saltinbocca. Tarantella—also Salmonella.
Annunciation hoping for a better strategy.

In the morning, after matins, we'll eat some waffles.
Evenings—why not taste the prolix of Rijkstoeffel?
Good times will come, you'll see,
when skating up and down—over's fine, but never under—
(best is going round and round)—
the cold indifferent waters of the Zuider Zee.

SCHOOL DAYS

One day, when I was in fourth grade, I was transferred to a room that had tables around which students sat, perhaps eight to a table, so that they could look directly at each other. This was a big improvement over my other room, the standard one, in which everyone sat facing front in those one piece chair-desks that seem designed to slowly but inexorably deform young bones. I'm not sure why I was transferred; it was the middle of the term, so I thought I was being promoted.

It had to be so; I had never seen a classroom like the one I now was in—large bright lights, with complicated smells of paint and paste, and pictures and maps all over the walls. The students, none of whom I knew, also seemed complicated. They looked better than the other ones, didn't seem afraid to move about the room, and were all doing different things. They looked like what are now called high-achievers.

I had not been achieving much in school; mostly I was being yelled at. I take yelling to be a more assaultive version of loud speech than shouting; the rare moments of physical fury in my later life usually came in response to someone's yelling at me. But back then, in public school, I mostly sat still until it stopped, or looked away pretending it wasn't directed at me. There was little point in trying to reach for origins, causes, reasons. The episodes erupted and passed by too quickly; they were natural phenomena as were the teachers, not to be talked to—but the violence of the sounds made me wary. Considered as language, the yellings were like parentheses around periods of droning—they didn't define these periods, but they did give them a shape—an early example of parameters. But watching out for them made it difficult for me to attend to the matter of the dronings in between. If what passed between the parentheses were the subjects being studied, I don't remember knowing what they were.

It now seems probable that my transfer to the class with tables was not a promotion, as I then thought, but a trial balloon: Seeing that I was getting nowhere (I was, but not their where) they sent me upstairs. At worst, two minuses (eventually) add up to a plus; in this (my) case, I was sent to see what a minus and a plus would come to.

The new teacher—although I thought that she eyed me with suspicion—gave me a place at one of the tables, said some thing about a project, and left me to the stares, quite self-assured, of the other students. Things were pleasant enough for a few days; I fiddled with finding a project, and practiced looking around. Then a girl at my table raised her hand: "That boy (pointing to me) is picking his nose. It's disgusting and makes me feel like throwing up." Well, how better to get at a Polish boy than to accuse him of nose-picking. I denied it, waving my hands and saying (I lapsed into my father's accent) that I was merely touching my nose—and there the matter rested for a while. I could not look at the girl, nor at anyone—but after some moments my finger drifted, to my amazement, back up to my nose. "There, see, he's doing it again." "I saw you this time" said teacher, her eyes beady as a bird's. (People often turn into animals when I get into trouble). Then there ensued a lot of "if you do this again," "not decent," "other people's feelings," "don't you have a handkerchief?" (another ethnic slur), and I was put at a different table. I remember after that I left my nose alone; I had learned something and so I was not transferred back to the yelling class.

There was another room with larger tables where, twice a week in the afternoon, we would go to "art"—but it might well have been "science." By that time, I could identify different subjects, although they sometimes got mixed up. The fault was not entirely mine however. In all our classes, teachers demonstrated success through tangible objects—"projects"—that could be spread about, pinned up on walls, and displayed to principals, important visitors, even to those occasional parents who had reason to come by.
So in each of our classes, whatever its nominal subject, we cut and pasted, folded and hammered, painted and drew. Although, in later years, I did a lot of cutting and pasting, I didn't then. With so many hands in the act, everything was always being covered with paste and paint; my fingers and clothing would get sticky, which bothered me and upset my mother. So I drew—on clean white paper with a pencil.

We must have been studying electricity in another class—but the word came down, because I was given the project of drawing a light-bulb. This was no ordinary in-class job, but an over-the-weekend, on white matte-board, large scale, soul-is-on-the-line job. I remember spending Friday night holding a lightbulb, like Yorick's head, in my hand, and thinking melancholy thoughts. Saturday I drew the shape freehand, stepping back from time to time to see how close to perfection I was getting. Much later I saw a movie in which an artist (Laughton as Rembrandt, I think) would step back to check on the progress of his masterpiece. I felt precocious. I drew the innards of the bulb very exactly: the filaments and coils, and the strange lumpy glass in which they were embedded—or emerging from—an ancient sprouting, as I thought. Yes, it was alive, my bulb, but with the eternal life of a fossil. I had, by then, been to the Museum of Natural History. My bulb was all bones, a dinosaur of pure form. Sunday I colored it sparingly using colored pencils that I sharpened with the kitchen knife. I used blues, greens, and grays, and I remember the result as cool, transparent, and distant, which I accepted as being what I wanted. There was a day of waiting, but I didn't touch the drawing again. I had stepped back; returned to look; it was finished.

But I must tell you that I wasn't the only one chosen for that assignment. There was another boy, someone I didn't know (a dangerous omen) who was also coming in on Tuesday with his own light-bulb project. And then teacher, a big bustly chickadee, put them, his and mine, up on the wall side by side. It has always amazed me how my paintings look when away from my studio. They look comparative; not showing what they are, but what they do not have that others have. Such "not-having" is not always bad, of course; maturity, as I later learned, is a lot about not wanting what others have. But at this moment, I felt vanquished. The other boy's light-bulb was yellow. He had painted the light, the glow, the radiance, the living life. I hadn't even turned mine on; mine had no movement, no personality; I had made a corpse. Teacher asked for a show of preference, and mine lost; light and life is where it's at, of course. Then she spoke at length about the impropriety of comparing (which she had just asked us to do)—and this because each drawing has its own qualities that are valuable—in themselves. But she didn't believe it—and neither did the other students.

For me, however, a value of "in itself" was a new and appealing notion. Art became a subject I could understand—a first lesson in the conflict between empathy and abstraction, and a primer in the politics of opportunistic relativism.

The drawings hung side by side for a long time. Nobody looked at them after the first day (another lesson) and when the term ended and I took mine home, I found that I had come to like it because of what it did not have.

NAMES IN PROSE

I lived in my aunt's house as a child. There were two Louis's on her block. The one Louis—it could have been "Lewis," I never saw it written—lived in the rental apartment that was the second floor of my aunt's house. His insistence on pronouncing the "s" in his name much impressed me, for in that neighborhood of alliances, prejudices, and envies—what others made of one's name—was a sign of one's prospects. The other Louis was "Louee," never an "s"—the name being a call-word, as in "Hey Louee!"

Compared to me, however, the two Louis's had clear nominations. My "Lucian" began in my mother's family's Poland—in a small town called "Mielecz"—and Lucian, when spoken in Polish, sounds something like "Lootzyan." But this was disastrous for the Brooklyn streets—what kind of bird is a "Lootzyan?"—and so other versions emerged. The one that distressed me most sounded like "Lucyann," and as—for immigrant reasons—my boyhood shorts and Buster Brown haircut had lingered too long, this version of my name carried intimations of "sissy" with it. Had I been better planted, it would have passed quickly, but there seemed an unending string of increasingly large boys to keep it going, and I had to revert to silence and cunning—this being the first seed of the estrangement that, much later, would have me want to write about my different names.

Legally, I had been given other names; my first middle name is "Wladyslaw," and the second middle name—a proliferation affected by those who enter the new world with heritage but no money—is "Edvard." My parents didn't tell me much about Edvard; oh, there were some whispers (children hear everything) about Austrian cavalry sweeping through the town; and there was uneasy mention of an ancestor who, for inscrutable European reasons, the family felt obligated to remember but not discuss. "Wladyslaw," however, has an older, non-familial—past. The name, as I was often told, recalls Poland's most successful king, Wladyslaw Jagiello, he who in ancient times defeated the Swedish armies on the ice (I struggled to find an image for that—they say he waved two swords) and it was even said that, at another time, he fought the Czar's armies to a stand-still. "Wladyslaw" is unpronounceable in Brooklynese, and at one Christmas gathering, my cousin Florence—the first of our family to go to college—suggested that the English equivalent might well be "Walter." I was dismayed, I am not a Walter; and my mother's usual holiday gloom deepened at the sound of it. So, despite the link between its heritage and my present state, "Wladyslaw" did not become "Walter."

The name, in fact, is a description: "Wlad-the-Slav." But its polyphony did not play in Brooklyn—so it was restricted to baptism and vaccination certificates until, much later, after Poland had been trapped behind the Iron Curtain, it came out as a patriotic conceit.

A woman on the block—it could have been the mother of the Louis with the "s"—started calling me "Lokshen" which is Yiddish for "noodles," and which, as I grew taller, became "Langer Luksh." This version presented an image of affable goofiness, which secretly I did not relish—but it was easier to carry than the anonymous images of Lou or Loosh. The woman meant well; she evidently saw the distress that an incipient "Lucyann" was causing me, and her substitution was meant to ease that. But it did something more: Being a Polish Catholic with, now, a Jewish nick-name, it put me squarely between the Catholics, who were mostly Italian and Irish, and the Jews, who were mostly Polish and Russian. What to do? The first Lewis, was Jewish, and although older and more sure of himself than I, did sometimes talk quietly with me, lend me comic books, and show me toy soldiers from his collection. The other Lou-ee, my nemesis, who was Catholic and Italian, could only talk by shouting—and systematically roughed me up whenever I showed-up on the street.

One day, he and some other boys grabbed me, pulled my pants down, and started beating me with a stick. The other Lewis was there too, as a charter member of the block—but he was appalled at this turn and loudly insisted that they stop. He was large, and so they let me go. I showed the marks to my mother who then dragged me to the house where Lou-ee lived and pulled down my pants again to show them to Lou-ee's mother. After much shouting, the mothers agreed it would be nice if we all walked—Lucian and Lou-ee and their mothers (no fathers were ever mentioned)—together to Mass on Sunday. This would show a solidarity, despite ethnic quarrels, within the common faith. The walk happened three times—as I remember. The mothers spoke in sing-song although they had nothing to say of interest to each other. Lou-ee remained silent and sullen—but he did leave me alone after that.

The anti-Semitism in my family was deep-rooted but passive, and it was voiced mostly through imported Polish cliches, quietly, indoors, after supper. But my social precariousness pushed the issue outdoors. I was first enrolled in the Catholic cub-scouts, but they also shouted a lot and fought, and it made for long walks to the church basement every friday night. So I resisted. My mother then did something the enormity of which I did not sense until much later. She went to the Jewish temple on the next block, which also had a cub-scout troop, and tried to enroll me.

Understand—this was an orthodox synagogue, rich in ritual and clothing, with a faith so demanding that its services were well attended. My mother never spoke to me of that experience—how she walked in, who spoke with her, what was asked, how answered. I still don't know what that silence meant, whether she felt ashamed, heretical, emancipated. But I imagine her walking up those heavy stairs with her threadbare coat, no scarf, no jewelry—so Gentile—to talk with a man in a double-breasted suit and white shirt with no tie, wearing a yarmulka; a thick man, more powerful and, yes, more sensual than any in our meager tribe. How did her voice sound? Did it crack? Did she speak English, Polish, or the bit of German she knew that let her communicate with the old ones on the block who spoke only Yiddish? Recently, I found my mother's citizenship papers and learned that she stood all of five foot one. What could she have said to those men, those large suspicious men—that her Catholic son Lokshen would be safer among the Jews?

However she said it, it was done, and in a few days she took me with her to the synagogue and turned me over to Mr. Moses, the scout-master. He was hearty in a somewhat unfocused way, had a constant bead of sweat on his upper lip and spoke in stentorian tones; but the troop—more precisely, "pack,"—was actually run by women. They were mothers of the scouts and I remember them as quick, plump, elaborately dressed, well-perfumed, and very verbal. Everyone, in fact, talked a lot, and so I began to talk too, and I discovered that it is a good way to make my way with people who will talk and listen. I don't remember what we talked about but I do remember learning how to substitute words for feelings as well as things.

"Lokshen" was the first of the many names devised by people who thought to make me more comfortable in my skin. A later example of this benevolence was "Luscious," a name awarded me by a woman in an accounting firm where I had my first summer job. She was, of course, much older—easily twenty-five. But I sought her out—although I didn't know how not to blush and stammer everytime we spoke. She had the secretarial tight skirt, and tan sinewy feet in high heels, and she wore a gold watch pinned to a scarf, and bracelets around her wrists, and she smelled like flowers in the early morning.

I think she somewhat liked my gaping sniffing fumbling. And, who knows, she might have fleetingly entertained the thought of trying sex with me—as I had just passed the age of first consent. Well, she should have, no matter how awkward. With her, I would have been the pupil who offers unripe apples to mollify the regrets that will come in her later years, and I would have quickly learned what usually takes so long—how to travel up and down the length of her, how to watch, when to leap, and how not to fear the closeness of someone else's flesh. But she was getting married; I was too gangly—all knees elbows and premature ejaculations. So she gave me the name instead—"Luscious," a name that had we actually shared it—said it to each other during all those hidden hours—would have been the catalyst for sounds and movements (and epiphanies) that we could both have had—for all the however many times to come.

As I grew older, my naming became more neutral—less wound or shield, and more the simple label I needed in college classes and among my now more friendly friends. The name that survived the early shifts of hope and pain and became my standard for those years was "Looshun"—"Loosh" for short. It was not the one I would have choosen as the exemplar of my qualities—but it did identify me without malice.

But sometimes, choosing a version for a naming is a serious matter. These circumstances are typically divided into whether the asker is male or female. When a man asks: "How do you pronounce your name?" I am on guard: Be careful how you answer; don't give away too much; make sure your voice is slightly growly. So what did I say? Usually, I said "call me Lou." Other times however, feeling more theatened than usual, I would roll out my heavy weapons: "Actually, when I was in the Marines they called me `Ski' —all the Polacks (heh, heh) were called 'Ski.' There was private Ski—me; there was a Captain Ski—Tarski; and there also was a General Ski—Dombrowski."

"You were in the Marines?"—the fellow would yodel. "Well actually I was drafted." I said. "I didn't know they drafted into the Marines," he said. "Oh yes, Korean war; when the Chinese came over the Yalu, they needed men fast you know, one out of three at the induction center—bam, bam boom—I was boom." "Did you go to Korea?" "Well, no, (heh), I stayed in North Carolina, missed the fighting—too bad, (heh, heh)."

On the other side of gender, I took a woman's asking "How do you pronounce your name?" as an opening to the erotic. It seems to me that the men ask the question aggressively and the women ask it suggestively— pronunciation as seduction. "Now that you ask," I would say, "shall I tell you, in passing, how interesting I am? The Polish `Lucjan' is actually a modification of the Latin `Lucian'—of course you know the Roman poet of that name." "Well yes," she would say, "I remember reading him, but that was some time ago—a little while ago in college." "Yes, yes" I would answer—"the French made the 'a' into an 'e' as in 'Lucien Lelong' and the Italians countered by keeping the 'a' and adding an 'o' as in 'Luciano Pavarotti.' But I would prefer that you call me whatever sounds best to you." "Oh yes, I'll do that, I'll try them all on you."

I have constructed—for myself as well as others—a real heritage, not entirely false but admittedly embellished, with a name for every occasion, with comrades both international and historical, alluding to a colorful and checkered past. It is a testimonial to the value of the liberal arts that my changing names became a way of life—a reasonable way to survive in war, love, and the confusing years that followed.

NAMES IN POEMS

Dearest Loosh, you are so louche.
But I'll not meet you in the hay today.
Perhaps tonight, when the bed-bugs bite—
although we must remember
that they like us best
those times we scratch and sweat—
before the light returns at morning.

So they do; it's true; and so do you—
like me that way too.
But a little blood and many scratches
are good for healing the painful swellings
of our hidden and forbidden noonday itches.

Shoosh, Loosh!
The dogs are listening to your laughter.
And Lokshen listens to me laughing too—
laughing at your scratched-up torso,
the flakey skin beneath my nails,
the blood-flecked sheets,
and the curious ways you have
of making love.

FIVE PROSE WORDS

Five words need attending to. They are: What, When, Where, Who, Why.

The first three refer to the world outside us—to that which occurs; to the time(s) of its occurrence; to the place(s) in which it occurs. The last two (who and why) refer to the ways we are in the world—so as to accommodate the recognizing of the "who" that writes about the world, and looks for reasons (if any can be found) that bring our particular "who" to a juncture with the "why" that has us write.

There are clear young folk as well as some older wooly ones—who have no difficulty in answering "where?" with a "there!" Such "there-thinking" affirms the value of the place where the thinker may contingently be. "There," they say, is neutral between any and no-where—a good safe place to hang out. But this affirmation of a "somewhere" can move (the rest of) us from the ecstatic uncertainty of free spirits to the analytic doldrums practiced by the sober and mature. The object for these latter, is to precisely find the "where" of their "there." But there are those others (myself included) who doubt there ever is a "there" that will stay put anywhere.

Consider, as an example, the current mind-brain controversy: Where is the location of thought? Why, in the mind! But the materialist view locates this "where" within the structure of the brain—the thinking mind just is (in) the physical brain. Such a thesis, dualists counter, is of only elliptical help in this inquiry, for it illuminates a consequence of brain-language infatuation—a neuronal "there"—a place where the more sceptical "who's" do not cogently—or comfortably—find themselves.

Views that propose multiple locations for cognizing existence do not include doubts that the brain is the structural arbiter of these locations—there is no brain-free (brainless) cognition. What is in doubt is the presumption that all our experiences can be located and explained by physical analysis (manipulation) of the brain, and its relevant language: It is a stretch too far, e.g., to find loving, hating, reflecting, hoping, etc.—embedded within discrete neuronal correlates.

The notion of "mind," my argument goes, offers more linguistic room for affective, lived-life, descriptions: We are "mindful of," "have a mind to," are "in" or "out" of our minds, we do not know our "loved-one's mind"—or the "mind of God." (It seems evident that God has no need for a brain—if so, brainists must all be atheists). The dead had minds that once were full but now are closed forever to our asking—but not to our remembering. It seems that fussing with nerve-endings in their lobal locations—alive or dead—gives us neither answers nor memories.

The answers preferred by "who's" —
at whatever place their "where's" may be—
suggest themselves before the morning pee.
They then come to rosy bloom
abetted by the wines of afternoon—
finding their evidence in the hand-holds
and foot-notes of an early-evening.
Later, they fade into the darker dreams
and tangled glades of memory.

There are also more extravagant views, held by some mind-speakers, that offer to "who's" who have no interest in their "where's," the comforting belief that they are free to not need a where—certainly not one located in the brain, and not even in the mind. This is the path to an ecstasy which requires that one be out of (one's) mind—a venture that also seeks a where-free location. Such "where-less who's" are, however, most vulnerable in the early morning hours—when, sitting on the pot, they find they do not entirely exist as fiction or spirit. But in other more fanciful times and places, they can avoid sharing the same modalities as do their more concrete selves, and so need not much bother with the evidence that upholds their actual existence.

There is a middle ground that has more general appeal to doubters of mind-brain identity, for it does not enirely reject the evident relationship between "who's" and "where's." Instead, it offers a view of their communal co-existence in time and place—the belief that for an event to be characterized as an occurrence, it must be within a physical framework at a certain time in a particular place. Thoughts in the mind and actions in the brain, on this account, are described as simultaneous events—and through formal equivalence, can be considered identical. On a different level of relationship, however, these may not be causally related—little can be assumed about mental function by evoking future findings in the brain: (Post-hoc non ergo propter-hoc). What can be said—is that prior brain findings (a tumor, say) will probably result in certain mental behavior. Taken more generally, however, "mind" (everything we can think) is not (yet) an entity subject to a causal explanation through reference to specific brain-events. The expansion of neurological research would need further reduction—and regimentation—of what we consider mind-events in order for an equivalence with brain-events to be reached. I hope that this will not (again) become the "true epistemic path"—as it was, say, with logical-positivism. Otherwise, imagination is in trouble.

One argument supporting the dualistic view holds that terms such as "events" and "occurrences" are merely codifications—and thus, abstractions—of times past or future. There is no denying that in every time and place, we face a programmatic uncertainty about the nature and location of times and places—even to the point where such locutions as "each" and "every," and "before" and "after," presume a totality that does not reflect a more co-responsive view of experience.

One solution—of a religious kind—to such uncertainty, is to suppose that all variables and possibles come together in a mind—not yours or mine—but in an ideal mind which contains all the possible variations in existence—past and future. This thesis, among its other virtues, provides defense against anxieties about the threat of nothing—the fear that when the physical brain stops, the mind just ends. It is a comforting faith to believe that one's individual demise is not a chance occurrence, but instead, a proper part of cosmic necessity—a necessity given its law (and reality) by the mind (not brain) of a necessary Deity.

Given this, we can look forward, when we die, to our small ripple rejoining the larger waves off shore—and so we continue to "exist." But this remains a considerable "given." Remember Kant's assertion that "existence is not a predicate."

The thesis of an ideal mind can also be found in a secular context—when it is considered to be—at least—co-extensive with a brain. Such a mind-brain reveals itself in the expansion of our (computational) efforts to encompass and encode the material processes of mental function. One aspect of such a program (the speculative aspect) would be to give us a this-worldly version of the transcendental mind: If we could get it all together—if we could put all the variables, past and future, that are implicit in experience, into one grand self-correcting scheme—we could then (progressively) grasp what knowing, and what knowing that we know (and so on)—finally comes to. In such a finality, there will be nothing left behind—or yet to come—that we do not, or cannot, know.

But we draw back from such improbability by saying that mind, like brain, is in a place—perhaps the same place. But the difficulties in locating "place" (more so—"same-place") bring to mind the old academic verities where acceptance of an existential thesis was gained through mutual accord in a true belief about what there is. But this attempt to fix "place" and circumscribe "existence" founders on the problems of delimitation and modality: "When is the place referred to?" "Is its existence actual (a there and then), possible (contingent-on-being experienced), necessary (but unknowable in its immeasurable completeness)?"

One solution would be to avoid such epistemic complexity and join (however reluctantly) with the forces that categorically champion places as being the concrete locations we desire: All spaces are places. It can then be said: There are no spaces in (that occur to) the mind (however absent-minded or far-fetched)—that are not places in the body, most notably, in the brain. But where does this get us? Of course, adherents of the opposing view—that mind is not reducible to location—can be dismissed as a grab-bag of myopic Hegelians, retired relativists, nostalgic flower-children, and other skeptics and visionaries whose interests are variously directed to undermining reductionist theories—and by so doing, to give credence to their preferences for wandering from concrete place to open space.

Such skeptics typically don't believe that translations between languages (mind-talk and brain-talk) can be definitive (salve-veritate)—because truth is not always the goal. They also don't believe that explanatory theories are cumulative (contra Hegel). What they believe, instead, is that theories are only richer or more meager—depending on how they explain what we use, flee from, or marvel at. Simply put: the analytic, pragmatic, aesthetic, when extended beyond academic civility, speak different languages. At stake, here, is not the notion that mind is "located in" or "the same as" the brain. It is, rather, the poverty of brain-theory's explanatory function as well as the weakness of its predictive power—when it comes to issues that are mind-specific—emotion, volition, appreciation, meaning, morality, imagination— to dredge up an embattled term—"subjective." These are issues that have different explanatory parameters than do "objective" ones.

The inter-translateability between quality and quantity remains a question. In cosmological theory, the hyphen in space-time is as uneasy as it is in mind-body or in inside-outside; "unobservable" and "immeasurable" are offered as attributes of real entities—as in "dark matter." In political theory, "freedom" and "equality" vacillate between support and antagonism, as do "progress" and "justice." Language, in such cases, stretches to accommodate them.

Advocates of separate theories of "mind" and "brain" are heartened in their beliefs when they peer across the fence and see how the advocates of "mind-as-brain" fare in trying to map the "soft" problems of ethics, aesthetics, private consciousness—as well, indeed, as the "hard" ones of incessant wars and observational indeterminacy—onto a neuronal matrix. The (soft) question: "What makes people act this way?" can be answered by the (hard) rejoinder: "We'll soon have an organic handle on all those differences in belief, and we'll be able to offer explanations (as well as cures) for every brain-place that is their origin. Unfortunately, we have so far been hindered by atavars (like you) of mind-speak—those poetic-psychologic-sociologic-spiritualistic-babblers—who refuse to come around to accepting the one place that (soon—soon) offers a full account."

In contrast, the mind—as the mind-ists insist—is not simply a location. Rather, it has places which it shares (physically but indeterminately) with the brain—but it can also be located (metaphorically) in spaces that are not (in) the brain—and it responds to questions that are not answerable by (perusal of) the brain.

The task of mind-defenders is to fend off the regimentists and reductionists who offer the dictum that we can locate all this flotsam of thinking, willing, feeling, creating, wanting, loving, hating, despairing—time past and time future—within the brain-scans etc., offered by neurologists in the laboratories.

Such an empirical fix can be seen as a laudable ambition, but its realization would create a brave new world that I, for one, would not want to live in. Theoretical advances can diminish as well as enhance the "quality of life"—in the sense that the "explained" subject is often smaller —definitionally impoverished—than the earlier one to be explained. In this case, the subject is conscious life. So (in the non-linear way of mind-ists) I look at the conflict from the vantage of a different place.

The study of physics (as I limitedly understand it) has gone far beyond location-in-place in its search for reality. Quarks, in experimental situations, appear in time-spans that occur only in our recordings— the accelerators, i.e., that produce ever-smaller, more basic variants of known particles, are increasingly subject to (or independent of) observational parsimony. One question is: How miniscule can these variants be before it can only be said that they are fictionally observed—although they perhaps are not really fictional—for they really exist as they are used—sometimes satisfying theorems, sometimes inspiring art—even when not observable.

Then we have string theory—a celestial conceit if ever there was one—which is offered as (finally) underlying the whole of material nature—no more problems reconciling the forces of celestial mechanics with the forces inside the atom. Although strings can be figured and reconfigured in theory—as being the most inclusive and explanatory ur-phenomena we yet have, they, by their very formulation, are not subject, being ur-dimensional, to perceptual verification in plain old time and space. They cannot, alas, be so strummed (by us) as to (adequately) sound the music of the spheres. They cannot even, so I'm told, account for the workings of our world's particular place in the new inclusiveness.

The notion of consciousness is analogously difficult. Consciousness, too, is a phenomenon in and of the world—but it is not reducible to the empiricism of place and time—even (especially) when it is purportedly explained via a tangle of firing neurons. Someday we may sort out each and every tangle—who knows? The ideal of adequacy lurks behind every scientific theory. But for now, the philosophically ambitious mind risks becoming a captive of the medically innocent brain. Acknowledging the value of historical error, we might call the brain the new pineal gland—the doorway (transfer station) through which we will bring body and mind together. Parenthetically, in a religious context, where we would accept another entity—soul—into our schema, we might then say that mind is the pineal gland between body and soul—a transfer between existence and belief.

Descartes' hope for a seamless transition between the ineffable soul and the matter-of-fact mind foundered, among other things, on bad physiology. But there is no doubt these days (do you still have some?) that everything the mind conceives has correlation with actions in the brain.

Where else? Well then, let's ask the metaphoricians:
Correlations can be found between cold toes and a runny nose

—

or maybe also in a field of ancient thistles
that prick your quick, but bloom at end of winter.
Or even in the hallowed courts that decide
(with diagrams) the proper pathways
between the what's when's and how's of lovers—
(recent courts have trouble with the why's).

There are correlations everywhere—look not here but there.

"Where else?"—that arrogant question—implies that someday we can cap it all: We will finally find the ultimate physical particle, match technologically advanced observation to the increasing expansion of the universe—and, at the same time, we will stuff mind and its misbehaving surrogate, consciousness, so completely into the brain that there will be no distinction left to pester us.

But some things, you know, are always left outside—those peripheral irritants that test the boundaries of every explanation. Think about the defunct certainties (just recently) that girded the attempts to reduce language to sense-data and then, through logical construction, into objects: "Erlebs" join "Qualia" (Carnap and Goodman) in the salon of benighted visions of transparent reference. But there still may be good conversation in way-stations with the older advocates of ether and phlogiston—not to mention the four humours—and think about the over-soul. Those folks knew how to party!

This overflow of certainty, these failures—if you will—I accept as travails of the soul. But here I give the term 'soul' a special usage—as a name for programmatic uncertainty about what is left over from all our attempts to squeeze mind into brain.

Soul, in this usage, need not retain a religious sense—although it may. I offer it as a way of marking the distance between what bedevils our present aspirations to become complete in our theories, and the conundrums that in time diffuse our every success.

Can we still be optimistic Hegelians without accepting Hegel's final stages for the achievement of spirit? There were terrible wars fought over that issue. Theories that pretend to such powers of explanation, have a way of insisting that you heed and do what they say they are right about. Everything that does not fit is irrelevant, unknowable, or unaskable—good grounds for dismissing criticism or denying citizenship.

But contrasting theories—those that attack the desire for certainty have had their own shot at being duly considered, and were also found wanting. To resolve this impasse is not a matter of theoretic equalization—but of contextual autonomy—agreement that accepting a theory requires understanding the language through which it is expressed. Realizing such latitude in present theorizing is a chimera, to be sure—but even chimeras have power.

To exercise this power, they need to probe the different logics of square and crooked dancing, and demonstrate the competing correspondences between the still of painted images and the rhythms of the moving world; they must empower the architecture of music heard from out a neighbors's window, and appreciate the scribblings on bathroom walls and subway cars that celebrate repressed or repressive longings. And, with non-sequential gloom or glee (depending on the place they're at) must undertake the task of writing both prose and poetry about all that.

HARD AND SOFT PHILOSOPHY

"Hard Philosophy" and "Soft Philosophy" is not a division between truth and error—nor between rigorous and sloppy thinking.

It would not suit the ambi-valent nature of my thesis to divide its principals as neatly as is offered in the academic distinction between Rationalists and Empiricists—endemic to curricular clarity from which few students emerge without puzzlement. There are, of course, the ideological prejudices—philosophical camps with which to ally one's self in the ongoing search for (warranted) "true belief." Clear oppositions also make it easier to teach undergraduates the subject. But which belief actually satisfies the wanted distinction, and which does not? What historical figures (without waffling) fully occupy the competing sides? To what purposes does one put this distinction now?

I have the same difficulties with "Rationalism and Empiricism" that I have with "Mind and Brain:" Each evokes a polemical procrustian bed upon which no event or observation fits without due stretching or chopping.

Here is my sense of the standard distinction: Rationalism views reality as a logical completeness theoretically but not actually attainable—except as a hope that the human mind will successively approximate the mind of God (the universal seat of logic). This, admittedly, is an infinite task. But the attempt is justifiable as a wordly search—a progressive capacity to explain the world's unity and latent perfectibility—and so, correct its behavior.

Empiricism, in contrast, finds reality in the organization of sensory experience, but variously locates that reality in the nature of perceiving, or—a dangerous move—in the object itself, independent of any given perception. This leads to a disjunction wherein the world has qualities that are not (perhaps cannot be) perceived, and other qualities that are dependent on (perhaps donated by) perception. How then, can we "know" the world?

I suggest that the opposing members in these contrasting schools of philosophy often find surprising agreement in the doctines of their antagonists. This depends largely on what one takes as the prime issues of disagreement and what other (sometimes compatible) beliefs are not, at a given time, seen as important. Philosophers have a plethora of belief objects that elude specification—especially those that are peripheral to their major theses: Those philosophers concerned with, e.g., value, soul, totality—will not focus on, e.g., sense data, empirical proof, linguistic accuracy. These peripheral issues, if seriously attended to by both sides, might go a ways toward developing a "unified" theory (on some modest level) of reality and its perception—but remember, this is still war!

My point is that reciprocities between these views, while not easily forthcoming, are needed for a larger intelligibility (if such is what we want). The undecidables in each school—the fact-value points of impasse—require language and curiosity from both sides for mutual accomodation. This is a salient point in my dissatisfaction with "mind-brain," "body-soul"—and other such dichotomies.

To briefly show this, I offer some examples from philosophers who have been traditionally assigned to the opposing schools noted here:

Rene Descartes, a Rationalist, argues that examining the coherence between ideas in the mind can be transformed into a correspondence theory between mental perceptions and the actuality of the world: If perceptions are not misleading—if no evil demon can totally deceive us (the irrefutability of "cogito ergo sum") then the world actually is as we experience it. Taking this further, Decartes holds that while sensory perception is not misleading, it is always incomplete in regard to the immensity of its (universal) subject. This incompleteness however, comes to light through an examination of mental function—that we can contrast the limitations of our knowledge of the world with our held idea of perfection—God's knowledge of totality. Required here, however, is the further belief that mind is up to veridical self-examination—that it knows it knows (the evil demon notwithstanding) that, as a thinking thing, it is not deceived that it thinks, and accordingly, that it exists. Such belief is based on the equating of a humanly conceived perfection (the reality of "clear and distinct ideas") with the actuality of God's and the world's existence.

Descartes' observation—that our having the idea of unlimited perfection even when in all other respects we remain imperfect, must have its source in a perfect being—and therefore may be taken as a proof of God's existence. But this suggests a regress—from a (hypothetically) enabling God back to a created mind that mirrors Him—and then forward—to that mind's (God-given) capacity for such mirroring as a guarantee of God's existence. Given that God's perfection is incompatible with deceit, the argument continues into its wordly consequence—the verifiability of actual existence.

Both the idea of perfection and, thus, of God—are based on a logical (mental) coherence between them—for neither is a sense datum. Descartes, however, justifies this further reach between the idea of perfection and other ideas—those of actuality and their subject—the physical world, within one theory. But this second pairing is between (mental) ideas and (sensate) experiences, and so requires, not coherence, but a theory of correspondence (as in mind-brain). Descartes does not see a tension between these uses; the intersection between speculative and empirical thinking is not a problem for his philosophy. Further, he does not posit a first, unifying idea through which the pairing above (if he would admit it as such) could be derived. Some later critics—notably Kierkegaard—consider the "Cogito Ergo Sum" to be a tautology: There is nothing, i.e., added to the "I am" by the "I think"—hence, no "therefore." Here again, a more fundamental proposition is needed to give a prior credence to the "I" which occurs in both parts of the equation. But Descartes does not give us this.

John Locke, an empiricist, begins—not with mind, but with sense perceptions which he calls "simple ideas." They are simple because of their limitations—in time, place, and scope. These ideas are the bases upon which our knowledge is built. The process requires an examination of these ideas to ascertain their origins. One set of ideas is determined by sensory experience which can be imputed to the characteristics of the objects "themselves," e.g., density, measurement, position. This echo's the Platonic notion of the underlying reality of such qualities: They are the qualities whose accuracy can be verified by rational agreement bolstered by mathematics—the enduring "form" of the object—which exists (as Plato has it) in "that place beyond the heavens."

Then there are other qualities that cannot be so measured—but derive their reality from the emotional subjectivities of mind—the unruly steed (as in the Phaedrus) which feasts on the changing grasses of desire and pleasure. These (lesser) qualities are experiences of, e.g., taste, smell, color. They are the romantic ideals, rescued periodically through history as being more "personal" (therefore subjectively more true) experiences—than their rivals of form and measurement.

This distinction—between "primary" and "secondary qualities," or as Locke sometimes put it, between "simple and complex ideas"—purports to tell us which of our perceptions are indubitably generated by things in the world, and which are "given" to things by the changing character of our perceptions. The distinction results in a dualistic theory in which knowledge is attained by different, although (for Locke) complementary ways—through the physical experiencing and measuring of sensory imput and the mental structuring, or embellishing, of such imput. Locke shares with Descartes the virtue of not finding difficulties in presenting this duality as a coherent theoretical analogue of the real world. Yet the distinction between these types is a basis of his theory, and it founders in the difficulty (which Hume later attacked) that both sets of ideas are based on a single perception—and to so separate them would lead to separate but equally absurd conclusions—that the world exists without perceivers, or that the world is formed entirely through our perceptions.

As with Descartes then, another—independent—judgment seems called for which determines, for any such idea, whether its origins are in world or mind, and how it can be brought together with its antagonist. This, in effect, would also constitutes a tri-partite theory—of which a non-derivable member (unmoved mover, perhaps) provides a prior justification that underlies the contrasting pair—and enables a theory through which we can envision the actuality of a single world—even as our perceptions of it are dualistic. But Locke—as with Desccartes—does not give us this.

Unlike Descartes, however, Locke does not base his religious beliefs upon his philosophy. He accepts the new testament as a reasonable way to approach the questions that empirical analysis cannot encompass: creation, immortality, sin, obligation, and the like. Locke's main concern with religion is that each belief remain tolerant of other forms of belief so that all, without interference or coercion, may ponder the limits of (holistic) reason—and enjoy the possibilities and uses of (partial) understanding. This is another of his virtues.

The next philosophers I compare are Benedictus Spinoza and G. W. Leibniz. Both these philosophers are typically identified as Rationalists, but the differences between their theories, notwithstanding, are as fundamental as the differences between them and Empiricist philosophy.

The Rationalist Spinoza, in contrast to both Descartes and Leibniz, admits of only one substance, of which mind and body are attributes, and individual beings are particular modes. Substance is everything that there is. It is infinite and encompasses both God and nature. God is not separate from nature anymore than is the human mind (or soul) from God. There are no distinct realms of Heaven or Hell—and correspondingly, no after-life. Human virtue rests in a conformity with God's nature—not through obedience to his will (as revealed, e.g., in theological dogma) but by thinking through the conundrum of rationality as existing in-the-world. This is the basis of Spinoza's Pantheistic effort to place both meaning and its justification within a single context of existence.

The attainment of truth (and virtue), in this context, entails a self-examination. Non-conformity (with God's nature) is not disobedience (sin)—but a privation (isolation, degradation) of potential. As humans share the aspects of thought and extension with the universe, virtue lies in a grasp (and joining with) nature's complexity through an increasingly adequate understanding of both self and the universe as constituting the infinite idea of God. This is a theology of "immersion." The human is an aspect of God—neither a creation nor a servant. Nature is not evidenced as primordial chaos but as timeless and totalizing geometry—and is therefore (progressively) knowable. As mind, universe, and God have (are) the same nature, there is no dualism lurking in the cognition of reality—only the task of (cognitive and affective) communion.

Leibniz, who knew and engaged with Spinoza, conceives of reality as an aggregate of distinct entities —which he calls "monads," and characterizes them as depending, for their interaction, on a separate and transcendent God. Monads are given actuality through the union with their physical bodies, and they gain their reality through their place in the divine schema—the "pre-established harmony" through which God structures the correspondences—the physical interchange —between monads. Humans are a complex type of monad which are distinguished from the simpler types by having the capacity for thought and self-consciousness. They also have the idea of free-will.

But this conjoining of human will with divine perfection seems to contradict Leibniz' thesis of God's master-plan—the strict determinism that it apparently entails. For how could a universal pre-established harmony exist if humans were free to do as they would (often perversely) wish? Is "freedom," then, defined by the (restrictive—but hidden) logical (God —given) nature of its possibility?

Leibniz here resorts to a somewhat counter-intuitive solution: God gives humans the illusion of being free, but through His infinite knowledge, all human actions are (pre- and post-facto) designed to be in acccordance with His dictate. This provokes the infamous thesis (Voltaire made such fun of it) that our world is the "best of all possible worlds." In this (best) world, despite its deistic regimentation, humans experience themselves as having free will, and so take the indignities of life as being a necessary part of living free—however unjust the experiences of that life.

In this sense, Leibniz' philosophy, in contrast to Spinoza's, is dualistic—a world composed of monads of varying complexity, whose nature and future depend entirely on the will of a separate, yet all-powerful God—but whose sense of life is that of self-determination.

Spinoza rejects the traditional trappings of an afterlife—of heaven and hell, sin, reward and punishment—in favor of a single Universe (the soul as a rivulet slipping back into the ocean) that includes God as an ideal of completeness, but whose location is within—not outside—the realm of nature. In Spinoza's words: "Deus Sive Natura." Where God is positioned, in this context, depends (as a friend once said to me) on what one wants from God.

Curiously, Leibniz' response to Spinoza's single-realm inclusiveness, is that the universe so construed, would give humans no choice at all, neither in thought nor action—for they would be subject—as are animals and stones—to the single-mindless (soul-less) determinism of nature. The (separate) Divine Will "just is" the source of human freedom—for that is where it originates. More: If God did not exist in His three perfections—omniscience, omnipotence, omni-benevolence—nothing imperfect (read: human) could exist.

For Leibniz, the divine plan issues from God's omni-benevolence, and so rationally "encloses" the amorality of natural freedom. Spinoza's God, in contrast, as He is "within" nature, becomes the impetus for the (developmental) unification of morality and natural freedom—without the imposition of a transcendent "Will." This impetus marks Spinoza's essential philosophic value of a transcendental (immanent, rational, and all-inclusive) benevolence. It has no place for Leibniz's transcendent (imposed and other-worldly) benevolence—given by a separate God.

There are always good reasons for devising a system that identifies what we need to know—with what, and how, we can know. Such systems are rare, but when successful, they are like ecumenical cathedrals in which—sorted out and variously assigned—are contained the needs, doubts, and resolutions that press on the lateness of their time—and so, present a new understanding.

Immanuel Kant's "critical philosophy" is one such—the philosophical masterwork of his (and, as I believe, our own) time.

When Kant began rebuilding the house he had inherited, it was clear that its outworn and overargued elements must be separated, refurbished, and added to. Only then could they be made to cogently address the bases of reality, experience, and the needs—possibilities and limitations—of thought. But Kant, interested less in housekeeping than in categories, offers a new schema which critically addresses the inherited array of intractables and incorrigibles, and so offers a system of both analysis and synthesis that would replace them.

This system is expansive —not reductive. It does not delete one member of an apparently opposing pair so as to hegemonize the other. Rather, it shows that the opposing claims—to both reification and explanation—are directed at different targets, and have different compliants in mind. The duality, once resolved, could then become—first a duet, then an oratorio. (Kant's "Critique" and Bach's "St. Matthew's Passion" are close in historical time).
Kant offers a system of reciprocal units which provide answers to his four basic philosophical questions: What is there? How can we know? What must we do? For what can we hope?

The first question is directed at our understanding of the world—the realm of what was once called meta-physics but is now called ontology, and is addressed through the empirical sciences; the second is directed to the nature of that understanding—what was once called revelation is now epistemology, and is taken up by cognitive science and psychology; the third pertains to our desires and actions—the continuing realm of ethics and morality—which is codified in theology, philosophy, and law; the fourth question is more speculative—for it is about beauty and sublimity, art and teleology—and asks whether there is a material basis for appreciating the world-as-rational, and how it instantiates our hopes for progress.

I simplify all this greatly—when the question veers, Kant weaves between the critiques; when it threatens to disappear, he provides new rainment and a differerent home—the argument is nothing if not complex—as is the world it presents.

The aspect of Kant's philosophy that here concerns me most is the question "for what can we hope, " which is taken up in his third critique—of "Judgment." This is where the concept of the "reflective"—as opposed to the "determinate"—judgment appears. Versions of the determinate judgment operate in the earlier critiques—as empirical (scientific) judgment in the first , and as moral (categorical) judgment in the second.

But it is in the third critique that Kant takes up the reflective judgment—primarily, in the apprehension of beauty, secondarily, in the appreciation and creation of art—and finally, as a sensory sign of the world's evolution towards rationality.

As regards "beauty:" For Kant and, evidently for us as well, there is no listing of physical properties that provides evidence for our judgment that something is beautiful. But we certainly do see aspects of the world as beautiful—we are moved by art—and we often give this a considerable (sometimes metaphysical) importance.

Kant proposes that our reflections on beauty give us hope that the world is harmonious, and support our expectations that it is rational. There is reason, good reason, to want the world to—cognitively and actually—become (be) a unity. There is a different, but compatible, reason—to hope that living will (increasingly) be grounded on an ecumenical morality—as exemplified in beauty. But reasons, however good, are not determinants. They are dependent on what grounds we have for hoping they prevail.

Such grounds can be offered (I expand on Kant's descriptions) when—on a temperate afternoon, we walk among the trees and grasses, inhaling their odors while looking up at the interplay between clouds and sky. We listen to bird-songs and murmorings of the wind, and we find ourselves completed in our own identity by the feeling that the harmony we experience justifies our hope that the world actually is as we then perceive it. We cannot know this—as we would be able to know the factual findings of experiments—and we cannot demand this—as we would categorically demand obedience to moral law.

But we can hope for a rationality that is also sensately exhibited—linking the holistic nature of the world with the variability of its changes. This is a hope we can neither prove nor demand, but one that is given credence (as Kant would have it) by our experience of beauty.

Kant makes clear what the perception of beauty does not entail—namely—possession, utility, factual analysis. We cannot want, use, or count the contents of beauty. Its perception, in his terms, must be "disinterested" (not "uninterested")—a knowing that is based on the purity and compatibility of feeling and experience, rather than on fact, use, or obligation—or even—the actual existence of the subject of that experience.

There is another side to the reflective judgment, which is found in the experience of the "sublime." This experience, like that of beauty, is holistic—but, here, it combines the elements of power, enormity, and fear—the power of a cataract or storm, the infinite scope of the heavens—the fear that our constricted life is not adequate to a threatening reality—so we retreat, in such cases, by fleeing from the perils of lived experience. But Kant turns this retreat back onto itself. The very experience of sublimity—when understood not as fear, but as awe—transforms fear into our capacity, even in dire circumstances, for reflection on totality. The experience of the world as sublime, becomes a capacity for distancing (and yet embracing) that which we fear. This capacity mediates the existential anxiety in our experience through our awareness that we, in fact, can reflect on what we fear. We are given a place, in reflection, for the experience of incompleteness—which thereby gives (our) reason a meliorating power over the limits of our lives—and offers the hope for a larger belonging.

Kant uses artistic creativity as the human model of the natural sublime. The artist, rather than assuming the spectator's position of disinterestedness in aesthetic appreciation, presents its opposite—a joining with (becoming) the power of sublimity through the creation of art. Here, Kant identifies the artist as a "force of nature"—a force beyond pedagogy or will. This force is instantiated by "genius" whose power transcends both instruction and desire. It is a power "given to" but a few, but through its consequences—great art—it reveals the source of, and compatibity with, the sublime in (human) nature.

The interplay between the experiences of beauty and sublimity brings us closer to direct intuitive knowledge about the nature and juncture of two realities—those of our world and our lives. Such knowledge subsists in the tension between unattainable perfection and overwhelming power—as spectator, through the appreciation of beauty—as artist, through the expression of sublimity. It is our capacity to experience and accept this interplay that affirms the value of our lives—our status (so Kant puts it) as "a member of the kingdom of ends." This status is also attributed (in the second critique) to the sheer "good will" of the moral person—and is probably as close as Kant wants to come to the experience of God and the immortal soul.

The experience of beauty, for Kant, is not a reference to Plato's Forms; it is found in the phenomenal world: The perceptive walk in the garden and the appreciation of an art-work are sources. But the quality of beauty—its completeness, its clarity, its timelesness—does not come from the world. Rather, it is through the totalizing capacity of a mental faculty—judgment—that we experience it.

I return here—with a suggestion—to our previous discussion of mind-brain. Reflection, as Kant has it, is a reconciliation of realms. But this truce has a curious turn: As the mental constructions of rules of (logical) coherence and of (empirical) correspondence—whatever their discrete subjects—are both in the mind-qua-brain; and if that amalgam is a proper part of the physical world—then the rules that govern our truths must exist in the physical world as well. I refer not only to phenomenal truths—those scientific truths subject to empirical verification—but to noumenal truths that are determined by pure thought—the a-priori, or analytic, workings of the mind.

I suggest that Kant anticipated a synthesis of the mind-brain duality when he posited the "synthetic a-priori judgment." There are two sets of distinctions here: The first is [a-priori—a-posteriori] —before (independent of) experience, as opposed to after (because of) experience. The second is [analytic-synthetic]—the predicate "contained in" the subject, as opposed to the predicate "adding to" the subject.

The first is about the nature of knowledge—whether we can know something (about, say, the nature of thinking) that is not derived from our experience in the world, but which determines (through thinking's very necessity of making distinctions) the world we do experience.

The second is about the nature of language—the tautology, say, of logical truths (2+2=4) as contrasted with statements in which the predicate adds to the knowledge contained in the subject (the towel is white). Here too, the formulation of a logical truth is not based on empirical experience.

I propose that the experience of beauty rests on a judgment (the reflective judgment) that, existentially, is a-priori; and linguistically, is synthetic. The content of the experience is obtained through the senses—its source is not other-worldly. Yet, its form is inherent in the mind—as it reflects on its (very) need for unity and harmony in the completeness of its thought, and finds an image of this need satisfied—in the reflective judgment that some "x" is beautiful. This purports to have us understand the possibility of the world through the nature of thought—a (developmental) notion that places our awareness of the import of sensory judgment within the process of (our) species evolution. Further, it places the notion of our need for completeness within this process—in our experience of beauty.

For our purposes, then, the brain is the world-in-perception (synthetic), and the mind is perception-as-consciousness (a-priori). We do not have theories that would satisfactorily place the one (either one) within the other. Yet we do have needs, physical and social—even metaphysical—that would reject (no?) the proposal of "identity"—that one "just is" the other.

BIRTHDAY BOY

Birthday Boy was born in the same old way—
at the break of day as they wrote it down.
But it was a different place and another day—
quite far away in an Eastern town.
It was some time ago—a time that's past.
But time doesn't pass away—not the way
he will, when his late time comes
in some other town at another day.

He sits here now—this very moment,
lounging in the early evening,
much opinionated and less than neat,
with reading glasses and an a/fib beat.
But he's a Hearty Harry notwithstanding.
Come by most any day you feel the need
to use him or peruse him.
He'll love it both or either way.

But choose your coming from among
the moments within the many times of life
that form the functions of our varied minds.
Choose the ones that happen
more than once—or in multiples of twice.

Remember also that the family thought
your visit was very nice—for him—not you.
They do remember that you once said —
you would prefer him dead.

KINDS OF TRUTH

Poems are like butterflies; they flit blamelessly to the outsides of the page—just in case they must hide—or otherwise protect themselves from the demands of a lurking prosy notion that took on the rule of power to profess the truth, but in the process became too dessicated to perform in places set aside for song, dance, and the sweeter sadness. There are few such places now—worn shelters that once resounded with old ballads—all the ones that overcame their rhyming to tell us what is important for us to know.

Prose is hard.
Is that all you have to say?
But, I say
I'm getting smarter by the day.

Poetry is harder.
Is that all that counts for you?
But, you know—
maybe that-there's all there is
to say.

When did poetry relinquish its affinity between telling and knowing? Perhaps when truths that come from knowing became democratic and lost their categories, when most any truth would qualify for all levels of profundity—and become suitable for most any use —whether in prose or poetry. But should we not, if we need a measure to keep our truths together, safe and in one piece, choose a good measure—the best we can afford—and then only mind the most potent truths? After all, there are so many that try to play the game, and increasingly they (both truths and measures) look less and less alike—unless we show them all we love them equally and dearly. But then—how can we choose between them—when love is made before its choosing? Well, we could avoid this riddle —and tell the chosen that some won't get paid (in kind) for being lovers—unless they're certifiably true-as-advertised, and also will behave themselves as stipulated.

This is difficult to do with truth, for the word hides many sentiments such that, if you listen carefully, can have outlandish applications—some of which you would not reference with friends at supper or when in bed with a friendly stranger. There's no stopping public sentiment, however. One can slash the pictures, burn the books, and ring the curtain down—even shoot the messenger. But, like Asian carp, presumptive truths will get through the barriers and proliferate down stream—by the very banks upon which you and your true love once were safely wont to bide.

Years have been wasted building barricades—but I say the day can still be won. The wars of truth are raging still. (can you imagine—after all this time?) So get off your fat ass and reach with me into the seamy places where truths of all persuasion comport and disport one with the other. We cannot love them all, for some are too sad and tired, others too mean and ugly; and many—more than we once thought—will not show themselves because they are already spoken for in hostile languages.

But some truths look familiar: They have grown to full discourse in adjoining neighborhoods, speak the same if differently inflected language as we do, wear trousers that buckle snugly at the waist instead of sagging below the butt, do not use wigs or multi-dye their hair, avoid tatoos, and seldom pierce in private places.

Such truths represent us better than do the others: Among these familiars are the self-evident truths—they come in all colors. When asked why they are true, they smile and wave at everything that now is and has ever been—and then quietly affirm that we and they, and all of that and them, are one. There is no point in arguing with self-evidential truths—but a glass of white wine at an outdoor table is comforting.

Then there are the logical truths—they are neither red nor blue (actually, somewhat colorless). These truths are more vulnerable to the question: "Where do truths come from?" than to the question: "What is true?" In respect and wonderment, we see them in their stern and subtle robes, but we also want to know what place it is that gives them their authority. They reply that they, of course, are from the mind—that is where they think up the rules by which they themselves, their proofs and propositions, are formed—a neat trick—the snake in full-circle with tail-in-mouth. But we can also suppose that they come from elsewhere—the mind of God, or maybe chanting on the beach.

We now retreat to go forward: As the mind is—must be—a proper part of the brain—then the logical truths, together with all possible rules of formation, must be there as well—assigned variables and firing neurons are kissing cousins. Indeed, one might imagine the brain to be (not merely look-like) a comprehensive (bio) logical system. It once was understood as a comprehensive (teleo) logical system. Both are true under certain conditions. But can we imagine the mind that way? It is (should be) too unruly to conform with systems—or parentheses.

If we poke around—dissect, scan, and otherwise illuminate—we might find those rule-forming places in the brain more easily than if we searched for them in the mind. Poets, it must be said, have done some good mind-searching—but have published their findings through their poems—which, as art, can be discounted but not disputed.

If we assume that the brain (unlike the mind) is a proper part of our physical extension, we can, as above, speculate that rules are somewhere there as well—that the rules of logic must be compatible with the stuff of the physical world—thoughts, their formats, and their stimuli must have a material basis and location. If logic can be found in the brain—as this story goes—we can seamlessly reach out from brain to world, and then return from world to brain along a parallel reaching: The world is logical—ergo—logic is physical—it and we all are rational.

Wonderful! But, of course, there are problems with this conflation of logical thought with a physical site: Logical truths do not justify themselves by waving at the vagaries—excesses and insufficiencies—of the world. They have an internal elegance—but are reticent, often shy, and show their external beauty only to afficionados. They gain their status through coherence in their rules—such rules as govern contradiction, negation, implication, necessity, and the like. But these rules do not show themselves through a correspondence with events which would demonstrate them in the world—they show themselves in language where, in various ways, they talk about the world—or about themselves. Indeed, logical truths need not have support from the outside world (although logicians do). They are in the mind—marvelous creations—and so, are unworldly or other-worldly.

But they are somewhere—everything is—and this brings us back to the choice of a creator God—who would give them infallibility—or to a primordial chaos that develops into quiescent plateaus—of which our world is one. (Is logic dependent on quiescence? Is there a logic of chaos? Is "God" compatible with chaos?) Help me out.

But we—as compendia of—dependents on—both mind and brain, do need worldly reference to give reality to our affairs. The beliefs we have in matters of controversy, that, e.g., "our arguments are better than theirs"—first need a logic provided by the mind—from which we migrate across the border to the relevant physical events. The world is actual—the mind is logical—the brain is the transfer station between the two. This is our reality.

Moving from mind to brain to world, then, involves having (increasingly) adequate measures of compatibility that affirm the completeness of the transfer between the descriptions specific to each. If this is true, then nothing—in principle—should be left out. But as long as the world moves in time—there always is something left out. As a counter to this worry, there is the optimistic thesis of development: "We are getting better at knowing what there is." True—but as we get better, the subjects of knowledge increase—the "is" changes and gets larger.

The movement from brain to world is easy; from mind to brain is harder.
To begin with: We would all agree that our thinking capacity—personal and historic—seems unlimited. On the other side—the billions or so of neurons and their firing pathways also seem unlimited. But the task of correlating these sets (whether they are infinite or merely indefinite) is formidable—even if we knew what the "correlations" are we want to make.
Are we, for example, trying to explain (as if the neural evidence, long embalmed, could show) why Keats was a great poet? Or are we trying to predict (to find out through her DNA) as to which now-surly undergraduate will write good music?

Or are we—for the sake of tidiness—trying to avoid the normative and aesthetic questions entirely in our thinking?

SYLLOGISM

All men are mortal

Socrates is a man

Socrates is mortal

<u>All men are mortal</u>.

Some men are also gods—take Jesus and Buddha as examples.
Then: Ask Parvati about the manliness of Shiva or Danae about Zeus.
Then: Sometimes, you can't tell man from god—ask the Magdalen.
Then: All gods are immortal.
Then: Some men are gods—and some gods are men.
Then: Some men are immortal.
Then: And what about women?
Then: Remember Mary's bodily assumption.
Then: Celebrate the beneficence of Kwan-Yin and tremble at the recurrences of Kali.
Then: Some women are gods—and some gods are women.

<u>Socrates is a man</u>.

My dog is named 'Socrates.'
Then: Socrates, my dog, is not a man—as are not some other Socrates's so named. Then: There is a large rock outside of town that the locals have named 'Socrates.'
Then: This rock is also not a man—although it resembles one when seen from a certain point of view.

Socrates is mortal.

To be mortal is to die.
Then: Socrates the man and Socrates my dog will die.
Then: Socrates the rock, does not die—although it may crumble to where it is an unnamed pebble. Is this loss of naming a form of dying? Are there different modes of dying?
Then: Some entities named 'Socrates' are mortal and will die; others so named will not.

'Socrates' is a name. (Commentary)

Names, like 'Socrates,' are not mortal.
Then: 'Socrates' is not mortal and will not die—although the name may be forgotten.
Then: If all the living forget the name, it will not die—but it will disappear.
Then: Disappearing does not matter—for "forgetting" is a matter for the living.
Then: 'Socrates' (but not Socrates) may—like the god—come back another day.
Then: Socrates is so-called by the living to name a something which, they feel, will inform, or save, or otherwise commemorate their day.
Then: The man, Socrates, is long dead, and will not come back—but his name 'Socrates' can still celebrate some special day.

"Socrates" is a memory. (Commentary)

A memory is not a person—but is sometimes, like a person, named.
Then: I remember "Socrates"—and often call him 'Socrates'—
but I never knew Socrates.

MEANING

The poet thinks, as he reads his writings: "This is what I mean to say." But he (that poet at a later time) might say: "This is not how I would now say what I then meant to say." How does he know? Well, the poet (as poets do) knows his mind—knows what he means as parsed by remembering and forgetting. Or should we ask someone else—a "neuro-philosopher," say— to find out the matter of the poets meaning that is embedded in the time-slices of his brain? This version of "finding-out" makes the poet's inspiration for the poem recoverable from an astute probing of said brain—the "original condition" of the writing of the poem (not the same, mind you, as the poem's meaning) as it is recoverable from the brain, in which all this poetizing (despite all that distracting "mind-talk") is taking place. This strategy, messy as it is, would then remove the gap between the physical rendering and the mental inspiration. But where, in all this, is the meaning?

What to do? If the poet did not (then) write what he wants (now) to say about it, then "intrusive, retroactive, elucidation" is one (hard) way to find out.

If, however, the poet cannot (now) write what he (then) meant to say, then the urge to write (call it creativity) is challenged by the obscurantism of memory (call it a deviance in recollection)—which is that increasing distance between the formulation of the poem and its future readings. The poet having realized this—and perhaps to spite his admirers, having willfully dropped dead—left "meanings" up to them. They, of course, will get it wrong—as he would predict. That's why he died.

Despite the various strategies of retrieval, living memory is always incomplete: On some occasion one forgets one's keys; on another, the ancient feeling of first-love returns unbidden. When the mind fails to recover everything the brain has putatively stored, aesthetic anguish, further introspection, and then surrender to the unescapable ineffable are in order. This is the Romantic solution.

But do the hidden links between the mind's remembering and the brain's storing need retrieving for the poet's or the poem's sake? What about us—the readers' sake? How do we know what it is being retrieved—and for what reason? Neither mind nor brain are immune to playing tricks on us. Mind needs love, and brains want nourishment—just a friendly competition—or a difference in taste, as it is often called. Is poetic value, then, a function of the success of such retrieval—as stipulated by some or other rules of success—neurological, psychological, critical? If not, then the poet (however mind and brain work out, and whether or not "meanings" are entities to be retrieved) may not be necessary for the poetry—at all. (the modern scepticism).

Worrying this dichotomy—looking for poetic inspiration in the poet's mind or probing for it in the brain—may be like the memories an old dog has of hunting when he is limited to chewing on an ancient bone. Some poets, however much they try to be buried in memory, are not dead-dogs in fact. Other poets are more accomodating and stay alive to join the nowadays. Then, writing-about and remembering-why, become unnecessary reaches for a talent looking for success. Focussing on the present, our new poet will brush aside retrieval, and say of the writing that it doesn't have the inside track of Jones's poems (Jones being a recent recipient of the "Most Promising Poet" award) but—as friends have pointed out—it has a better be-bop rhythm, and it uses more dirty words.

MIND AND BRAIN

The passage from brain to mind is metaphysically easy; the passage from mind to brain is politically easy. The second, in fact, may not need the visit of the first: Some brain champions would be happy with an excommunicated mind—get rid of all pretenders! But other champions—old afficionados of the mental—still care for their relatives who have come upon hard times. If we believe that continuing to probe the interplay between mind and brain is an issue that can lead to something other than the inconclusive skirmishes of our present border war—then we must rescue that some-time mind, now under threat of imprisonment (without sufficient reason) in the brain.

It (the mind) is these days the weaker of the two—but still feisty. We minders can say to the brainists that the duality need not be overcome—clear borders make for different languages (and practices). But these respective languages—mind-talk and brain-talk—do need a disinterested observer to give them some advice. Mind, at this point, should be asked to cede to brain the necessity of showing (before the fact) how thinking occurs. To this, a brainist might deny that mindists have indicated that they care about such things. In rebuttal: Mindists could say that brain-thinking is more concerned with concrete specifics than with open vistas, and in their turn, will demand probity for different questions—determinations of the subjective kind—of beauty, goodness, love, the meaning-of-life —to name a few. The disinterested observer, in his turn, will (surely) say that two distinct languages are better at reaching accord (or, at least, partition) than is the admonition to remain silent.

It can be noted, when we look at the controversy, that there are now many languages vying for attention in all sorts of places. Quine's fabled "indeterminacy of translation" (and local interests) keep them safe from the parsimony of "adequate translation." But even when we venture to the more formal levels of thinking, we find competing languages: Physics speaks differently than does Biology; the proposed reduction of the latter to the former (once a great project) is now too embarassing for, even, cocktail chat; Anthropology and Cultural History will not either become one-nation

POETIC TRUTH

To tell the truth, I have no idea
how it feels to tell the truth—
or to rejoicing over telling it.

Truth, as I suspect, is a shell game
that we use for quelling doubts
that you or I can tell the world
something, anything, about how it was—
that might help our knowing how it is.

We tell the truth through "ings"
like know-ing, verify-ing, annotat-ing, correlat-ing.
These hide the world's indifference
to the truths we do not tell, and (sadly)
to our best reasons for not telling them.

The world has it's truths and we have ours.
Some think they're both the same.
But truths that occurs within the mind
some others think are also inside the brain—
which we now all know is in the world.

The mind we have is in the world as well—
but you wouldn't know it.
Because, for instance, you can't see it
in the way you can see dissected brains
when probed for secrets they once had—
before they became dead.
Minds engage the world by hoping it will tell us
what we need to know about the way things are.
Tigers also need to know, as do rats,
salamanders, gnats, and kangaroos.
Brain is all they need—but there are dogs
who use our minds to know—I had a few.

How far do you think the quick will go —
with all its brains—when we are gone
or do not have a mind to know?

POETRY, PROSE, AND TRUTH

Can poetry tell the truth (about the world)? Sometimes it can by happenstance—as when a Pelican's bill is too engorged for the bird to fly—or whether the comet at tomorrow's dusk will illuminate the sky. But these are only empirical truths—even if fancifully put. Perhaps the more salient question is: Does poetry contain its own—special—truth? Poetry—it can first be said—wants the poet to see the world as truthfully poetical.

But it also has been said that poetry cannot be sure it truly says what the poet means to say—nor can poets truly know what it is they mean to say. The poem says what it says—no guarantee needed of "meanings" that transfer back to poets—and none from poets, however attractive they may be, to tell their readers.

A poem is easier to end than prose, for the descant of historical memories and the knockings of imported common-sense, signal the poet that it, the poem, now has reached its end. Some (those boors) might very well say that it could have ended sooner. Long poems—after Dante and Milton—that tell large stories and end at a greater distance than these-days poems do, are difficult for us these days to read.

But prose, too, has its problems. It can be deadly dull because it usually is too long—and even when short and to the point, its reading is tainted by the drowsy anxiety of neglected chores. Most things, these days, move faster than their readings, and so, as paragraphs grind inexorably on, prose writers worry—about what they, back then, were saying.

But however the readings come at you—in script or on the screen—few of us now have the fortitude to slog through others' memory games—especially when the authors say that what they purport to show-and-tell, in the fickle here-and-now, fast becoming there-and-then, is really about us all, dear friends, in the spaces allocated for tonight's frolic—which, as we also know, took place a while ago.

Mind-brain identity need not be taken as a denial of mind-body duality—much less a rejection of the soul-mind-body trinity. The question is really about whether there can be an achievable completeness of explanation—specifically, the notion that explanation, when systematically pursued, and given good will and ample time, will merge with the subject of explanation—namely, itself.

If mind and brain indeed could merge, the explanations that define the circumstances of their union, would, to my mind, (always) have to face the charge of question-begging—of ignoring what other stuff this particular merger needs to set aside—ignore—for its own success. The soul, however, is pleased by incompleteness:

Whether one trudges along the trail to reach the final pass, or one climbs the ladder rung by rung until it can be kicked away, incompleteness contains the promise of a coming together of anxiety and actuality. Coming when? When completeness is all—and everything—there is. (Before something else shows up.)

Explanations all require a supervenience which acts to support them by gathering past memories, present descriptions, family attitudes, forebodings about the future—as well as accounts of pain and pleasure. These do not supply "a" meaning, but rather precede one—by presenting an arena of shifting interests in things that we, from time to time, notice enough to want to explain—to give meanings to.

This sounds slippery, I admit. How does one do explaining without clearly circumscribing the landscape of concern? How do we delimit the aggregate of possibilities, out of all we can surmise and dream, to what it is we want to explain—and to what we are explaining? (These latter two are not always the same).

Art and its practitioners have had little problem with the lack of limits. Both exclusion and inclusion signal a change in style—thereby revealing the new attentions that configurate a given historical time. Change in art is a signal that extant efforts are exhausted—not devalued—not corrected—only done with.

Philosophy, however, has a different take on historical succession. Systematicity is an exercise in philosophical greed. We attempt, in explanation, to correct the errors in the theories we have discarded. Philosophy, given Hegel's prodding, has had hopes for a theory of everything; but these hopes are as much metaphysical (perhaps aesthetic) as they are potentially demonstrations of how the world (really) is.

Art wants a world; philosophy wants the world. But philosophy also has a habit of avoiding the part of the world that is not susceptible to accepted modes of explanation. Art, in contrast, is irreverent, wanting and yet dreading the incommensurable that becomes actual, while offering itself seasonally (sacrificially) for a new mode of appreciation and criticism. Neither art nor philosophy should be vocations. Arting, in its practice, has no way to win or lose—only to be (contextually) better or worse. Philosophy depends too much on its seductive powers when it gives the sources of its arguments the gloss of reason, truth, utility (or some current alternative).

There is, of course, the ancient quarrel between art and philosophy, between appearance and reality, truth and feeling, the world as it is and as it is perceived.

This is a quarrel that will not be resolved. Nor should we, on pain of boredom, want it to be. Accepting the inevitability of this quarrel is an insight reflecting the ancient wisdom that not all things can be brought together, that human existence is not a whole—rather, it is stitched, raveled and unraveled, as on a multi-generational tapestry-in-process, through the efforts of its successive (and often contrary) weavers.

TWO WORDS, A POEM

Who is what (that one which) I'd like to be
when the smell of being just a What—
especially when it's old and musty—
is more (on a windy day) than I can bear?

There always are the many others—
all Whats—but reently washed you know.
They wrinkle their noses at my dirty toes,
and denigrate my clever prose.

So why do they come to where I am,
sitting solitary on my rock?
(I chose it long ago —when rocks were cheap).

The Whats I know come trilling
as they always do, about art so new
that it's a bargain—if you know someone
who can really tell which artist is a What
and how to avoid the one who's Who.

I once rummaged through the village
to see what I could pillage from out
the heap of now discarded pretty ones—
mostly Who's who stand and preen awhile,
then sit and argue with each other
about the river flooding more
this year than ever.

Some go swimming in the swollen waters.
I'm not interested in them—they drown too easy.
The ones l care about don't care to wash their feet.
It's God's will they say, and a damn-fool thing to do—
except in spring when the winter logs get free of ice,
and come floating down to bump the rump

of pretty biddies like your friend Clarice.

Oh! I like you all—Clarice and you and others too.
But the river's got more dangerous than it used to be—
so don't swim too far—stay close to me.
Stay right here—where I can keep both eyes
on just the two of you.

FIVE WORDS, A STORY

A Who is the antipode of a What. To be a Who is the stuff of extravagance, illusion, loneliness, and—now almost forgotten—the sickness of the soul (before "soul" was left behind to become the "mind"). Now, they say, the soul is back—infecting mind with its older sickness—just to keep the What's away.

We've seen that happen once—it didn't take long—just a cosmic instant in a lifetime. So we can now assume geriatric privilege and unload our Who, without shame or pity, onto those once-luscious other Who's who still come to eat and drink at our stained, unfashionable table.

They are all my friends—bumbling long-humbled stumblebums, truth-finders and sometime pleasure-seekers, long-disappointed artists and their plumped-out models, and the dear-old-others who will always come for bread and wine. But they are now outnumbered by errant gossips and malformed critics—the usual irritants—who are there to gloat (they are all so young) over the ugliness of pretentious old age, and if that's not enough—to spot some smidgeons of my outworn worth they can vilify and macerate in tomorrow's section of the Arts-And-Entertainment-Daily.

But because they have come to eat our food and drink our wine, we are free to lecture them about our sense of What and Who—and baste them with the hot-sauce of disputative barbeque—so that (for once) they can taste the acrid (and yet curiously refreshing) distinctions we make between the good and bad, and suffer our indifference to their choosing between the ins and outs of arty contraband.

Why, anyway, should those creeps just sit and smile when I show them what they are and who I am? It's a difference, they might say, that is only important for the age-old, old-age exercise of taste and hate. But as they regard specific-me as taste-free, and yet have come to hate (and be hated by) the universal me, they cannot believe there is a difference between my Who—when compared to their What—when they were offered it at a tasting of the first cold pressing of my inner olive. Of course, they do not know the weather and the soils which produce the best of oils. They do not know what it is like to be hand-picked and then hard-pressed. But in my refuge, partying with my faithfuls, I care more about eating olives before they're pressed. I do not tell them that—but if they are not more caring about what they think (and taste)—they will soon be buying olive oil that is a blend from out of Texas, Kansas, and Hoboken.

Consider now, the difficulties in linking a What with its Where—which linking was once considered a fool-proof way to distinguish What's from Who's: A What needs a Where (to be somewhere) more than does a Who. Who's are never sure as to where they are. But it does matter to a bona-fide ambitious What that there are Where's—inhabited by pundits, moguls, and promoters—developers of the latest circular about the straight path that shows the fastest way-to-go. Such documents, although expensive—are always there for the What in you.

Who's, alas, have become unfashionable because they contribute more to obscure journals than to the real-life interests of a What in search of a suitable Where.

So it is surprising that there are still Who's brave enough to step into the fluorescent light and proclaim that the controversy between them and What's continues to make a difference. Surprising, also, that there are Who's—despite all physiologic evidence (trepanning, truth-serums, electric-shock, lobotomies, and the like)—who (in their essence) proclaim independent from their What's. What is an essence for—but to make a distinction that is a difference?

And then there are the What's (now in the majority) who believe that a What is to a Who as brain is to mind—the latter term, in both cases, signifying an atavism of only historical interest, and now ready for discarding—or redistricting.

This ancient battle between the inside and the outside—between Who's and What's—has been won many times by one side or the other—only to come back into contention in the guise of new and different imperatives. Believing that my Who is embodied-in—yet supervenient on my What (or the other way around)—is a way-station on Hegel's grand dialectic journey aimed at bringing Who and What together in a final synthesis.

This completed synthesis, one that transcends the two-ness of body and mind, will not occur until the cessation of the big-bang expulsion—that (finally) time-free moment, coincident with Armageddon, when the cosmos no longer expands, Adam and Eve have stopped quarreling, and dialectical development ceases to be a necessary modality for spirit. But as of now, we are still moving. The play is between our present antagonists: physical brain and immaterial mind, inner feeling and outer form, history as progress or as random change, time as inexorably linear or reactively variable.

Some say that believing in a What is not a belief but an empirical matter of fact, and that believing in a Who is not even a belief, but an instance of wooly fabrication.

If it should happen that you come to my party, you are free to believe in Who's and What's in any configuration you like: Take a look at those partying over there—all races and religions—they're real nice. I encourage you to drink wine with them—beyond the limits of the dualistic propriety (property-line) that infects their separate selves. Indeed, you are free, as the night goes on, to reject any one or another self. (Do not reject them all—or, without another self with you, you may no longer be). Then you can walk away, if you still are able—with no further obligations, but with, perhaps, a companion of your dreams—an unanticipated pleasure of resolving formal differences.

Introspection is a venerable method of searching for the Who in us. Its signs are familiar in academic circles: furrowed brows and undirected frowns, a quivering at the corners of the mouth, and excessive sweating beneath your mortar-board during graduation. However, these signs are not always reliable, for they can also be imputed to gastric upset, or to chigger bites.

Looking for one's Who is as reliable as are the measures for interpreting the physical signs of its theoretical presence. In the absence of clarity, successful clients, having earlier solidified their What, might approach avaiable Who's in a health-spa style: They will want their private Who to emulate their public What—to be depilated, re-structured for greater perfection, introduced to sex at an early age—while remaining unfulfilled and still in search of the perfect orgasm. This is the belief—more prevalent among What's than Who's about what counts in a civic society.

But we must all be cautious: Do not prematurely throw your hard-earned What's, or long-suffering Who's, back into indifferent waters—to swim again with the obdurate and antinomic anemonies (the Who-less Whats and the What-less Whos) that occasionally emerge, still-quivering and always hungry—lusting for any vitals they can eat. Yes, they thrive and wait and hover—in the breakers just off Malibu, and even in the unexpected deep of Golden Pond.

EATING

Why do pimple-picking and chicken-flicking come together
in my time and for my story?
And who do I ask this question of and why?

Not of you my dear—don't worry—my infirmities are not yet nigh.

It is more my need to resurrect the finger-licking that could join us back together—
if such is now acceptable to you—who once told me that you know
what matters, and will not stand for me to tell you what is left to say.
What is it then, despite our differences, that I can still speak with you about?

There may be many words or few or none left now.
But, as I have also said to you, the truths we seek
are residues of old pus and long-dead heroes.
How could we any longer admit them to our mouths?
So stay with me and eat the fresh take-out in the fridge.
I bought it for you and me—for us to eat tonight.

I was raised to commemorate the nut-filled strudel
sitting on the kitchen table.
And to praise the great kielbasa lifted dripping from the pot
where it has lain long simmering.
We must celebrate before it bursts—as they did back then—
with a slop of grainy mustard and a heap of boiled potatos.
Very filling—sometimes killing—we ate it anyway.

BELIEF

Belief is everywhere—every soul has some beliefs through which they put the world to bed at night. But in its more singular philosophical versions, "belief" becomes more (or less) civilized than does knowledge in that it escapes the arrogance of its cousin —"true belief"—that real knowing purports to need. I propose the following: All beliefs need warrants that they hope would have us hold them. There is no true belief without a warrant that upholds its being true. Further, there is no belief—true or false—that does not have a warrant that permits its being entertained. Warrants are second order beliefs—permissions to believe—that minds give themselves when they venture into the dangerous question of why they believe.

But there is no belief without a believer, and so no belief without reflective reasons—sometimes considered adequate—that support the believing. These reasons constitute a warrant. Warranted belief, then, requires introspection—an action which supports the effort. The reasons for this may themselves be good or bad—and so warranted belief may be true or false. Such reasons range from data generated by scientific experimentation and research, to habitual responses in local contexts to familiar situations.

No mind is immune, in its maturation, from having entertained warranted beliefs that are not true. So, to bring belief and truth—mind and world—together, we must go further—to "warranted true belief." Such belief has its warrant, and what is there that is warranted turns out to be true—a correspondence between that belief and the actuality of some state of affairs. "Warranted true belief" then, is often simply called "the truth."

Belief, however, even in its manifestations as "true," contains uncertainties—hidden memories, peripheral doctrines, skewed anticipations—such that, if we were to accept them as part of a belief, could cloud (bring a programmatic uncertainty to) the judgments confirming that belief. Then, what we believe could be seen as not absolutely true enough or almost false—an indeterminacy that, if persistent, could indicate the futility of adopting that kind of belief—or, worse, any belief—however attained. Warrants of warrants can always be called upon: however, they can accumulate and show a corrosive regress. When do we stop? When do we just (want to) believe in our believing—more so than in any of its contents?

Assurance in belief, then, needs another ground when introspection itself (which had promised so much) becomes the issue, rather than the belief that it reveals—when the function of knowing replaces the subject to be known. Then there is a rush back to simplicity—to the comfort of first belief—or to scepticism. Historically, simple beliefs usually have the advantages of community: sceptics, having put everything around them into question, often die alone.

There is a ladder (not Wittgenstein's) to be imaged here whose first rung is an early yet uneasy fullness—an actuality of an anticipated meal, but one which is followed by the increasing anxieties of not knowing when the next meal arrives. The climb (for us) continues until the final rung is reached (by future folk) whose nourishment—however minimal and dessicated it would now seem—is offered with the same flourish (but less anxiety) than was the meal eaten at the first rung.

This marks the exchange between belief and faith—the last achieved rung concludes the effort at overcoming perplexity through our climb from insecure belief to assured faith. The warrant for this realization (although the faithful seldom need such) is an epistemic merging of belief and actuality that marks the prediction as a success. This can result in a faith (Hume called it "habit") that such will be the case in the future. Often, this faith is expanded to include a deity—one that, as Einstein once said: "does not play dice with the world." Such a faith transcends reason in that it is a knowing given outside of warrant—except through (our participation in) the rational mind of God.

But there are problems: Faith comes closer to the vagaries of belief when we venture to ask whether there are false faiths (as there are false beliefs). The faithful believer would say "no"—false faith is not an error: it is a deprivation—or a prevarication by evil spirits.

Yet, many dreadful wars have been fought—between believers—over the issue of a "true faith." The epistemic distinction between faith and belief remains clouded.

To believe that what one has faith in is true—is not the same as to have faith that what one believes to be true—is true. The warrants come from different directions: To (come to) believe in the findings of faith is to (self-admittedly) diminish the adequacy of belief for knowing without faith. It also implies knowing the difference—and the history of interchanges—between having faith and entertaining belief. However, to offer faith as the self-evident and primary guarantor of belief, is to have a ladder with only one rung—whose continuing ascent (not itself a matter of faith) is based on the verities of untrammeled thought, infinite time, and the irrelevance of doubt and pain.

DEEP DIVING

To admonish Who's—that they need not
wallow in the sweat shop of their
mind-less bosses—should speak as well
to What's lusting in the aisles for errant Who's.
For both: Depending on
neural networks is not the best way
a libido can (without condition) be enjoyed.

In every age, there are divers for whom going deep is dangerous—not just a preference or point-of-view. Those afraid stay shallow and do not (much) consider what they're missing down below.

For some, however, deep diving is a necessary response to a deeply nested, however exotically imagined, reality. The effort to dredge-up demons, despite the probability of their non-existence, is preferable to paddling toward shore with friendly minnows and other surface-riders. Those who go obsessively down below the warning signs on the rope (deeper than the limits of clear thinking) are just those who will tolerate the darkness and the pressure, while looking for the bubbles that signify the location of another needy fish or diver—even when, because of proximity to the unspeakable (such as the loss of discerning up or down) location-location can transform mere drowning into a grand performance of the Liebestod.

Deep diving in the psychic waters provides access to the excess of nitrogen that counters the oxygenated clime of surface truths. The inhalations of air when our heads are above water is at one with the rational middle—while the deeper mixes, because of their narcotic content, are deemed antithetical to rationality by sober surface critics.

(Imagine offering, at 400 feet down, your limited air to deprived fishes and friendly mermaids, and come to consider it to be, before you die, the proper way to run a country).

This feud—between surface sippers and deeply infused inhalers—is a version of the ongoing quarrel about the way to achieve a self—to distinguish between the "what I have become" and the "who I really am." Such acrimony can be traced to the schism between the tribes of Cain and Abel (warrior vs. poet). It shows up in the tension between Plato's love of the beloved and the austere needs of his Republic (lust vs. order)—and it figures in the latest attempts at mapping poetry onto brain-waves (creation vs. explication).

Who and What are the contenders in this conflict of identities. Where and When are the determinants of the terrain and the strategies of battle. We ask: Where? And, in answer, someone says: There—the place beyond the trees—although the getting-there has become harder in these passing years. But this is so because What's have so greatly proliferated that by sheer number they deny the importance of their own Where's—by, for example—chopping down the trees of their technologies. (It's only, they say, a response to free-market necessity). But, really, What's don't care. They, in principal, are eternal optimists—waiting only to be proven right, however long it takes a tree to grow. In the interim, they need remuneration—lots of it—as stipulated by prior agreement. They are the legitimate constituents, as they themselves say, of the consumer world—and so, are entitled to its rewards.

Included in this celebration (of legitimacy) is the When of a What—for certainly, a What needs an appropriate When just to be somewhere at sometime —preferably at the right time. But the right time is not always a given—it can be another time that does not contain the smug assertion that identifies a "now" as being the right time for the expanding ambitions of a What. Without a "now," then, whats a What to do?

Our What, as described above, functions through its claim to our attention during some highlighted When. But Who's don't often care, Yet, not attending to the wants of What's by a bunch of Who's is financially hurtful and socially impolite—Who's can be uppity, too. Nevertheless, snubs do not make a What's ambitions disappear—they only call for harder work to get the message through.

A What's proliferation in time depends on showing up—as is expected—at a projected When. A Who's' neglect of acknowledging a What at some given When may be attributed to the disregard, in general, by Who's for the importance of attending to the times of Whens. But such disregard may also be more specific; it may cover a hidden envy—a covert rejection—of the life-style of a What. This leads to the politically fraught situation of What's losing the attention of communities of Who's—who, all this while, seem to have been their faithful customers.

But it is not simply inattention to market-changes that threatens a What's existence. It is a matter of the When and the Where of a What not having—schematically—been brought together. This is a matter of What's wanting to show themselves as essentially the same in various surroundings, comfortable in their identity—so that errant Who's would have to see them as self-sufficient entities—happy in their work—not really needed a Who with whom to flesh out the world.

It is quite different with the existence of a Who. There is less concerns with external identity. Being there in place—as, say, a lawyer, banker, potentate, policeman—would not satisfy the needs of Who's concerned with discovering all the things they may not yet know they are.

A Who, unlike a What, has more Where's than it inhabits, or When's that can be remembered. The Where of a Who seldom satisfies determinate location; the When's of a Who do not always have a particular Where. But they always have an anywhere, within which they find a somewhere, on which to map the changing times and places that Who's tend to occupy in order to affirm, within a particular sojourn, the entity that they sometimes are: "I am the one, my dear, you have looked for all these years; let me, after we have talked awhile, lead you to the barricades—or my rumpled bed."

We were sitting on the dock when she sang our song before the ship began to sail—
to where I did not know or care. I never knew what she called herself, and I remember only moments of how rough the journey was—and nothing about the place that we
in passing came to.

The answer to "When?" is an easy one for What's: Just look at the calendar and mind the clock. The world goes by in two-step time—which can be fudged a bit to accommodate an early bid. The When of a Who, however, is more quicksilver. When did it happen that I spurned my sweetheart for the Jezebel across the river? It began in the genetic protocal of the egg and sperm that I was born from, and as things go, it is still happening—as I write it here and now, and whenever I buy plums to give as sweets to another Who who hesitates as she passes by.

We then, as I tell it, are caught in this ménage-a-quatre of Who, What, Where, and When. All participants in this performance vie for dominance—for a leading role in the theatre of success, remembrance, and pleasure. That such acrimony in casting will not end until the death of language, should show that there is no hope (except in the self-sufficient realm of Forms—in which When's and Where's are kept around as comic relief) for a coming together of truth, beauty, and their reasons, within a mutual and transparent reading.

This leaves us with Why. To ask "Why?" is usually a manegeable question if we just want information: We look it up, ask an expert, or wait for further advances in technology. These are procedures familiar to What's—it gives them what they want to know—they already have the reasons.

If, however, we bare our faces and ask the existential "Why?" (Why, O Lord, am I smitten. . .? Why is my brother taller. . .? Why did she run away with Ralph. . .?) then we are in the territory of Who's—where a Why never has an answer, but must nevertheless be asked —if only to clarify the content of a barely choate need.

ALLEGIANCES

Who's and What's are the ancestors of Mind and Brain.
They each have done their time in the stockade—
accused of trying to pervert or overturn the natural order.
The first is a sin found mainly in the soul.
The second is a crime committed by the body.

You can be hanged by the neck or denied tenure for such infractions,
unless you are astute enough to anticipate a change in governance.
Then you can watch your adversaries in turn be humbled
by the consequences of their historically objective errors.

As I am too old to err, I pledge my allegiences to my Who and its admirers.
This is not to say the material world does not exist—only that it can be pushy.
Who's are of a mind to let the flowers bloom in tandem with unplanted grass.
The competition for this view is pavement—which can be disastrous to the belief
that walking is good on grass—and even better if you strain to pass
on rocks, through underbrush, and across the fast and foaming waters.
What's, however, need pavement for the fast-pass to their power-place.

It's not disastrous to dwell on old and inert categories—only boring.
What's—however much their lowers tell their uppers to be Who's,
will not meet with any one or two up-front—and seldom at the end.
Do you think, you What's, that by pilling down your pains and
acquiring every costly bauble, this world will be more knowable?
You should know that knowing brings unknowings with it.
There is no finality to this—only a ranging rage of controversy which,
if engaged in with a modest grace, could lead you back to pleasure.

INTERSECTIONS

At an older time and in another place, I wrote a story which has a similar content to this—namely—the division of people into opposing categories according to their behaviors, beliefs, bodily characteristics, sexual interests, social status, political connections, eating habits, wealth, ancestry—and so forth. I called it "Crooked and Straight." The categories, I present here —"What and Who"—also also offer distinctions regulating our recognition of and attitude towards people. By bringing the two together (as I do below) I project the hope (a long shot, true) that such overtness might give some reasons given for wars, subjugations, intolerances, prejudices—and so forth —impetus for re- examination and, perhaps, change. It is why I name this chapter" Intersection."

Categorizing people, it may be objected, can be an immoral as well as a conceptually flawed endeavor: Categorization is often looked upon as imprisonment without cause—more based on fashion, prejudice, and power, than on empirical criteria. Actually, I agree with this—categories are always ripe for overturning—but also for reforming. A world described by a category—free language, however, is an inchoate notion.

Categorization —whether done formally or in-passing—is one of the basic linguistic functions. Nothing is immune from such imposition. Everyone is" an x" or" the y." Such designations follow from birthing-place to school-hall, from marriage-bed to after-life. You are something other than just you in the board-room, living-room, hospital-bed, bedroom, and even in the peopleless-void where you would go to avoid all this—but where (you find) that a specification of" yourself" is still given to you by you.

There evidently is no " you-pure" (without you). You are multiple—identified and packaged through (changing) categorical identities—which are the" story of your life." Categorization is the story-teller of human consciousness. It also is the bell-weather of historical change.

To return to the intersection of schemata I propose above: I submit that we are all children of the Straights and Crookeds—although the battles between us show few signs of abating. If you are unsure as to which side you're on—look behind you. But remember that categories—even at their most adamant—are like the changing landscapes of mountains, sky, and water. Be grateful for new perspectives—for time has the proclivity to dissolve old categories and a capacity for creating new ones. Don't be surprised, however, if any new incarnation is not to your present liking.

The prophets of progress sing that the resolution of all conflicts is just around the corner—dialectic gives to time its determinate content. But in our time, such prophetic chants cannot long remain in simple plain-song. Look around! Young curiosity will soon fold simple opposition into the tantrums of rap—or, if teleology is still with us—the new complexities of neo-counterpoint (thank you Miles and Monk)—or music as attended noise (thanks to you Varese and Cage). These, et-al, will push the songs along.

I have travelled through some lands contested by hostile factions—they do not engage in war right now, but they still throw stones when twilight makes recognizing friends more difficult—and disagreement more easy. I was younger when I made these journeys, and was more fascinated by differences in the changing costumes of taste, shape, sound, smell, feel, than I was in polemical disputes. Also, I was gratified by the evidence of composite minglings—a more subtle set of changes—even as grievous enemies to the idea of change continued to emerge. Back then it was harder (unless you got real close) to determine which passer-by was a Straight or a Crooked—or some of both—and would or not be waiting, when you turn the corner, for someone more or less like you.

After living eighty years or so, and despite my early influences—I was born and nurtured simple-straight—I have always been inclined to swerve. From childhood, I have had crooked proclivities—as is still evidenced by my interest in curves, birds, and unstable people. Recently, I went again to those still-contentious lands where I was born—just to see how it is now—but I couldn't really tell the changes from the aberrations. I am back now—a little tired from the trip—and I find changes around me that one could live with—if they were not so prevalent, and so intent on being aberrations.

So, in defence, I sit—and consider vectors : Looking back, I see that the straightest roads were once those that everyone in power took. Looking forward, I expect that straight roads, however continuous with the old, will be avoided. But wouldn't you know it, few of my friends will listen. They say that" road"—as a metaphor for belief or purpose—is boring. I reply: Don't you want (deserve) to know the best way to get there? Conundra are boring too, they say!

I now see that many of my old-time buddies in the market-place, one-time scratchers at insurgence and disheveled seekers of excess, have gone straighter than even geometry can provide. They now insist—for hallowed reasons they won't reveal—that they are enemies of the Crookeds.

One cure for obstinacy, is complexity. So here, I again take up the other schema explored earlier in this writing—that between Who's and What's—between external and

internal ways of correlating self and world. I now propose to bring the two schemata together—not just as explanation—but to reveal some hidden fruits of complexity. To be fruitfully imposed upon one another (confront, dispute, confer, conciliate) the two must run, not parallel—but at right-angle intersection with each other. The aim, here, is to show the possible locations (degrees of intersection) of actual grades of belief.

The Intersection of Crooked-Straight with What-Who

	WHAT		WHAT	
S		8		C
T		7		R
R		6		O
A	I	5	II	O
I		4		K
G		3		E
H		2		D
T		1		
8 7 6 5 4 3 2	1	0	-1 -2 -3 -4 -5 -6 -7	-8
S		-1		
T		-2		C
R		-3		R
A	IV	-4	III	O
I		-5		O
G		-6		K
H		-7		E
T		-8		D
	WHO		WHO	

In referring to the diagram—notice the following. (If not, you can skip the following.)

I install the intersection of the two schemata through an equal subdivision of a square along its vertical and horizontal axes—which delimits the field by generating four equal quadrants—and thus gives us four subject categories: Reading clockwise from the upper left, we have a territorial population distribution of (I) Straight What's; (II) Crooked What's; (III) Crooked Who's; (IV) Straight Who's.

But the purpose of this schema is not merely an illustration of position, but a dynamics as regards change: It allows for successive degrees of convergence between the opposing populations—thus indicating that their extremes are plotted to hybridize as they approach the opposing quadrants.

To show this, I assign numerical values (8 to 0 to -8) along both the vertical and horizontal axes separating the four quadrants. This gives us 16 points for plotting convergence between each of the two systems. As an example—using the notation StCr for Straight Crooked—a reading along the StCr axis of +6, indicates a pattern strongly affirming doctrinal Straight beliefs—while that of -1 indicates a tendency to compromise with a small emphasis on Crooked (flexible) beliefs.

Along the other axis, I use the notation WtWo for What Who. Correspondingly, a reading on the WtWo axis of —5, shows a clear but still-partial affirmation of a Who (subjectivist) attitude, while a reading of +7 indicates a strongly contrary (objectivist) What attitude.

Such readings can also be understood as points on a scale of purity (+8) to admixture (0) to contrary purity (- 8). Note, however, that this delineation (8 to 0 to -8) is not fixed; it can be numerically increased or decreased—depending on the precision in attribution that is desired, or possible.

Bringing the two systems together vastly increases the potential for (and dangers of) categories using numerical designations in identifying character traits. But, if not taken too literally, these may sharpen our acuity in making the distinctions we must make to separate out the entities that compose our designated world.

Consider the example: The intersection of [StCr—2, WtWo—3]. This points to a moderately private introspective individual—while [StCr + 2,WtWo + 3] shows a moderately aggressive public individual. But then consider more extreme distributions, as: [StCr + 8,WtWo + 8].

This fits a fanatic with doctrinal obsession but little actual regard for the people to whom the imperatives are directed; while [StCr +8, WtWo -8] fits a fanatic greatly interested in the effects his dictates would have on the lives of its recipients. Another set of extremes—but on the opposite side: [StCr + 8,WtWo -8] suggests a self-righteous libertine, while [StCr - 8, WtWo + 8] suggests an opportunistic politician. Then there is [StCr 0, WtWo 0] where no-one (living) wants to be.

The specifics of any such attributional scheme have characteristics that are both complex and may be patently unquantifiable. This does not mean that the undertaking is worthless—only that the intercession of fiction and poetry—the distaff sides of" Mind"—must be brought into play before a subject actually emerges from a given attribution.

My previous narratives surrounding What and Who—and the ones that continue on with Crooked and Straight—give some such distaff materials with which to fill in—or flesh out—the categorical structure I offer here.

But then, you are free to introduce personages and events to these categories—however they show up—even if they don't easily, or consistently, or dependably, match their designations. Attend (as you yourself see fit) to the prolix possibilities of Mind as it bypasses Brain to make common cause with Spirit—or as it refutes Spirit to find shelter from the infinite with Brain: Indulge your loves (most always); skewer your foes (the weaker ones); ignore those (as best you can) who do not live in your world; bad-mouth those (if you must) whom you despise for reasons you need not divulge; avoid the ones (when you dare) who are young and have good lawyers. Be free to change your mind as the world changes (yes, you must be free).

To return to my story: I recently came upon a club across town that caters to a variety of ecumenical folk—who call themselves "The Crookeds." They party well! Why choose a single way to go, they sing, when one can do the double trouble, and play it too—at once sashaying with a crooked gait, while standing straight when you are still. What with life so short, and worthwhile goals all near in mind but yet so far from hand—why not try a cosmic combination where-in you will both succeed and fail—die and be immortal. All you need to do is avoid adamant conviction. While doing all of this, it helps to bend and sway. Come—take a walk with me.

Do you not see the hills without valleys and the ponds that are neither deep nor shallow? Look both ways: There, lurking in the twilight just behind the prickle bushes are the lions and tigers and bears of olden days. But they, come now-a-days, are welcome even when they bite—for fleshly blood has a way to pass beyond its seepage of becoming into the free-flow realm of being. When the bad-snake bites, however, the blood congeals—and the poison travels through to eat your marrow and still your heart. Then what will you do with your remaining time? In that special case, you had best say to those who hover, that there are no good reasons left to live as they still do—and then you must affirm, with your remaining breath, that there are better reasons to live as you once did—until that snake got through to you.

If you are careful and ambitious, reply the passing Straights—you should, of course, at all costs avoid the irrationality of bad-snakes. But you should avoid, as well—slanted shadows, inchoate whisperings, titterings that evoke obscenity, the fleeting glimpse of naked thigh, and non-Euclidian geometry. These are the signposts of evil in-our-time. Your slightest interest in one or other will cause the demons to pull you down before you have reached retirement age. And demons, for ancient reasons, also choose that innocent moment when you have stepped off the straight-away onto some beguiling patch of dewy grass, and you are happily wetting yourself between the toes. But other demons—the younger ones—are more creative, They might choose instead, that leisured time when signs are good and you wade further through the softly swaying reeds—and, while watching minnows, you see the limbs of wantons moving in the water—then you're gone.

Such visions (the Straights will say)—whether by the shore, during the morning shower, or in your night-time solitary bed—have perilous consequences. Realize that they are contributions from the demons of infernal theatre to the script that defines your essence when it is most captive to your appetites. If you relish appetitic-essence, these demons will bake a cassoulet so plump and fully fashioned that, when finally you are stuffed, you will be content to just rest there, not thinking, never praying, farting along with friends. But then, after the last gas has passed, and all the friends are gone—you will be alone again, emptier than before, in the moonlight that shows only a coruscation of dead leaves.

Using my now-crooked breath, I say back: Look to yourself—you scold. You put my (to you) unseemly passing together with such devotion—not omitting a single word—that I am tempted to offer you (through my own designated God) the fate you assign to me—and take for myself what you think is rightly yours. Then I will patiently suffer the wispy clouds of dull, chill, abstemious, salvation that should float me far above the burning, fuming, yet eternally hopping flesh, that will (surprised?) be yours.

But in the meantime, scold-o-mine, you might think further upon the resilience of evil—not so much as exhibited in me—but in the configurations that appear to show the nature of all there" Is"—beyond the" Seems," that is.

For example, there is the notion that a straight line is the mark of the Devil. This, of course, is found in the program of our older Crookeds. They ask us to consider that the posture of a striking snake is a straight-line (moving, to be sure) just before it bites. But after—its purpose having been attained—the snake reverts to the crooked-coil that it had been before you stumbled and disturbed its search for little furry things—so it had to bite you instead. A mistake for the snake, you might reply. The snake has spent its venom and not got food—and you (incidentally) are getting dead. A straight line, then—in this practical sense—is a failed assault, a mere mistake—not harmful to the category.

But in a theoretical sense, I continue, the snake's straightness is also a shallow way to address a complex question: To ask" what is the meaning of life" should be answered by how fully we live it—and that in turn, entails the divergent factors we are willing to learn from. Snakes cannot do this—they just bite, lay eggs, and produce other snakes that bite. But you who could—straight friend of mine—don't want to—(live fully, that is). Your full is my empty, you say? Enough! We're in this together—till book's end.

Imagine the spokes of a particular wheel that is moving and turning. Its direction is erratic, determined by occasional tiltings off the vertical of straight and narrow into all sorts of diagonals and, yes, occasional horizontals. A flawed wheel—the Straights will call it—caused by the caprice of chance, human weakness, or the will of God. Crookeds prefer a different explanation: Straights, they insist, leave out too many of life's tilts and swerves, and instead, try to convince the undecided that never falling—by assiduously avoiding the what-not of moisty glens and hidden valleys, will make the straight-path safer—if not (in its earthly time) more enjoyable to traverse. But for the Crookeds, such probity puts off the advent of pleasure until the (uncertain) eternity of after-death. The Straights, however, will continue to maintain that this later pleasure is the real pleasure—

Heavenly Bliss, as they call it—certainly worth waiting for.

Such a dispute can be confusing to both sides: Consider the recent Sunday sermons by our new minister who says he tries to demonstrate (with fulsome anecdote) the practices of evil—so as to fix them as negatives in our minds. He is much taken, as he admitted at Friday's communal dinner, by the spectacle of Bosch's sinners rent and rendered by fearsome lizards. (He also likes to consider, in detail, the torments of Saint Agatha). Some parishioners have objected. They say his hidden purpose is pornographic, and that representations of evil can themselves be evil, for they cast a too-revealing light on what should remain forever hidden—out of mind and away from the frailties of body and the consequent vulnerability of soul. Even some of my crooked friends agree. In the evenings—in atonement—they bring out their old collections—tattered magazines and fragile film-strips that display the sounds and pictures, the lamentations and writhings of old evil—which, however artfully conceived and faithfully rendered, will bring us nothing—they say—but obsession with new evil.

Away—we will together cry!
As the clear crow discards the gloomy night
and flies into the morning sun,
so must you and I avoid the pricks and poesies
of both satanic and pietistic porno-graphy.
And we take with us only those who fit
into the sack of enlightened affirmation—
anticipating, as we should, celestial adulation.

But this does not always satisfy the peace process: Someday, say the straightest, evil will assuredly come back. But confronting it—as you can see beneath the rictus of my soon dead once deadly face—are the spare weapons—the rigorous demands of consistency, abstemiousness, and righteous anger. I got there, I did—I got to the gates of Heaven—unlike those crooked-snookered souls who say they also journey there—but hit every motel en route. My way, in contrast, however calumniated by the opposition as boring and too-narrow is, I assure you, on the right side of the ancient direction that shows (to those willing to see) the real road to eternal bliss.

So, dear my kiddies, don't listen to the dirty stories of that misbegotten preacher. (I suspect that he's a Crooked's plant). You must instead be clear about the way you want to go. It's getting to be your time now—you are older—it's around that time to proceed to the beginning of the end—what with your shiny faces and firm impassioned tread.

But what is it I hear? After all my teachings, you are not quite ready? Speak louder and come into the bright light. Yes, oh yes, I can see the quivering of too-early fatty cheeks, the blinking bloodshot eyes, the flaccid pudgy limbs—none of which bodes well for a commitment to direct ascent. Too bad. So sad.

But, well—you are allowed (these later days) to be afraid of true-belief. Neither the world nor I (and I say this to you in strict confidence) really knows the right direction of the Straight-of-Ways. Too-firm belief on this score has been the very devil for our given mandate—and it makes a muddle of our attempts to pin down the self-evident path of righteousness. But times do change—although true belief of course should not.

Yet, I do fear: Rather than seeing you succumb to the greater evil of non-belief (often caused by the excessive rigors of true-belief) I say to you: If you just can't stand it here (sometimes I can't either) there is a different path which, in its unseemly way, claims the same rights of origin and final goal as we do. They call themselves the Crookeds—in contrast, as you know, to our calling ourselves the Straights.

Although the distinction is more a difference of practice than doctrine, you can spot a Crooked easily. They are less steadfast in bearing than we (they being mostly fat and often short and easily winded). They eat too much—and they are, in principle, accommodating in theory but sneaky in their politics—not a categorically pure imperative anywhere in their heads.

In fairness I must admit that, despite their flat feet, and the sweet-and-sour smell of their ambivalence about distinctions, they too are bona-fide members of our most-comprehensive club of aging oldies which, for various ideological, historical, and prudential reasons, has recently (at a meeting in Austin) named itself " The Straights and the Crookeds." But some members, as always, are calling for another meeting.

When pressed, the faction to which I once belonged describes the term" straightness" as indicating directness, clarity, abstemiousness. It does this to confirm its claim to the best seats in Heaven. The other faction calls itself the "Crookeds"—which (to them) connotes multi-directionality rather than deformity. They do not see themselves as irretrievably (or even slightly) deviant—certainly not as is sometimes insinuated by the most pointy-nosed of Straights. It's just that they have a different way to go.

Crookeds react to accusations of their way-wardness by insisting that Straights should seek a middle ground between doctrinal inflexibility and directionless relativism. They also insist that they be counted as members of the loyal opposition which, while not agreeing with all decisions, yet did contribute—when war with the Shapeless-Formless seemed inevitable—to the cadences of the Long March.

If you are interested, my dears, in taking this more devious route, you can find the dwelling place of Crookeds by crossing the street directly in front of our old church, and then bearing left. Those folks have built a new and shiny temple, whose outer courtyard includes a coffee-shop that serves European blends and sinfully exotic pastries. If you go further back inside, sweet-smelling smoke celebrates a barbeque emporium which, they insist, provides the best ribs to be found this side of non-belief.

But my advice to try them out—I must tell you —has generated trouble for me at our temple. Listen to the comments of my peers: "balderdash, poppycock, blasphemy and bullshit" is the cry—even from my dearest friends among the Straights. "These Crooked leftist rascals," they say to me,"to which you would so blithely send our children, will soft-sell their hedonistic ways and promote a no-sweat path to get to where we, through our efforts to make the Straights more narrow, and the Crookeds Straight, refuse to take. We—not they—are headed directly to the only source of purity and righteousness."

But, here, I disagree with my friends. A needed reformulation of ancient verities always brings criticism—particularly from the old folks of worn belief. But there is hope: Just look up the road, I tell them—there are no Narrow Straights to be seen out in the suburbs—except for those still living near the trail-head that leads toward the stagnant bogs that reek of that old-dead smell. If you are interested in sadness, it's worth a trip to talk with those forlorn creatures. But after days of dry and musty natter, you may ask yourself why anyone would choose to face the mosquitoes and the muck and mire of narrow choice —without the consolations of barbeque and poetry?

In contrast to constant mortification, the Crookeds offer alternatives (such being their stock-in-trade) that are flexible and up-to-date. The main exit from the Krooked-Klub Motel is a well-paved, recently-marked road. If you decide to go that way, you will find that it eventually merges (yes it does) with a cross-country super-highway.

But let's pull back a bit. I may, for fairness' sake, have over-vilified the opposition. Actually, it doesn't really matter which road you take. You'll eventually get to where you need to go. But be careful. Take particular note of the friction factor in your decisions on both belief and travel. The Narrow-Straights seek out roads that go interminably up-hill, and they are often undermined by the painful rubbings of bunions and dry penance. The better lubricated Crookeds don't do pain well—and will cry for help even before it hurts. And this especially if things get too uncomfortable between dogma and interpretation, and the food runs out.

But in the long run, roads do cross. Caravans that came from opposite directions in the early times, found companionship in places where only strangers used to meet. So it was with the Straights and Crookeds who reached the juncture where unbelievers would not venture. They first came for mutual protection, and then to sit and eat together—of course, much else followed. Some still attribute such meetings to coincidence—but if shown the old photographs, they will recollect sharing beds and trading goods. For are not we and they—the wise ones on both sides say—really of the same persuasion? Not quite—not yet—but it could be so with some more work.

Sadly, the wanted union has not yet come. It's an old story: The Straights are dualists. For them, there is a never-ending war between good and evil. Evil, even in disguise, has no access to true belief, because the acrid smell that identifies the source of evil (despite the new detergents and perfumes) has remained undiminished throughout eternity.

Evil—the narrowest of the Straights insist—is the other to everything that should be, and it fills its eternal time by chewing on the out-lying shoulders of the narrow way so as to make it rife for falling. No problem, the broader Straights reply (they are more familiar with the geography of evil)—we always lose a few, but it doesn't happen often.

Evil was once considered absolute—by Straights of every persuasion—but when looked at within the wider swings—and styles—of recent times, some evils (in good faith) might be shunted into the more malleable context of the merely undesireable. Once there, freed from the onus of the truly diabolical, evil can be further nudged to where what was once sinful will be swept into the outermost rings of respectability—the suburbs of the Good.

The Crookeds, while they do not deny the presence of evil, yet do not regard it as absolutely other. They are not dualists, but monists—for them, all oppositions eventually become one. The spiral is their alternative to the straight and narrow, for unlike its single-minded competitor, the spiral has expanding latitude within which to envelop different interests within its swirl. It is also less direct—less brutal—more accomodating—more gracious—a shape to party with.

All this comes slowly, mind you, as in the digestion of a big snake's catch. Evil can fulfill the needs of a new world-view by diminishing its contrast with the Good. In this transformation, evil divides into positions of varying, even contradictory, schools of malfeasance: Necessary evil becomes contingent—in keeping with the transcendent good which turned absolute obedience—as it opened up—to prudence.

According to the grand plan of the Crookeds—when evil is brought into the subtleties of discourse about right and wrong and in-be-tween—and its proponents exposed to pedicures and steam baths—it will (never completely but increasingly) shed the scaly skin of intimacy with its Satanic source. Crookeds want to smooth things out—to make evil into an energizing variant—a gadfly of the stationary Good. This way makes evil into a player—a participant in the next stage of forming a better (more enlightened) Good.

But this is wearying: Goodness knows where the Good resides. Kant hypothesizes only a good will—as achieved through a self-examining measure that provides, but cannot mandate, a universal for moral action. Schopenhauer holds instead that will is destructive and yet all-pervasive, but must in any case be overcome—in order for individuals to achieve an a-historical goodness. If you are so inclined, he says, listen to music—it's all there without the pain. Hegel thinks that Good comes out best in the end—where it corresponds to the final achievement of Spirit. But in this achievement—without the solace of flesh, or art, or even religion—only philosophy and mind are left. And what kind of solace is that?

For uncommitted travelers (and philosophobes), the road to follow that gets you to goodness presents a real conundrum. There are the dark trails in the forest, with demons twittering in the bushes. Finding your way can lead to enervating wallows, full of biting insects and suffocating slime. Fleeing up the hill, however, exposes one to brambles and unrelenting heat—not to mention unsettling glimpses of retired show-girls who live in trailers perched on patches of high but barren land. Some of these now saggy beauties can still give a good semblance of kicking up a heel or two—but they will not leave the sunlight (even for you) because they prefer its warmth to dank and stingy crotches. After all they've been through, they say, sunburn is no problem—and they've come to like the smell of yesterday waiting for tomorrow's repast in the sun.

Yet, all these are ways of arriving at a destination—that most comprehensive place of getting-there. But where? Certainly not anywhere! So why choose there? Wait! Calm down! We should agree—if we want at all to play—that there is an acceptable there for all of us somewhere. So, after the many centuries of across-aisle scowling, the Straights and the Crookeds came to agree that they share the objective of going to that essential-quintessential somewhere—the Place of Good—the Form of Beauty—the Body of Truth.

Evidently—all going is going somewhere—one-or-another way. The going that the Straights propose is a long-hard-way, and as one grows older, the legs tend to soften and we lose balance—the requisite development requires a stable admixture of crookedity and straightitude. The rest of us, however—whatever shape we're in—may take comfort: There are, as with martinis, many styles of travel—generated by long debates over purposes and ingredients. A martini, evidently, is not simply gin and ice—there must be the civilizing presence of vermouth (just a few drops) and a salutary consideration of garnishes—olive, lemon twist, pearl onions—to encourage our having more than one.

So maybe you'll be carried there.

There have been some ancient and a few recent clashes between our factions. But do you not remember the times when skinny scarred and stiff-limbed Straights would wander through the outside dark—sniffing at the chic and well-fed effluence that coats the gestures of their crooked adversaries?

Then there were the nights—some others might remember—when the coiffed and softly rounded Crookeds, normally reliant on an all-volunteer army, but suffering from their pent-up need for penetration without words—turn on the front-hall lights. At which time the spare and bony Straights—attracted like moths to the zapper—will foresake both envy and vituperation, and mutely acquiesce to the giving and getting of a four-hand massage.

At history's end, all such frolics are forgiven. When the journey's over, each side, without penalty, can inhale the vapors that emanate from the other side. The young and curious who were conceived along the way, might want to combine these ancient fragrances and arrive at a new scent which greets them when next they come together.

This scent, centuries in the making, is indeed an admixture of new prurience and old hatreds. But it also exemplifies the irresistible waft and taste of communal barbeque. Oh, how those tips and slabs, first dry-rubbed and then well-mopped, can smell after hours of slow smoking. This is our modern contribution to the loaves and fishes that are a celebration of ecumenity.

We begin our celebration by stretching the plumpest of the Crookeds, brushed lightly with a red-wine and tomato marinade (adding a bit of oregano and some garlic) upon the grill of penitence. Heavy groans and sub-rosa pleadings emerge—asking to do them till they're finished. Then we throw on the rinsed-off Straights, slathered with honey, cumin, and hot pepper. When, on the brink of browning they start singing, they are mixed together with the chubbies in a comprehensive menage of fragrant flesh and willing bone. Deep squeals and diminishing denials; serial stroking in negotiation with spasmodic shyness. A full chorus! The caterwauls that sound till late at night are orchestrated by the contrapuntal logic that reveals the inadequacies of separate voices—which, if left to only sing their selfish tunes would never know what can be sounded in an all-together that discards the need for separate styles.

If you are still concerned with missing-out (or opting out)—consider that the standpoint of eternity is not always critical of a lost campaign. Failure in a good cause is usually due to overreaching, but the debris of failure need not be discarded—it can be sorted out for valuable artifacts. The shards of great failures are, after all, testimonials of fervent trying. Eternity (unlike modernity) is quite benevolent—even though ecumenicity is a political not a formal art, and does not flourish without some historical gestures toward completeness.

Slow-smoked barbeque assiduously basted, is where we all should come together at road's end. All conflicts about the Greater Good, whether they start in the head or gut, and however much they are separately meant to reveal another's sinful ways, are, when pressed, like pomegranates giving forth their seeds—too many to count and no good way to eat them all.

So the philosophical attempt to create certainty continues without fail, to fail. What would adjudicating between the appetites and beliefs of Straights and Crookeds come to? Is it the dry rub, the slow smoker, the careful aging, or the winy marinade that gives the best taste when the rib is offered for its eating. Does our patience and taste sometimes falter in mid-cooking—and we reach impatiently for the secondary sausage, the sides of cole slaw and potato salad, and, yes, the ubiquitous pre-cooked corn? Should we not, instead, wait and have a drink or two before such leaping? The setting sun is the best time for eating barbeque—tomorrow is day enough to count the ribs.

After all these years of separation, and having glimpsed the value of the joining of the roads, no-one now needs reverting to the path of early discord. So let us, as our elders say, declare an ideological holiday. They, being old and optimistic, think that this is a good move. Also, being old, they have fewer consequences to face if they are wrong. So they instruct us cheerfully: We should begin the festivities at both the far-left and far-right of our once acrimonious bazaar—as these have traditionally been the places that foment discord. Now, reaching out to steady one-another, we will build walkways filled with promises of universal satisfaction, from which small paths branch off—each dotted by faux-grottos with pumped-up beauties in six-inch heels tempting you to buy what you do not need. Yes, a bit tasteless—but commerce, as we all know, is good for both sides.

If you can—avoid buying too much of what you cannot use—there are other ways to go: Turn again and take the path that leads uphill. You will soon hear a drone of chants inveighing against cooked flesh—whether eaten for sustenance or for pleasure. The women chanting all wear flowered skirts and plastic sandals, and distribute free handouts of veggie recipes which include cautionary tales directed to the old folks about how to avoid the fall—the last temptations of animal fat. The men go barefoot and play guitars.

If all this makes you uncomfortable—continue walking. There are other paths that will lead you back downhill to where you can find a different cuisine: In a large hut made of rattan and straw, women smelling of fresh perspiration offer trays of felafel and egg-rolls that cohabit shamelessly with offerings of jerked goat, fried ants, and smoked eel. The men are hairy and laugh a lot. In the center, there is an inviting sit-down place with a full menu of couscous, garlic-sauce, lamb-shanks—and, from 6 to 10 pm, tattoed belly dancers. When you've eaten your fill, go further down the road. You will find an area, somewhat hidden by leafy brush and pungent smoke, where one-time flower-children—now mostly in their forties—veterans of the wilder days of civil disobedience—relive their best-of-times. They speak in parables and smile a lot.

But if, instead, you veer down and to the right—be cautious! There are other roads, privately owned, with hidden cameras, that lead to nowhere anyone would want to go. These are the scary ways—far away from the optimistic, albeit still-contentious pathways of both left and right. It may be —yes, could be—that the intrusion of such dangerous roads into our privileged times, signals an end to the very notion of right direction. For why should one take a road that goes to nowhere—to where one will not exist—except that going nowhere might (just might) feel better than continuing on the obligation-laden path to somewhere.

Reason's imperative these days is so enmeshed in destination that it generates few wondrous findings—such as (chosen at random) the Eternal Form of Non-Being in cohabitation with the contingent form of being. Wonder, which over centuries has been the devoted companion of progress, is now estranged. Both, as a consequence, are in danger of mindless dilution. Progress has become the incessant drumbeat of unnecessary commerce. Wonder which, like a single-malt scotch, once went down with spirit and roaring—now offers nostalgia but only little bite. I myself, these days, do penance with cheap wine. But now that wonder and progress have separated, wonder should not—even when it leads to dangerous places—be diluted by nostalgia for the nostrums of progress.

RECONCILIATIONS

How is it, despite all categorical conflicts, that we still want to find a reconciliation?

There are openings which encourage ontologically ambitious daredevils to move between the worlds of sense and sensibility—between their What and their Who—deciding that they are either Crooked or Straight before they learn the manner (get the feel) of reconciliation. Nostalgia is an ancient remedy for bruises to the brain and inadequacies of mind—it is a folk remedy, an age-old salve for painful bifurcations. Nostalgia also wakes old memory—of a sea that once parted and opened a path to the opposing shore—which blessed way allowed the worthy to come across to their salvation—only to be disappointed, yet again, by a farther sea to cross.

The lone and level sands you see, eventually
end in another sea—but don't despair.
The troops are in the brambles, slaughtering the heathen.
The king is in his counting house, attending to the tally.
The queen is in the parlor, receiving pricks and honey.
God is in His Heaven, planning Armageddon.
Beasts are in the armory, devising crueler weapons.
I leave this paragraph to search for better leaven.

Imagine a world in some undivided past where the good-folk celebrate the union of once separate identities—the coming together of tribes and the diminishing fear of incest. That world and this are not incompatible—but traveling between the two, across a non-parting sea, is indeed precarious. Be careful of the battering of the ancient waves —they will suck you down! Look ahead instead, and ask the elements (they are eternal and should know) which players in this contest between mind and brain have already won the game? The winners are the ones (check it out) who embrace the historical strategy of "no contest." The mind, when under-nourished, runs out of solace; the well-fed but indifferent brain prefers action to communion.
For the latter—winning is better. But either way you play the game, you lose: Maintaining the separation between mind and brain evokes the distinction between thought and things—between descriptions and the world. But

denying that distinction puts our (sometime) cherished attributes of introspection and imagination into the unfeeling hopper of stimulus-response. Translating, for example, from the impasse between mind and brain once prevalent on the continent, is the following: "Der Konflikt zwischen Geist und Gehirn" where "Gehirn" is brain, and "Geist" can be understood as "spirit" as well as "mind." This is a skirmish that precedes the later 20th century battle: "Der Konflikt zwischen Kunst und Leben"—art and life—representation and reality.

All such conflicts start, so says Meister Ekhardt, with the medieval skirmish: "Der Konflkt zwischen Dasein und Istigkeit"—existence and essence—Aristotle vs. Plato.

So you see, duality continues (is always with us) as the goad to ongoing war. It is a war based on the need for a totality—choosing one wing from among any of the polar oppostites you pick, and relegating the others to the scorn and the penalties for being both inaccurate and unfashionable.

Peace (maybe even "perpetual peace") is based, I suggest, on the acceptance of—not only "duality," but "multi-alities"—as the new path to Enlightenment. The old path foundered on a lack of attention to the anxiety in such parables as: "et in Arcadia, ego," or "waves or particles." These parables do not predict victory for the powerful, or species ascendent. Instead, they are symbols of a need for harmony between worlds based on the (trans-world) realization that war is hell—and that its feverish rationales eventually find their way into the catologue of historical error.

Choosing a particular language for reality is committing an attack of linguistic supervenience—and so, by extension, injuring the compliants of the victim languages.

"Brain-talk" is welcome in the peaceable kingdom—but not when it asserts its primacy in deciding between the inhabitants. The same, to be fair, must also hold for "mind-talk."

People on either side seldom understand the language they deride. Yet for appearance sake (the show of well-roundedness) they will often dip a toe into foreign waters. But this is risky: Brainers might prefer Mantovani to Vivaldi; and mindists may confuse scientology with science. Then, what do we disinterested expatriates say?

CODICIL

Shadrach, Meshach, Abednigo.
Each has much to offer to the other.
Satchmo sings the story.

Shad is authoritative on May-Day marches.
Mesh is prescient about the Ides of March.
Abed is expert on the rhetoric of contumely.
All are familiar with the Fiery Furnace.

So you see:

The dialectic has been germinating early.
It started about the time when time began.
The three-form provides ways-out passages
when two-form thought becomes
too sticky-set and static—
using only local edicts for its rhetoric.

Our heroes are three instead of two.
Each was born at break of day—years apart, some say.
But they are, or can be, brothers.

That is:

If they shed their skins of clashing color,
renounce the disfigurements of servile certainty,
and avoid the wounds that come with mindless valor.

SOUL

Speaking of the soul can indeed be poetry, but that does not exclude it as a way of telling truths about (us in) the world. Soul need not be a theological scold; it is rather good company when it is offered as an enriching collusion—rather than collision—with the mind.

This is a worthwhile offer because it provides movement—if not a present solution—for the political impasse between mind and brain. Such movement should become triadic if it is to divert the present war of all against all into a framework of even fragile peace. To do this, it must propose new directions for all three—brain-mind-soul—in the hope for an enriching trade between their individual worlds.

Mind and soul have often been lumped together as a superfluous category in the analysis of brain function. But they neither are the same nor are they necessarily hostile to each other. Nor is either hostile to the workings of the brain. The mind mimics the universe in it's expansiveness. There is no limit to what we—individually and historically—can think. There are no logical safeguards that can obviate the varieties of reference and image in thought—nor are there neural explanations that show or predict the origins, cogency, and consequences of what we think about. I suggest that brain function is not mind function. The first is system building—indefinitely large, yet constrictive according to its rules. The second is expansive—bound only by circumstances that we are never entirely aware of. The brain can be mapped for its location of bodily functions. But it does not have a place for the location of "personality." We can (statistically) predict what we (all) will do—but the changes in our individual sentiments are not the same as, say, the diagnosis and cure of an organic abnormality.

The soul has a special place: It is a conceit of ecumenical promise—it is the great peacemaker. Let me give this a poetic transference: Soul is firmly for the mind to the extent that the mind is firmly in the brain. Soul is (partakes of—leavens) both.

A secret pact seems to be afoot! Soul and brain together, in serious negotiation with the mind, can present a strategy towards mitigating the uncertainties and impasses that afflict each separately! Mind, in this pact, does not have to choose exclusive alliance with either soul or brain. We may agree that mind is a phenomenon of brain, but this is only to say that the fully explained brain will take some time (don't wait) to account for all that mind can be about. The soul is the faculty of offering continuity between historical efforts at explanation; it encourages the transformation of the residue that bubbles up between explanations into a narrative of becoming—the first premonition of a new idea, the psychic itch that cannot yet be thought, the first indication that not all is well—these are the contents of what I call the soul.

Appetites, ambitions, loves and hates, are indeed rooted in both mind and body—good and evil is there, ugliness and beauty too—as are ideals, pledges of allegiance, blasphemies and travesties of justice—as well as the ordinary mindful or mindless acts of living. Also present is the notion—given through a categorical ascent but with doctrinal disguises—that everything located in the mind and body is in the soul as well. If we want to be stubbornly empirical and insist that all this containing is only to be found in the brain, we forsake the richness of the soul and its ecumenical task. Then mind, having lost a friend, leaves in a huff—and we are back to partisan strife.

IDEALS

A ski-jumpress suffers trauma
(ruptures, tears, with no workable repairs)
to the tendons of her knees, her ankles,
only sparing her pink embooted toes.

But I don't much care about her healing.
For jumping, I prefer a languid poetess
with creamy thighs and almond eyes
who, under duress and reciprocal coercion,
will tell me all the truths the world entails.
And, if further pressed —
with just those truths I need to know
to have me help her reap and sow.

When pressure fails, she can eat my cockles.
And if she's good at it, I'll pull her pigtails.
But if that briny substance is too filling,
I'll feed her softer shrimp—God willing.

Yet, to end this poem with such scatto
would not be what I mean to do.
The impulse for my writing, given what
I've done, now needs retelling.
It needs containing all those truths
that let me say I love you too.

BIFURCATION

Mind and body are a blessing when allowed to co-inhabit,
despite and notwithstanding their distinctions.
But some prefer spaghetti plain, luke warm, without distractions.
Tomato-sauce, these say, confuses clarity; and meat-balls so encumbered
hint darkly at immolation within forbidden realms of cheese and hypertension—
marked by the error of tasting goodness without concern for truth.

Watch them now, those others—obese prophets for the good—
sprawled on dunes that once were ours when God was young—
feckless slurping of bounties that the soul alone should have.
But look further, across the river, to where the rival pedants sit,
morbidly nibbling on the crust of real-truth—hoping so
to guarantee their privileged places in the protocols of death.

It would be easier for reality if empiricists were skinny—
and more suitable to cosmology if rationalists were fat.
But this has never been the case, you know.
The world is full of pudgy in-betweens.

Like hand-made chocolates in laquered boxes,
the coating hides from view the cherry, nut, and cream.
You have to bite to differentiate between a What and Who—
to find out when the taste is of a juicy Who,
or if the harder chew suggests a What.
Have another if you need to.

EARLY DAYS

Despite weekly mailings from the ministries of Who and What,
and daily importunings from both Straights and Crookeds,
I remain divided.

I once believed that art helps us find our special place by offering images of historical contention for the meaning (if not the facts) of life. But as I look back from my vantage in the morose present, all this arting is mostly pain-in-the-ass memories of allegiances to causes that (had I looked more carefully) showed themselves as spittle-stains on the chins of advocates when they declaimed (as they usually do) for the latest best-way-to-go.

When one is young and wanting, watching spittle form on bearded chins can lead to admiration and even emulation. It clearly is better to embrace a cause (however vague) than to wander the Brooklyn streets from dry twilight into foggy morning without finding an opening, not a glimmer through a shaded window, for that much-needed glimpse of pink.

Don't get me wrong. Such a deserving Who as I, wants only simple soulful things: I want anointment by multiple loves, all showing me—step by step and drop by drop, kissing deeply as we go—how to enter that world where one can be a Crooked Who, and famous too.

My chance to climb the ladder of redemption and true purpose, came through the (then) free City University of New York—where I was shown how to compare my opaque darks, however much I loved them, with others' multi-colored brights.

I became a locust in an early swarm, buzzing fitfully by day in Brooklyn—but come evening, I would join the other locusts who dared to cross the river and invade the seedy bars that then separated the Bohemian village in Manhattan's downtown from its ethnic neighbors.

Two beers in Cedar-Bar is what all night you need to buy; and for that you gain access to the latest exposition of worldly strategies affirmed by all the other boozers—art as final freedom or just-past dead—which, when assiduously adhered to, will for sure dreg up images to resolve the old (and old-world) traumas of political and stylistic change. The final reconciliation between Brooklyn, Art, and History! For two beers? What a bargain!

Also included were ad-hoc demonstrations of gesture, arrogance, and the skittish aura of immanent talent. And then there were those girls with the radical badge of hairy legs and long dank hair. Real freedom. All of us were artists—girls and boys together—sex, sexes, sexing everywhere. We danced under the penumbra of art and life—within the protection of the anticipated end of style, and the coming of a finally free art and a just society. We were told, as we whirled, that this end, this freedom, will last—if not forever (as someone said)—at least a thousand years.

BLOOD

The day before my wedding, my mother bought a jar of chicken blood
from the kosher butcher down the street.
She planned to pour it on a sheet and in the morning
flaunt it like a pennent from a war just won.
A flag to wave at unbelieving neighbors—with priapic sons
who had all been there themselves to turn the trick.

My mother said: You don't know how hard I worked.
I put down our best sheet—the linen one—to catch the blood.
I spilled it because I thought he might be small—
too small—one never knows—to bring it out of you himself.

Never mind he's short and has splayed feet.
You'll get used to that—the main thing is the basics.
You'll live in a better neighborhood than this.
And if you leave him, you'll have alimony,
a house paid off, and a child or two to comfort you.

It was the morning before my marriage
that I told her I am here because
the blue pills your doctor-cousin gave me
put me in an all-pink bubble—replete
with wine and roses, a blender and a Cadillac.
Where and when I was deflowered last I don't remember.
It might have been before a blood-stain became
the big deal it now is in Bensonhurst.
Or perhaps it was just after I was told
how much power a two-time virgin holds.

However it was or might have been, I do not know.
I must now free the remainder of my soul.
I want to live downtown and be an artist.
I want to leave red flowers on a burlap sheet,
grow long my pits and pubic hair,
put paint beneath my fingernails,
and wear sandals in the snow on Bleeker Street.

But most of all, I want, I want—
listen Ma—
I want to go.

THESE DAYS

These days—I don't much think about the early days.

But I paint a lot: Just the other year, I wrote wordy notions on my paintings, and sometimes I glued good-things over wanting splashes. Then, when all had dried and some talk between the sides began, I painted further—to see if the brushy natives, having been forced by clever invaders to hide in the tall grass, could reclaim their homeland by matching their ancient craft with the newer strengths of intruding words and glued-on photos. These intruders—some quite ancient in origin—have, through art's migration, found the courage to come across transgressive borders. Sometimes they behave like colonizers—presenting challenges to my painterly complacency. As to whether this dicy dance of sun and shadow, wet and dry, original and appropriated, can bring together the painted, photographed, and written—not to say the smelled and felt and tasted—is a question for the Who-What, seemingly straight couple that first met long ago (was it Eden?), and were told—by a perceptive angel—that they would look better together if at least one was crooked.

But through decades, centuries (or is it now millenia?) they peered critically into the clear-cracks that progressively lace the obfuscating shadows of true belief. They came slowly to believe (Adam and Eve, Venus and Adonis, Heidi and Peter—there are others) that they do look good together—even though age and changes in the weather bare the blotches, stoops, and wrinkles, that suggest the new-found form of ugliness.

The trick, I think (at least in art) is to keep them, the natives and intruders, mostly separated but occasionally assimilated—living austerely for themselves and yet, from time to time, engaged—trading mates and strategies—with each other. My own efforts go to mixing intruders with my fondest native memories, yet insisting all the while that they reveal (to each other) the secrets of their own ways. It is easy enough (for any of us) to scribble words on paintings, or paint over photographs, or paste exotic images to juice up wanting passages—all in response to the sound of hoofbeats on the up-town pavement. But if you think to make these into a happily consistent world—unsettling but believable—it gets harder.

In both art and life, the war between inhabitants and invaders has been couched in terms of style: Representation vs. abstraction, formalism vs. expressionism, fine-art vs. post-art—and also in terms of outcome: Success vs. obscurity, lust vs. love, life vs. death.

Memories of old conflicts, and strategies for winning recent wars, are a good resource for determining the acceptable parameters of one's aesthetic outreach. The extensions of the canvas, when they include a palette of memory and a need to change, become more fluid—more concerned with permeability and diffusion than with the priority or demarcation of borders.

To guard against the dangers of transient seepage (broken dykes or unregistered aliens) one must draw-up estimates that map the further limits (my limits? yours?) of bearable cohabitation, and then post warning against excessive dissonance or heedless littering. There is a difference (really) between a fecund confrontation and a casual dalliance. I used to like both—but I've changed.

We are in the here and now—my cast of characters and I. So we will enjoy our strolls—ogling and preening as if we were boulevardiers—cravat and cane—imagining the coming-together of classes, races, sexes, ages, and their (sometimes unspeakable—often enjoyable) preferences—even as we walk the changing streets that used to be the village green.

LISTENING

There is no louder listening to the ringing in my hearing
than the natter that surrounds the chatter, which in turn
transmogrifies into matter that is purportedly adequate
for evolving into cogent thought.

I was once more optimistic, listening to the natterings
that said progress will occur in time—
in its own good time and mine.

I now expect the chatter to remain in a sequestered place
and not pretend that it will lead us to that soft location
where, even now, there is a bare glimpse, a flash of flesh and
fleeting words which, if we were fast enough and nimble,
would refer us to the prized content
of which we could be confident
that God or History (I'm not sure which)
told us would be there.

That-there, after all the time and work, is where
we would want to see it—listen to it—taste and smell it—
as it is and some say was always there.

Because, soon, soon, it—assuredly—will not be there.
Not for anyone—not for us.

ART AND VALUE

It is good to enjoy art—but you know, of course you do—that artworks, whatever their inherited ambitions, have become less important than before—when they were more important than they are now. On a cloudy day, I say: These days, the best of art is in thrall to visionary architecture or to radical theatre or to forms of silence, or to calculated naughtiness. When it finally rains, I realize that we are surrounded—for all their Boom-Ba— by timid and ingratiating works which can no longer find contentious or transcendent images with which to please the Pope, or shock the Bourgeoisie. These-days artworks are everywhere abundant: Everyone I know knows an artist who makes works of art. In this way the porosity between notions of work and non-work increases—private doors become communal passages—the soul becomes a sieve—and the wanted distinctions between contrary ways are lost in the hustle of a secular and ambitious time.

Non-works—those weekaday foibles that sometimes dress up on weekend holidays as art—are now more in demand than are works that continue to seek exclusive status in the coming week or century. A non-work is something that can be found or sometimes made (by humans or by nature) and may, or may not (depending on the hour, day, and year) become art. But no matter: All distinctions are retractible—all attributions are refutable—ambition is always fungible.

Non-work works are usually made by those we know and love—the free gestures of giving and taking that bind the ties. But if our friendships sour, their donated tokens can be disposed of without guilt—just throw the knitted mittens in the dumpster where other objects—carapaces, lamps and cookies—none caring much for being art, can also be found.

As to the other (real-art art-work) kind—beware: Anything that insists on always being the same something is disturbing for these days. We no longer have a cogent critique of "always" and what such beliefs would entail—and we have lost our better ways of paying due respect to the continuum we once supposed lay before and after us. "Before us" is now anachronism—and "after us" is only speculation.

"Premonitions of immortality" is one of the more fanciful stories that artworks tell in order to be noticed. True; the term 'Artwork,' has, for a long while, had a sacred ring to it: Artworks, like "good-works" or "work-before-play" or "The Devil's-work" are important to the distinctions cherished by believers—distinctions between what is deeply meant and what simply happens. But it could be that 'art-work' is now just the wording of a solemn con-game: a guarantee (seldom honored—but often used) of safe passage between rational, accidental, and hostile worlds.

Early works, those that have survived and are now indubitably art, maintain their importance for us because they celebrate the historical accomplishments of culture: Usually of power and glory—sometimes of beauty and virtue—other times brutality and vice. But recent artworks, in this democratizing surge of our time, often want to be like ordinary folks—not much up to titles or formal celebrating, but interested in fun.

If such a notion as "good-art" still has currency in this context, its proponents must contrast the mere attainment of status (that of being "good") with those historical works that carry with them the premise of transcendent value—of "greatness:" From the first moments of their making, masterpieces strive to go beyond (often around) what is then taken as good-art—in their awesome efforts to be great. Main street, in contrast, is cluttered with good-art.

If we were to line up a few heroes of the greatness process, say: Giotto, Van Eyck, Michaelangelo, Rubens, Cezanne, Picasso—we could (with some caveats) sensibly ask the question: "Who is the greatest one of all?" But this, as a question in the context of "The Judgement of Paris," or "Cinderella," or "Ms. Universe," is evidently spurious. But it still carries with it a challenge to sensibility—if not an answer.

The hope for inclusion within the canons of aesthetic value is part of the received history of art, and is a basis (strategy) for the conjoining of art and greatness. It is located in the evolving pact between masterworks—which are always insecure in their ascendancy—and the most talented aspirants (often-time apprentices) who hope to confirm the older ones as undeniably great. Wanna-be's then join together with old-masters to form specific pathways of historical value—leading to a shared greatness in the future.

The extended script goes this way: Aspirants assure the old-ones that by acknowleging them (the young ones) as their anointed successors—they will both secure their proper places in the system of "begats" that regulates the succession of valuable art-works within the history of art and culture.

Personifying the works themselves as agents in this process, the wanted transaction can be described as follows: New works will say to the old works (of choice): Your maker was a genuine old master—this is corroborated by my emulation of the procedures that made you. We can both benefit. If we are adamant, they (my own admirers) will propose to the uncommited fledglings that follow us (get them while they're still in school) that they too should emulate the historical procedures we share, so as to become beholden to us as we are beholden to you—the old and famous ones.

In a lineage so established, the consquential procedures of an ongoing tradition can be developed—by finessing among those to incorporate and those to let go—which will make each member historically unique, and yet beholden to the others that come before and after. This continuity establishes a "Tradition-Class"—a historical sequence of style that embodies value—and so distinguishes between the successful ones and all the others. In this way, the old (masters), new (disciples), and promising (aspirants), together create a system of "begats"—a reciprocally indebted, evolving style—which ensures their mutual presence within the chronicles of great art.

The denial of the desirability—or possibility—of (continuing) to build such tradition classes, is—as I believe—a characteristic of the new art: Now, antecedents are selected for their contributions to the present agenda of novelty; descendents are those who deny, or equivocate about, any influences the others might have had; physical works increasingly become virtual (and easy to discard—or replicate) in keeping with the seductions of the moment. But there is something other than art-making at stake in Modernism : Mind requires memory; memory sifts the present into experiences we are most or least affected by; the present faces its past and future with anxiety, bravado, or indifference. This last, "indifference," is, I suggest, the present alternative to (and critic of) the notion I put forth above—of "tradition classes."

Indifference is the stance, inter-alia, of Duchamp, Warhol, and Koons. It is a criticism directed against the influence of history on the uniqueness of a particular time. The "coolness" of this stance is actually covert rage, often hidden under a show of unseemly manners, but directed against the aesthetically controlling demands of earlier art. Nevertheless, it reveals the poverty of it's own subjects—and expediently recommends avoiding consideration of subjects that still matter. What "matters" concerns the (moral—not only aesthetic) content of art at a given (say, our) time. But such mattering requires a public context of concern, and an artistic sense of vocation, that can express the range of imperatives—the difficult and contentious beliefs—of its (our) larger time. The aesthetics of indifference could be a hindrance to this by showing the futility of present art in addressing these concerns—or embodying these beliefs.

SOUNDS

"Natter" is a solitary noise.
Mosquitos and Chicadas make it by
rubbing themselves into a buzzing.
Peoples' natter emanates from out the mouth.
But neither of these noises is directed at a self—
for they evoke no such, as yet.
Natter is the sound of empty spaces —
prior to personification.

"Chatter" produces word-like sounds.
Monkeys chatter as they swing through trees,
which gives rhythm to their mutual passing.
People chatter with (not to) each other.
This sound is made by teeth and tongue—
by too-old friends and cell-phone addicts.

As it happens, there is good matter to be found in chatter.
It transmogrifies natter into ruminations
that tend to stay in place—despite the sonorous syllables
wafting within recorded space.

"Utter" brings words into a sentence.
Sentences join bowel and brain together—particularly
in those who are with, for, or against each other.
Utterances may begin in solitary places—but then
they spread to where their sense corroborates
another's need, anger, or gives a little pleasure —
whether above or just below the feet, reaching slowly
past the middle juices to the brain
then wafting sideways to the soul.

To "ruminate" places memories within thinking.
Rumination is re-thought—it also has the sound of silence.
Cows ruminate by regurgitating food for further chewing.

This makes food fine to fit the udder for the calf's delight.
People ruminate by chewing memory until that
which once was done becomes re-done.
Or until what was never done, shows up as done—
which memory will then accept as its own calf.

HOW TO PAINT A CIRCLE AND HOW TO PICK A STONE

I would like to bridge the gap between words and things by writing about something I did a time ago—namely, painting circles round and round a canvas with a brush.

These paintings are testimonials to a reconciliation between my favorite opposites—the family feud between the doers and the knowers—that has kept me going these many canvases and some pages. Before I did them, I had not done a pif of circle painting, not even a drawing; I only talked about it. But I promise that before you complete this story, you shall have something that shows a circle—not of my life; I am not that good—but of a thing that if looked at properly can be a worthy path for life to follow, if life—like circles—were to go around again.

But before I go a-circling, I must first talk about picking stones—for that topic shares, and in some ways precedes—my infatuation with circles.
The issue is this: How do you decide when picking a wild stone, say on a beach or from a field, which one is the best (more perfect, more beautiful, most stonish)—a stone that will hold its own among the domestic bric-a-brac that surrounds your life?

It is not an easy question, for I must say right off that every stone one finds is perfect, complete unto itself, adequate of its kind, needing companionship but not comparison, slated to outlive us all if left alone. All stones—as we are not—are beautiful in themselves. This is self-evident—if you would just back off from your Arp and Noguchi (good artists—both) and stop trying to find a stone that looks like sculpture inspired by notions about the "essence" of stone.

I once asked a class to visit a beach and find the one stone—among all the others—that is most beautiful, then bring it back for communal judging. We faced the array of stones, compared them, got mad at each other, and often wept. The conclusion (inevitable as it now seems) was that every stone—in its own way—is equally beautiful—an improvement, we came to agree, on how we look at people.

But, after that, there is something else. Each time I take a stone home (and I have taken many) from beach and mountain and construction site—I apologize to it for its loss of freedom, and the tedium it will face while living with me in my time and performing in the pageant of my tastes. Stones, unlike dogs, are not joiners. True, they like to lie around together in the all-together, but not when forced by select company to sit beside the coffee-pot or be laid down to make a wall. A stone will tolerate, begrudgingly, a neighbor who is friendly—a prickly bush, say, or a scraggly tree. But keep your distance—don't crowd me—or I'll begin to look like a brick or rubble!

Strangely though, it is hard to return a used stone to the place from which it came, for like an animal brought into captivity, it loses its ability to cope in the wild. If you don't believe me, just visit a discarded stone (one you've belatedly returned to where you found it)—you'll see how strained, how afraid of the winter waves it is. In captivity, it has become vulnerable to covering by snow, and it fears cracking in the cold. Like we the living, a domesticated stone needs shelter too.

Slightly more cracked is my effort to paint circles. I will tell you what I did before I tell you what I'm doing—and after that I will tell you why painting circles and picking stones belong together.

Among my stacks of long-ago drawings I found some raw sheets of paper (rawness, here, being an echo of wildness in stones) and I cut the papers into squares that would house my circles. I had become more interested in circles than in squares because circles go nowhere—even when spinning one can't tell them from the lazy ones at rest.

A square format can itself be dull—yet nicely holds a circle—whether spinning or at rest. Whatever else my circles are or do, I want them to be comfortable within their places.

So I found a dinner plate that fit happily within the area of my square, and with a pencil traced its circle. "Happiness" here, means something like Baby Bear's measure of appropriateness: Not too large and not too small . . . just right.

Then with a smaller plate, I traced another circle symmetrically placed within the larger one. I now had two circles with space between them—form and progeny. In the basement I found a paintbrush with ten years of service painting pipes and moldings.

Its hairs were coarse and uneven, they stuck out in all directions and bore the residue of many colors. With such a weapon, I could exercise control yet forego prediction.

I placed my sheets on a round table, one that my brush and I could seamlessly traverse without confronting corners. You may ask why I didn't cut the paper sheets themselves into a circle. Well, I didn't want a format that is itself a circle—rather, one that holds my representation of a circle—upon the neutral, even hostile matrix of its square home. This offers a battleground upon which great deeds can be attempted—and maybe accomplished. As with a stone, my circle (because encapsulated by the traced ones) will itself be perfect—however the first ones happen to look.

Further, I wanted to be as one with my circle in its representation. Before and behind would be wherever we both turned. There is no up or down. A circle has no Heaven or Hell, no gravity pressing down upon an unwilling rigidity—nothing but going around and coming around.

Grudgingly, a circle will tolerate being in a square—less so a rectangle, and not at all those funny forms coming out of triangularity. As for matrices devised from blobs and splashes—they are totally intolerable because they suffer from parochial ignorance of the ongoing debate between geometric purity and personal freedom. A circle, whatever else, has pride.

To go on: I dilute some India ink and dip my brush. But before I venture forth to draw, there are some rules to review—imperatives I give myself in order to protect the act against both spasmodic flourishes or cooked-up efforts at perfection:

Keep your brush within the confines of
the circles drawn in pencil.
Do not transgress an edge at any time.
Careless stroking has always faced
the charge of unrepentant posturing—
which is an Eastern criticism
of aesthetic disgraces in the West.

The space within my two geometrically drawn circles is the locus for my travel—the Scylla and Charybdis of my journey—requiring optimism and tranquility to brave the waves and venture through the narrow passage. As I look back, they were my early guides—but in the long run they became superfluous. I no longer needed a boat or pilot—for I had learned from fishes how to swim without fearing hungry sirens or angry rocks.

If you are diligent, you will heed the fish
and find
you no longer need the penciled marks
to guide your brush.

You can:
put the bristles down direct and right
on the virgin paper's waiting-place.
Then watch your brush go round with you—
to make a circle as perfect as the one you made
when you walked on freshly fallen snow.

You may:
Stop and go in clarified directions.
Press down or touch lightly,
stoop, fall, stand tall, run fast or dawdle—
stumble, slip and rest a bit, but don't stay put.
Yours must be the spirit's will to go.

But always:
Follow your brush—don't let it follow you.
Finishing must shape a circle without end.
Not much of a play, you say? But remember:
The music of a merry-go-round,
however loud it sounds,
but faintly echoes the music-of-the-spheres.

Well, in truth, you're right: Not much of a play. It would take a truly entranced and stoned appreciation to follow the faint blots and squiggles—brave the lurking presumptions of free-hand perfection—and make a sufficient world of them: Too much for me to ask—of even you.

So let's abandon niceties and go further: Take a stick of charcoal (a soft one that can be erased) and, without looking, trace the journey you have made while circling onto another sheet. Do it many times. You will then have learned to sound the soliloquy of a solitary man in a wide-brimmed hat as he travels around the rocks and gullies of an endless land. That is perhaps a better play.

I have taken this journey; I am one who has meandered along a circle's endless line.

Sometimes I had a good trip. But from the outside—from another point of view—this trip, as compared with the one up Saskia's leg or across Bierstadt's mountains—now seems too tame for one as old as me.

That is just the point, my man; art these days is uneventful—no goddesses to paint—only circles. But I tell you what. Tonight, instead of eating supper, try this: Mix a spoonful of dry bread crumbs with cold Crisco; then chew it slowly—don't you dig it? No? Well, that's the point.

Making a circle takes place, as it should, just beyond the inner space of competing voices. In their own defence (against the perfect imperfection of a perfect circle), Philistines offer the following (quite trendy) advice:

Let loose, Loosh—push the big gesture, the stentorian squiggle.
Deny your progeny and release at random
your semen, spittle, and your spoor.
Let them know for sure that you've already passed their way.

But the tremors of my beating heart, my need to breathe,
are squiggle enough for now. I do my best by circling—
for there is no braver best I have
that I can do.

They (those shits) then answer back:

Unleash your guilt; act out; thrash about.
Transfer your living from the point of pen and paper
to the persuasiveness of persona.
Worry about what happens after it is done.
Of course, you will, in later years,
as do your silly circles,
return to where it all began.
But now believe that you are free.
Run and have some serious fun.

I look at the faces of those beguiling voices as I circle: All races and religions, flushed and round, pasty-pale but never pointed, intoning the lines of perfection without a plan, showing scrupulous obedience to the arbitrary, arguing for the disavowal of hindsight and foreplay. They have been with me before and are still my biting pests—advisors, beseechers, yea-and-naysayers, micro-prophets, straight-laced vultures feeding on my circled leavings—midges waiting till I scratch to blood.

But listen: There are some much worse than these. They are the sly ones who appear whenever you need them least: "It's just a game, Lucian: Circle-while-you-wait. It's not about art at-all a-tall—just about playing at making choices when it doesn't matter what you choose. It's like picking stones. Tomorrow you won't remember what you saw in the little ones. Once, when you were optimistic, you made your pick by size—as big as you could carry to the car. Remember? But now you're old. Why strain?

We had built a little house on some land back east near the sea. I was operated on that early spring, on my left lung for what they thought was cancer. Just a shadow on the plate they said, a small one, no way to know without going in but too risky to leave alone. So in they went; two holes for drainage, another one to check the lymph nodes, and the big one across my back, full assault, to see what they could see. Well, they saw nothing much—good show I suppose. As the big man said: "Thrilling to be shot at and missed."

Well fuck you Jack, you started the war. So I lay around for a week, spitting blood and looking at the grey faces of lung transplants and at nurses' asses—thinking about how all these scars I now sport will affect my image as a sexual worthy.

No, I felt no gratitude, no new humility; nothing like that. As soon as I could I drove away, alone and a good deal skinnier, to the little house back east. I remember sitting on the sand dunes and stripping to a bikini although the weather was still cold. I warmed my scars in the morning sun and poured sand on my leg, then walked to where the waves would wash me off. I watched sea gulls and kicked at clam shells and tried to regain access to my invaded body and to the outside world from which I had been separated.

But all this was too passive; I needed action to regain my world; I wasn't sick—just wounded. So I went in search of sea-stones, the biggest I could find, to carry back and place around my house. The best stones were always furthest from the entrance to the beach, and each day I tried to find new wonders in some cove far away from the summer folks. It was the lifting and the pulling on my scars, the flash of pain across the numbness, that showed me I was coming back—able to stagger across the loose sand: "Just two more steps before you put it down—there's the car—try to get it all the way." No one was at the beach that time of year, only me, shameless in my weakness, and happy in my search for large and perfect stones.

Over the years, I have brought back many stones to the places where I lived. I look at them during morning coffee, setting down the cup each time I think to move one here or there, or replace it with another. There are now so many that they have taken on different occupations: They have made grottos and befriended bushes, hidden house keys, and given shelter to beetles and worms. In each place, the stones have regained some possession of their once-wild selves. But it is clear that they are tamer than they were when washed by ocean waves. I apologize for colonizing them, but then point out some advantages: "There is no sea to grind you down," I say. "You will last longer—and I am here to admire you." I think they agree—they seem not to mind my laying on of hands and walking around to place them in a different space.

As with circles, I sometimes—when I am dulled—reduce them to their arrangements, forgetting that each stone is perfect in-and-of-itself, and so needs a singular, specialized, admiration. Luckily, I do not have good taste, so I show them that I love them all—just as they are. Fortunately, my ventures into compatibility do not last long—no longer than does my memory of what and where they were.

But on the whole my stones seem happy with my uses of them. I expect they are grateful for the cognition of the time of life we have come to share—although, after that passes and the seas rise, they again will grind away—much more slowly, of course, than I—and will celebrate their autonomy by stubbornly greeting the latest style of incoming waves.

Painting a circle, like picking a stone, is making a portrait of an impossible demand—to fail at art in order to successfully represent a self. It is an arrogant act, this prideful documentation of a failure; and also aesthetically perverse, this replacement of a painting with a likeness of its process. But perhaps the act is merely selfish in an antiquarian way; for what is achieved—that intimacy with one's quirks and quivers—has been out of favor for some time: It no longer is a revelation or an indictment, not even a symptom of a condition that was once diagnosed as "authenticity."

Some who write about such matters think that the realm of the self is on the inside—gaining substance through layered memory and desire. Long ago—when God still lived—this realm was also located on the outside—the place where deviance could be noted and traced to demons against which only the exhibition of true belief and constant prayer—sometimes exorcism or immolation—could give protection. Later, it became propitious for the soul to stay inside and leave the outside to the creatures in the meadows of the body—where ecstasy invites ambivalent flesh to enter the valleys leading to the mountains where demons dance.

In the version I know best, the inside soul,
well-suffused with faith,
dries out when it climbs into the sun.
Once there it finds it has to merge
(what else can it do?)
with the moist yet unbelieving flesh—and pretend
it, too, likes the sway and swish of fornication
seen everywhere along the city beaches—
better than it does stiff prayer.

There is little art that can now be found inside, so I do not ask my circles—which come from inside-out—to be art. It is enough that they help me in remembering—offering their timeless comfort to my time of life. I opine that art, these days, is made on the outside by those who have merged their separate interests into common zones—within which these interests are presented (without much question) as joint compendia of once solitary inner selves. This is either false or regrettable—probably inevitable.

However, in a better world than mine—a more benign society—the values I care about could be dispensed with as guides to the general good—because they aren't needed.

It might turn out that once separate interests will generate communities that identify their otherness through designators of themselves—a mandala of many faces for each neighborhood—liberated monads flashing at an opening—show-girls on vacation.

The arrangement of faces would of course be circular—as the practice of navel-gazing dictates—and the whole of interchange could take place in the center of the village square, shielded from the weather by overlapping parasols and protected against assault by guardians chanting the admonitory rules of righteousness. Each painted face would designate a region, a tribe, and a way of sharing whatever interests that are not foreign to the others.

In such a world, all races, sexes, and religions will be treated equally—even those in favor of uncollected garbage or against school-lunches. For we all are artists now—with ad-lib hours—although it is permissible to delegate a bit when one is busy.

Circles and stones are still viable in such a world—if only for post-conceptual antiquarian-celebratory purposes. Their sizes and locations will be assigned by committee—thus ensuring moderation. During holiday seasons, all groups are required to bring an appropriate stone—as beautiful as

can be found, and as large as two can carry—to be set in a circle, and thus provide a resting place for dalliance, meditation, and free-trade.
General participation in the afternoon walk is to be encouraged. The prescribed route traces the shape of circles, one within the other, moving counter-clock around the center—a post-modern promenade modelled on the traditional "do-si-do" in which private needs are made to bear the interested scrutiny of public faces. The new hope is that the movement of well-turned ankles and sweaty t-shirts, in a climate of modest leers and muffled snickers, will mollify any age-old-rage of separate-souls who might be lurking there. Now, if such were to actually come to pass, I would be glad to venture out myself and give some free advice on the formal aspects of the art of circling—for I know some things about the balance between geometry and gesture, and I am well-attuned to the changing rhythms between round and round and in and out. Call me.

A dream peculiar to the inside self is of being naked—at a late age on a public stage—to show how things were done back then—when such things were still worth doing—and then to lament their absence through self-confession, and as a lesson to the younger ones who now do other things—not near as well, I'm told.

The prospect of such an invitation to reveal the ancient truths, is what makes a guru out of a failed banker. It also vindicates a continuing faith, however out-of-date, in the value of an inside effort to go traversing (however briefly) to the outside—then back inside again to hide—until the universal "we" comes to like both sides, and will codify the rules for benevolent passage between them. It is a historical test of stamina (and progress)—to see how often the passage is traversed. It is an existential test to see, for each of us, how well the journey is accomplished.

THE CASE

It is important to know what is the case before you die,
whether you remain renowned or will leave us little trace.
Dying in disgrace needs only knowing that your story
will be told, tut-tuttingly, for years—not each telling true.
The universe is always true—but may not be right—
as in this case—if it is not true that
a dastardly deed was committed by you—
to the detriment of good Tom Clancy
and the widow Sarah Jones.

The given case is always true—there are no false ones—
although cases are not exempt from asking when and whether.
Yet, to proclaim "This is the Case"
leads unbelievers to seek solace in a downtown place-
such as where the lissome widow used to sit
before she was shot in the back by that cowardly hack.

No one believed him when he showed proof
of Sarah's duplicity, perfidy, and greed—
and then described her deformities in bed.
When provoked, he said, she performed
with sighs and farts in rapid concert.
Her clitoris was less a blossom than a hazelnut,
and she smelled much worse for that.

All she wanted from Tom Clancy was his bottom-land.
She was mine before she went with Tom.
I had to shoot him too—he didn't understand
that she had taken from me everything except my shoes.
She started with my gold-mine
and didn't stop 'til she had my cattle—
and my mother's jewelry too.

I present my case, your honor, in the sense that
in this case, it is the case that I am right
to have done what you say I didn't do—
namely—to kill those two as proper retribution
for their denigration of my capacities in bed.
What I didn't do is what you say I did—
that is—kill them just because I wanted to.

The judge looked down and curled his lip.
You got no gold mine and you got no cattle.
You were from your mother's womb untimely ripped.
And she didn't have jewelry worth a shit—
only baubles given her by carpet-baggers
in payment for her prattle.

The case is closed; Sarah was my daughter.
As the good book says—
you'll get no quarter.

WHERE ART IS

All art-works are objects of some kind (for those of us who have placed the mind firmly within the brain) but only some such objects have been anointed by history's quarrelsome judges as incidentally objects but consequentially art. All such anointments, however, can be reversed when a something, once deemed to be art, is no longer art on the occasion that the designations of "object" and "work" no longer overlap. The tension between such occasions is shown in the conflicting demands of epistemology and fashion: "It once was beautiful" he says—"that's because of when they said art should be beautiful." "But it's so ugly now" she says— "so maybe now it isn't art, and maybe likely never was."

But why—we ask—should art be beautiful?
Why cannot art be ugly too—or better—
be somewhere where—or a thing to which —
such words no longer fit or matter?

Heroic images, once undeniably art, can lose their historical claim and become pigeon-glazed effigies in some central park. Patriotic anthems attesting to state victories, are sung to general indifference at base-ball games. Parades commemorating saints and heroes float down the avenues of large cities on kegs of beer. Pricy concerts sound-off until they have played their music out—a short time, really—and then subscription holders wend their ways through the fugue of honking taxis, while the cheaper seats, still beating time, wait for the allegro of oncoming subway-trains.

In film-land, there are movies about barbaric executions where sullen stars are interrupted in extremis by flashbacks of their previous lives—where they once played hardy hunks well tended to by lissome ingénues. In other movies, the characters talk so fast and smile so broadly, that the storyline never gets beyond the content of the pleasant present.

Then, for the latest private tastes, there are roles played out in silent first beginnings—before the noise is heard. These, transferred to tape, are shown on weekends for the delectation of audiences who want to see another past less tepid than is theirs—and make a wish that what once was could be again—in this present place at once so ephemoral and so cruel.

The joining of the slipperiness of "present" to a concept of "place," is indeed difficult. Place-concepts, as I have described them, are not sturdy. To consider all artworks as having a place (however "place" is modified by the niceties of "editions" or "performances") leaves one open to the possibility of "no-place" works which—by self-dispersal—threaten the identity of other artworks, and the very ontology of art.

Are there artworks of the kind that are never
in a place that's there? And where then
are they? How are we to appreciate them—
without their being somewhere
where we care?

Well, find some (make some) as you walk along,
Yes, yes, I'll do that—show me how to care.

But tell me:
Where was that street and when did I walk it—
and why do I think that what I find nowhere is art
when I don't remember being in a somewhere place
where there is no art.

Listen to me:
Don't fret—don't go back—and don't despair.
No-where art is everywhere.
Just look around
and pretend to care.

There are works that disappear and reappear—they must be disassembled and reassembled—after which they are the same and yet not the same.

In one Anselm Kiefer sculpture, shards of glass are scattered around its base. When the piece is moved, the glass is swept up, later to be re-scattered in some approximately similar order, in an often dissimilar location.

In constructions by Eva Hesse, strings of latex tubing coil around each other eventually to be pulled apart and re-entwined by unknown others in a new installation.

But she was partial to her own twining ways before she died.

A recent work by Richard Serra comprises massive sections of steel (torqued elipses) plunked ponderously down onto the reinforced floor of a masochistic museum—which, it seems, has long been waiting to be despoiled by this latest enormity. When passion fades, the hope remains that another place will give refuge to the aging balabuster and so prompt a further move—perhaps out onto a cove where its rusting and the rust of old abandoned ships can form a neighborhood.

But there are other works—still in the majority, so they say—that cannot do without a place of their own. Such works resist a move—even a walk around the block can upset stationary art. Instead, they hole up in the studio until they are assured that the new place offered them is really more comfortable—and so befits the change from a dirty pad of shock and awe to a place all lit up by informed regard.

But as public attention shortens and art proliferates, maintaining place grows more difficult. Serra's museum pieces in New York weigh more, I suspect, than any artwork this side of the Sphinx. Conceived in Manhattan, cast in Germany, shipped across the wide Atlantic, craned aboard waiting trucks, and then re-craned—while traffic stops and people gape—into the place where, once the installation is deemed secure, the curators and others of significance can gather, drink, and softly cheer their triumphant entry into a new art-history.

The sphinx, eight stories tall, has stayed in its place for millennia—it is a matter of religious mystery and national pride. Also, it is in the desert—populated more by sand and camels than by art-lovers. The Sphinx's present place is in books rather than on real- estate. A photograph and some commentary will do—no need to go and see it for yourself. In a few thousand years, if someone is still around, the Sphinx, as with the glories of Ozymandius, will be as one with the desert sands, sustained only by myth—but remaining intact in the future's confluence of images and memories.

The "David" in Florence was dragged through the streets amidst cheers that he had become so large after his biblical victory (not to mention the triumph of the Renaissance). But Michelangelo's sizing was small potatos, handled efficiently by a horse-drawn cart. He (David) got safely to his place, where he still stands, and where he shows his splendid proportions to the many viewers who prefer him to the Sphinx—because, in addition to all the other art around and his arcane cock and balls, the local food is better.

Some nay-sayers consider all distinctions between works and non-works to be elitist—in the way that impinges on the enjoyment of advanced living.

Among the complainers are anti-art artists and dyspeptic social critics who are always ready to spot collusion between art, advertising, and high finance—a malevolent brew, they insist, which undermines the real aesthetic deal—that of enjoying what you already have learned to like.

But art-works, as things-in-the-world, move around to find their best niches as avidly as do people. The aesthetic version of the historical imperative scatters its pieces over the landscape, and each piece, like a seedling, takes root in the soil in which it finds itself—and then mirrors both the nutrients and privations of that soil.

Serra and Christo challenge the power-builders—with whom, quixotically, they are kin—through their own intrusions into public spaces. Architect-manqués they are, presenting themselves as giving new instructions—more pure and to the point than do buildings or cloistered art-works—about how to live and love within the extravagances of a great city. They have forsaken frames and pedestals—and for that we should be thankful—and they are at home indoors or out. But in being this way, their art requires, more than older art, that we appreciate it by collectively paying attention—even though the moments may be transient. Also required are patrons who need not be collectors, but who pay the bills.

These days, art can have a populist way of taking public root in poor and mixed communities. The aesthetic impetus to deface is both celebratory and critical. The celebration is in walking through the colors and windings, scatterings and splashings—as if a band of neighborhood children had taken to festooning the streets while skipping class.

The criticism within such efforts is not apparent, but it is there—directed at the rote learning in schools and the repetitive dullness of the housing projects where those children must still live, when their art is over for the day.

The art-attack is seldom frontal; it mostly comes in swirls—red and black and green are favorites. This art is no respecter of categories; large colors may part to reveal a small homage: "I love Conchita"—or a declaration: "Third Avenue Tigers"—or just a patch of mottled splashes over a once-neutral surface.

Agitation is essential.
Despoilation does the Trick.
Decoration is Revolution.
No need for Representation.
Watch out for plain-clothes Dicks.

Graffiti are the urban traces of a dark clandestine collectivity whose members do not think themselves as culture heroes. The young-one caught and brought to the courts is not an artist self-professed, but only a poor vague kid from down the block who has no art-talk to speak of nor social program to enact. The arrest is a cultural clash and, usually, a personal tragedy: "He's just trying to express himself, Your Honor."

There is also an issue of cultural colonialism here. The recent urge to collect graffiti art and mount it above the sofa in the living room, can be as categorically obtuse as absconding with the Elgin Marbles—or collecting sea-stones and expecting them, newly arranged and gentrified, to glow with the same radiance as when they lay scattered among the moving waters. Sometimes, with massive infusions of "good taste," the glow of stones seems brighter in the home than on the shore. But look harder: The smile of (even benign) captivity soon becomes a glower—a dark objection to being snatched from out the beach or cut away from the subway-car that was once called home.

Stones I've talked to say they feel colonized when separated from friends and neighbors—their extended family on the rocky beach. Colonists, in the main, don't care about such sentiments. They expect the natives—whether stones, scribbles, or slaves—to preen and shine within prescribed dictates, and to spend their days without complaint among that awful bric-a-brac—where they have been placed to show what money, power, ambition, coupled with proper breeding and occasional slumming, can look like.

WALKING WITH HANDEL

There are ways and other ways to go.
Listen to Handel's "Semele."

> "Where e're you walk, cool gales shall fan the glade.
> Trees where you sit, shall crowd into a shade.
> Where e're you tread, the blushing flowers shall rise.
> And all things flourish, where e're you turn your eyes."

No ambiguity, no irony—only corny lovely mysogeny.
Such walking requires nudity—and is best sung-to by castrati.

Wouldn't it be lovely, though, if you could sing this song
without guile or learned regret—but with open voice, well placed—
to the one you love?

THE NATURAL SUBLIME

Graffiti on subway cars and nudes in bushes, are like stones and circles—they can be painted or discovered. They each bypass the aesthetic beauty that informs and seduces acquisition. Instead, they bring us closer to the natural sublime which, as we have come to know, is more immediate and more frightening than taste.

There are many outsiders—retired graffitists, lovers of nature's nudes—who live in places where the forms of things around them need no aesthetic or polemical instruction.

The "Lightning Fields" and the "Spiral Jetty" are art-places out there in the West—but they function more as lessons for visitors about how to (distinterestedly) view—rather than how to (intimately) live with—the wild surrounding country.

One can still find places where the primeval urge to differentiate has left its traces. There are the rivers which flow within the channels that they themselves have carved; and cliffs whose early smoothness is furrowed by the insistence of wind, rain, frost, and baking sun—which inscribe a character of age, wisdom, and endurance onto the faces of once fledgling rocks. These elements of change are not evil—they choose survivors from among expectant trees, give the rivers water for their flow, and alert animals to the coming seasons. Also, they present their ancient rhythms for our instruction and use in poetry and prose.

The red cliffs of Capitol Reef, the giant sequoia trees in California, and the glaciers that preen just off the road between Banff and Jasper, have been there long before the rise of acquisitive appreciation. They precede our earliest ambitions to make them into settlements, and are bemused, I expect, by our later ambitions to chuck it all and be "as one" with them.

But humans (some) do live in and reflect on nature—and from this arises a competition between our intentions of living as nature, our need to find out how (or whether) we are part of it, and why both we and nature (the separation varies) are here to begin with. For, upon reflection, we humans are both in-and-out of nature—whether we will it so or not. The very exercise of "will" (unless we subscribe to Pantheism) is located not in nature but in the psyche. Appetition ("willing-that") pits privation against excess on occasions (in both human and animal domains) that go beyond the contingencies of survival. But a considered fear of dying (Freuds "thanatos") places will into historical time—and separates human and animal sentience.

Human will affects the future in ways we try to anticipate, want to control, but cannot know. There-in lies the vaunted malevolence that Schopenhauer ascribes to "universal will"—its inherent indifference to human needs. The will in nature is indeed indifferent to the needs and desires of its human counterpart: It shows no appetite for stylistic or cultural change—it has no mind through which to be in fear of death. Nature's willing has no history—it does not dwell upon the past and has no interest in the future. It functions as does natural beauty—in the eternal present.

Arid cliffs resist human intrusion—the lessons needed to survive in waterless wastes of cold and heat are too hard for most of us to learn. Not a pity—there are the good times in Spring and Fall.

I sit on the cliffs at sunset, and and watch the crimson and pale ochre of the waning day revert in the late light to faded umbers and worn violets. The coming of night is restrained from abruptness by the glow the sun leaves on the higher rocks even as it sets beneath the lower hills. The night of nature, when free of contamination by city-lights and car-radios, is molded only by the wind and the stars.

The roaring of the wind as it funnels through a distant canyon becomes a rustling in the tree-tops—my companions of the night. The thick-soup of starlight in the wild-west sky seems spilled there through an agreement between divine and natural right.

But for the human seeker, this purity and seeming permanence is also enigmatic: The stars are in motion but seem quite still; the wind moves through, ceases, and returns again. A camera's time exposure gives the lie to the stillness of the stars. And when the wind returns, it is not the same wind that came before, nor the one we feel in daylight. Night-winds blow away incipient morning breezes—before yielding to the way the sun of morning comes to hide the light of its companion stars.

CLEMENTINE—A RECOLLECTION

In a cavern, in a canyon
excavating for a mine,
dwelt a miner, forty-niner
and his daughter Clementine.

Oh my darling, oh my darling,
oh my darling
Clementine.
You are lost and gone forever.
Dreadful sorry,
Clementine.

Light she was, and like a fairy,
and her shoes were number nine.
Herring boxes without topses,
sandals were for Clementine.

I first saw her in the moolight
talking to a porcupine,
not to eat him but to greet him.
I thought that was mighty fine.

Drove she ducklings to the water,
every morning just at nine.
Hit her foot upon a splinter
and fell into the foaming brine.

I will miss her, didn't kiss her,
and the fault for this was mine.
I felt bad that
she looked sadly
when I told her it's past time.

I admit I am no swimmer.
I can't keep my ducks in line.
I prefer pickles to fair maidens
when both are soaked in brine.

This (my choice) is not a crime.

There's nothing for it now
but whore it—in a brine-less
place along the Rhine.
Resurrection is no answer
for erections such as mine.

Oh my darling, oh my darling,
oh my darling
Clementine.
You are lost and gone forever

. . . and so forth.

LIVING WITH NATURE

Kierkegaard asks of "academic philosophers" that they include their own condition in their attacks on faith and belief. I agree. My condition is of placing my now-old self in a purple-painted house with an open view of the Mississippi River. The river sometimes floods, but when it just flows by I sit on the porch and watch the barges pass, drink cheap chardonnay, and write what you're reading. When the weather cools, I go to a shack that my love turned into a studio, and I make art-works that you are less likely to see than you are to read this. I have little reason to assault an empire that chooses—because of strategy rather than benevolence—to leave such as me alone. There are benefits to this mutual neglect. I am indubitably myself (no one around to doubt me)—dependent only on an academic pension that I have some reason to believe will last me through my span.

Being free, the zealots say, is an acquired value. I say it's a good way to scratch your ass and do what ever else you can think of doing before the sun goes down.

The red-rock canyon in Utah is a good place to find one's freedom. The rocks don't care—for they no longer have a soul. They are too old to chastise the trees and bushes over the infernal goings-on in the ravines—millennia of scraping and sighing, of sprouting and withering, to no particular purpose.

You should know, however, that in such an incurious place you won't be getting any praise for being free. They're all free out there. The chipmunks and the rattlesnakes are free; and yet they sometime seem jealous of my freedom, which they suppose to be less regimented—more broadly circumscribed at least—than theirs. So they bite if they must, or eat my grain if it's not safely stored. I began by guarding my freedom with a shotgun—but over the years, I never have managed to shoot at any creeping, running, or flying thing. I swear.

My resident snake knows where I walk and I know where he hunts his mice. We both keep our distance; I kick some brush to give warning; he no longer rattles at me but wiggles slowly across the path so that I can admire him.

Did you ever see a storm race across the roofs of ghetto tenements? It skims the surface as if it doesn't want to get involved in the deeper social problems underneath. The buildings picked by ghetto storms are mostly three stories, but the top story has long crumbled into the rubble that takes the place of once well-tended gardens.

There are many hidden places in all this sadness from which to see the darkling clouds and lightning streaks as they give notice to their arrival with barabooms of thunder. The crumple and rubble, when washed by wind and rain, will glow—showing approval of nature's attention to their new-found beauties.

But strong storms, especially in the mid-west, are more insistent than are the spectacles we would want for our enjoyment. They often overdo their stay, and we the living are grateful when they finally move past our spaces. Not that we don't like storms—as I say, they can be beautiful. But storms, much like the rest of us, are insecure; and once they've preened and strutted, will notice the lateness of time—and remember the long way they have to go. So they give a last boom-ba, and move to impose themselves on other places—whose inhabitants, unlike us, may consider them to only be a threat.

Storms are not like divas—they are not affronted by audience hostility. A stormic sense of place and time is not ours—although, if one were to ask a storm to stay longer or leave earlier, it (the storm) would wonder whether we (in the human way) seek to mitigate its role and make it into art.

But we already have much art, I say,
that wants to stay forever.
If you please then, storm, just go away—
and thanks for showing us that
there still are spaces
between the arty places that are grounded—
when you pass them on your windy way.

The storms we have inside are much like their outside cousins; they both realize their clearest form when they are over. "So, how do you feel now that you've thrown—up, peed, and had a bit of breakfast? Let's take a walk; it'll do you good. But look, the sun is coming out—soon you will want to go to where it's cool."

But inside storms, beneath their sometime need for expurgation and fresh air, have an intensity that is differently calibrated than the tempests that occur outside.

Their assigned space—the inner place—avoids the clouds, and is situated within hailing distance of the gateway to insanity—and not far from the path to immortality. This inner place has at least two gates—but just one john. It is small, modest, but well furnished. It is in a nook once thought to be located somewhere near the pineal gland. But the location is no longer certain—there is so much individual variation—some even say there is no such place.

But I disagree, for how could there be storms inside without a place for them to blow and rumble and then go away—as they often do?

Inner storms are more circumspect than the ones outside. "Tief wie das Meer" they may be, but what we see are only surface ripples. Inside feelings should never be fully expressed, the good-folk say: Those sounds of fear, lust, hatred and despair, are shameful—unnatural and ungodly—and are best muted, for all our sakes.

Shush, what will the neighbors say
when they hear the sounds we make?
Will they let their children play
with ours at bake-a-cake?
Or will they tell them
just to stay away?

If such storms should surface, they usually subside but sometimes do not—the psychic weather, like its surface counterpart, can always worsen. The large and powerful storms—tempests of the prenatally doomed—will elude all talking cures, and generate more turbulence than even rocks could stand to suffer.

Coping with such disturbances—despite the pain—is a task for culture-heroes of the mind—those who will dive deep, brave the psychic bends, and bring the weird-fish wiggling and biting back upside. Then they can eat them—let them rot—or coerce them into being sanity or art.

The red-rocks in the canyons do not want translation into art. They are made of outside storms and have no regard for feelings. Proposing an ontic unity between the still duration of cliffs and the flow of living, brings together entities that today have only the faintest whisper of a common place and time. Some of us do indeed talk familiarly, lovingly, even conspiratorially, with rocks—and our feelings about these conversations still stay with us when we come down from the cliff and drive back to our warm and comfy homes.

But because rocks have no feelings, they don't miss us—and they will endure for eons if left alone. In their desert sanctuary, rocks protect themselves from aesthetics. Wild rocks need no art —neither to be nor be around; they are not subject (as we are) to the transient batterings of criticism. They do not need to change.

One can deplore this space between us and rocks; but whether our human quivers of vulnerability show in the thighs or lips or tender toes—or in the place where noses want to go, we must not be so proper as to ignore those quivers—or, worse, take them back to our talks with rocks. This fastidiousness, however, limits the pleasures of living life: Whenever we feel the threat of our own mortality, we can exercise our "Schadenfreude" in knowing that these red and green encrusted sentinels—those massive silent age-old personages—will (on a terrible some-day) succumb to human avarice: They will catch the eye of a vile developer and face the talons of a tractor. Developers do not talk to rocks; they move them, crush them into gravel, or make them into ornaments.

I think about the places we almost bought—places that we thought could bring the stoic rocks and our own domestic quarrels into a satisfying union. Perhaps it would be better, sane-man says, if you just visit the cliffs from time to time. Better? Maybe si, maybe no. There is an old-fashioned metaphysics lurking in my aging bones—a wish to protect primeval nature before it is too-late corrupted by post-human uses. If we had bought that decaying cabin beneath the cliffs (it's not there anymore) we could have said with satisfaction: "These rocks are really real and we will be rocks among them." But we didn't know that rock-talk would soon become the fashion in the city—and then, just as quickly, be replaced by irony: "Are you (ha-ha) still talking to your rock?"

Where I am now is where no one much wants to live. Oh, it's a beautiful place, down by the banks of the Mississippi with sandstone bluffs on either side. Rafts little changed from Jim and Huck compete with barges along the river; catfish and deer are staples enjoyed by the old and inbred families. But there are no jobs to bring in more people, and few poets left of the kind that would probe the hot and sweaty river-rat infested, perennially flooding land, and push their toes deep into the mud along the shore. So here, a far-from-home boy takes his geriatric stand—telling stories, and waiting for the next ten year flood which, they say, will only submerge half the house.

There is no direct way to describe the trip that brought me here; my attempts at consecutive memory are waylaid by fictions of how I came to be—to be in this place.

So I write and you read, and we both face the mix of memory and embellishment that took eighty-odd years of highways and backroads to gel into a pudding of one old Lucian. Well, however it happened, it happened, and now I sit and watch the Mississippi flow by—a river quite as indifferent to me in its passage as is the sedentary stillness of the desert rocks.

The river flows—as the song says—past the troubles of old-folks stretched beyond their time; and it sometimes drowns the young ones, three times divorced, with children they have not learned to love.

All rivers, I am told, are like that—living close by their banks can be perilous. But on a winey summer's night, we all—loners, losers, slackers, strivers—gain absolution from this our own big river—which mostly shows a forgiving face, and gets angry only when the winter melts are more copious than usual. But low or high, the river has much to teach us. The wisdom, slowly given, is ephemoral, seldom practical, and yet eternal—as we are not.

One eventually learns to sit, leaving the moving for the waters, and watch the boys and girls on Harleys ride the river road—especially on weekends in the summer. They move against the current—the river's and the world's—and they use their small piece of freedom in a weekly search for ribs and fights and other forms of local wisdom.

I like ribs—but prefer the barbeque I make to the warmed-over stuff served at the emporia of beer and broken noses that line the river banks. I like fights too, but now, alas, only to watch from a table in the corner. No-one gets hurt much here—but oh my, there does come a mighty preen and swagger—the threats of mayhem well-soaked with beer and sweat in motorcycle leather, greying beards, and out-sized boots. Rank perspiration and foul breath are the condiments that grace the action. When the preliminary roarings are exhausted, there's nothing for it but to scuffle a bit, knock over a table or two, spill the ribs onto the wooden floor, and hope the owner breaks it up before the cops arrive.

But it's the language—the river-cussing—that is most notable. Denigrations of birth, family, and sexual preferences have priority. The adversary is typically a "mo-fucka, sum-bitch, pussy" who's also an "ass-lickin, cock-sucka"—as the case may be. There are lots of pauses—for more beer, yes—but mainly because the hurtful language that is needed for a larger fight hasn't yet been thought of. It is hard for even bad-ass river folks to find that language in the flotsom of their brain—and then fashion it into words.

HAIR AND THE RIVER

Tiny tufts top off your head—
baby blond and streaked with red.
Down below, the curly whirls of pubic hair
are moistened with your own elixir.
But unlike the tufts that grow on top,
these are black and show some silver.
How come?

Color doesn't matter to the river.
It has drowned them black and blonde
and even razor-bare. It doesn't matter
whether coifs are bottle-streaked,
or look like old-time tresses
made of down-home hennaed hair.

I told you a canoe's no good!
It's too light to bump-past a floating log.
The water's swifter than this morning.
It's still cold from winter snow—
and now it's pouring.

Hold tight to the log and kick your feet!
Maybe we'll get to reach the shore
before the locks will pull us in—
and mix us with dead fishes.

DAMNATION

There are categories of interest beyond those that sustain our ordinary thinking. They speak to the continuation of life as myth; they are the creatures of addled rumination gone back to nature.

But myth does present, however implausibly, multiple directions for our mortality when it most needs continuing beyond nature—when it fears a straight-on ending.

A major fear in ending is the anticipation of a last judgment. Doctrinally, such judgments occur when we die—they perform the summing-up of lives, and show our prospects for eternity. Historically, the theatrics surrounding judgment were liveliest in the early days—when belief was strongest and most visual. The further back in time one goes, the clearer is the distinction between those who make their final journey by climbing up to Heaven, and those that trip and tumble down to Hell. Of the Hell-makers, the Flemish are best, especially Bosch and Breugel. The fiends they assign to tormenting the damned are a colorful lot—shiny spikey amalgams of scorpions, lizards, bats, dragons, who all seem to take great pleasure in what they do—a perk of having been created evil from the start. But those flayers, stokers, and prickers are actually rather simple workers, part of the service sector of Hell, not really up to the subtler job—assigned to sadistic succubi—of tempting the dissatisfied here on earth to come-back-down and enjoy the pains of Hell.

Nevertheless, what they do they do well, these jolly torturers, and their duties are sufficiently varied to call up the best efforts of those artists whose task it is to document the wailing, weeping, and gnashing of teeth. Hell, after all, is one of the great artistic subjects, far more apt to stretch the imagination and spark the libido than, say, apples and pots arranged on a checkered tablecloth. And then there is the additional benefit of medieval creativity: Dante gives us a sanctioned trip through the most grievous perils of the soul, and shows them in clear detail, before he turns to the paler glories of salvation.

He himself, has the poet and the virgin—Virgil and Beatrice—to keep him safe. And he has his hatred of all who wronged him—to keep him writing.

Looking at:
The ever burning, never consummating
Flesh.

Listening to:
The abjectly glottal, multi-lingual
voices.

This, for all eternity:
The torment of my lost beloveds,
is the pain of Hell.

But what is the attraction of damnation and its practices for modern times, where Hell is disbelieved but its cruelties continue to be tasted and progressively embellished. Audiences come from far and wide—mostly in electronic journeys—to watch and listen to theatrical descriptions of the horrors—unending pain coupled with perverse pleasure (the "witches brew" as Nietzsche called it) that they themselves will (hopefully) avoid if they stay faithful to the Word. But they do like to watch all that happening to the others on a large screen in living color.

It should not surprise us that even they, the faithful, are as partial to the richly woven sadisms of this final drama as they are to TV terminators and soft-core flagellators. You see—there is a lot of sex in Hell. The dead, especially the evil dead, wear no clothes—so prurience is mixed in with the pain, just as it was when they stretched grandma naked on the rack, or when the ingenue got sliced apart while in the shower. Hell is populated by nakeds—howling jumping grilling boiling nakeds, boys and girls together, all wicked, and all finding out, at last, lastingly, with the nerve-endings of their souls, the penalty for the orgies that used to play in their early dreams and later assignations—those portents, now unreturnable, of their fate to be among the damned.

And we the clothed living look on in fascination, glad it isn't us, relieved that we're not there stripped bare—and wouldn't want to be of course—now that we see what it's really like. But wait a bit before you shut the door; let me look some more—a little more at that one clutching the ice floe while her foot is in the monster's mouth and the rest of her all hanging out, dangling this way and that. The play of torment has a casting call that never ends: Virgins and dragons, sullied country girls, and alien rapists from outer space, Faye Wray and King Kong (poor guy).

Say, I ask you: Do you suppose that I could get a real good look without buying in—that someone, a certified guide, would take me across and just show me around so that I could actually see the damned and listen to their complaints—even touch some in their most painful places before I have to leave?

Why sure! I'm glad you asked. The Devil always has itineraries that fit all needs—just ask Faust (with all his learning, alas—he didn't know the price differential between illusion and temptation—and he had to pay more). So you too must not expect to get in free. But anyway—do take the trip. We'll be glad to help.

SHANGRI-LA

Just when the lissome sybyl,
retroactively and inferentially,
seemed ours for infinity to love and hold,
the conductor showed his scowl.
And in a voice made hoarse
by millenia of telling time, said:
You are now departing Shangri-La.
Please grow old immediately.

The warts and wrinkles, the sags and blackened freckles
showed up clearly on my true-love's face.
Then, quickening, they popped-up in random places—
until her breasts and buttocks, elbows and pudenda,
were covered thick by growths from ancient sources.

She said: It is particularly important that you love me now.
These were words, as I remember, that she spoke
when she first took me to her bed.
I replied: It's different now—the horrid way you are today.
Your voice reminds me of a wart-hog's grunt,
and the rest of you is like an armadillo hide.

But this was indeed too much—she showed the pain
beneath her scars. So I changed the wording:
Wait, wait, I said. On second thought
I didn't really mean it as you heard it.
And I'm sad, yes so sad, that it's unfortunately true.

But please look here: Some one, in retaliation
for my alleged indifference to your suffering,
has put the Mark of Cain on me as well.
The mark first showed on my upper thigh
near the right side of my testicle—
the long-one hanging by the left side of my pecker—

where it clearly can be seen by the inquisitive.

The mark was black but now it's turning blue.
Some sunny afternoons it fades to white, and then
come night, it shows a greenish face that's smiling.

This mark, as you can see, is nasty—
worse than a scar or tatoo.
I can't get it off by washing or by willing—
so I asked some people that I knew:
The doctors poked and prodded, then scowling
filled their forms and went their way.
The mark remained—so I turned to see the priest.
There's nothing for it but to pray, said Father John.
Oh c'mon, I cried—you're just putting me on.

SALVATION

The other side of the great divide—salvation as we know it—although perfect, leaves something to be desired. The upper reaches of Last Judgments are not as pictorially interesting as the lower ones.

What can be interesting? Plump souls in white robes who forever sing the same old songs? Heavenly bliss is undoubtedly attractive when sounded by a neighborhood church choir—willowy sopranos, matronly altos, shallow tenors and rotund bassos. But painters never seem to get it right: The look of eternal happiness that is not-ever boring is hard to specify while fear and lust and hate—both here and down below—have much more going for them to show.

Consider Dore's illustrations for the Divine Comedy: His Hell is full of twisty hairy tortured limbs—one can hear the pleas and lamentations—yet when he tries for Heaven, it has only some few lines emanating from an invisible center and winding symmetrically around the heavenly host—a capitulation to the ideal of perfection. Rauschenberg's cool solution is to make both realms—Heaven and Hell—equally boring. Michelangelo is much better. In his "Last Judgment," he uses Hell to take revenge on his enemies—by depicting them there in full realization of their fate—sent to their come-uppance by the most vengeful Christ in all of art.

The "School of Athens" by Raphael is the best Heaven-picture I know, with a serious play between verticals and diagonals that shows, marching down the temple steps, the two ancient (dead) Philosophers who vie for our conception of the real. When we first look, we are taken with their gestures and the virtual content of their conversation—a trans-temporal invitation to eavesdropping. But the surroundings are not as interesting—standard Greek columns decorated by the placid obeisance of onlookers—and a sibyl or two for harmony.

It may be that these inequalities in picturing show that Heaven is best for describing and Hell better for depicting—a reciprocal (and unending) battle for superiority between verbal and visual realms—between words and pictures. Until recently, words (given their post-sensuous nature) were winning. Now that reading faces electronic competition, pictures—presented as public spectacle and instant imagery—have become the primary sources of both information and titillation. Hell—by way of the "Walking-Dead" and sundry other TV malcontents—is back again.

Some questions for the bemused: There is a philosophy of everything these days, so why not a critical philosophy of Heaven—an inquiry as to why eternal bliss should be deemed sufficient in answering our search for the complete meaning of our incomplete smarts and hidden fate—when Heaven's attractions are themselves so hard to express?

Why, after-all, is bliss so desireable? Have the responsible members of the Heavenly host tried mixing in a bit of pain (a touch of errant spice to all that in-place pleasure)?

To counter the Heaven-talk, I feel there should also be a philosophy of Hell—or is that, in contrast to a philosophy of Heaven, merely an oxymoron? Not so! The nether realm, these days, is richly presented through collage and film. But while Hell has been well inveighed against in sound and picture, it is not too well described in words. The theatre of Hell's agonies, has been best presented in sensuous—flesh-infused—pictorial images. Hell may have its modes of being known—but it needs more writing-about for a serious new consideration.

An aside—apropos final judgment and its consequences: Why is the bodily assumption of the Virgin into Heaven (a late doctrine) so important—except for keeping the faithful happy in anticipation of a bit of earthly joy mixed in with Heavenly bliss—and for exacerbating the fear of dying sinners that flesh as well as spirit will be consigned to the unremitting pains of Hell?

Something I have noticed about last judgments is that salvation is pictured sparely—just a line of souls on each side of the page, trudging upward twards an apex. The damned are treated differently; they are opened wide into their swift descent. Nothing is left for them to hide —not their scrawny bodies—nor their capacity for screams, pleadings, blasphemy, wailing and imprecation.

In contrast, the candidates for salvation—those clever, faithful poodles—they carefully pick their way up past the slippery-slope just before the pearly gate. On top (once chosen, they will never fall) they meet a formal greeter—a representative of their maker. He looks up from his ledger and says to one much like, but perhaps somewhat better than, you or me:

"I don't know, but I see nothing damning listed here: There is some mention of the time you pushed the sheep off the cliff and almost went over yourself, all-the-while spilling your seed upon the ground. But well, only a sheep—and you did bear your marriage like a cross, wore your hair-shirt until the pustules ripened, and prayed a lot. So we'll let you in. We're merciful—that's our motto you know—only wipe your feet for heaven-sake."

I cannot be like that, a supplicant for an eternal pension—although I had once smiled a bit at higher-ups, didn't pinch a single bespoke behind (oh, maybe one or two) and demonstrated much good will and understanding to my charges. But I have always, I insist, scowled at art-patrons, looked askance at positivists, regarded curators with stony disbelief, growled at censors, and never made a lot of friends or money.

I do admit, however, that I found my heaven in tenure upon the earth and did what was needed to get me in. I have eaten the crow of academe with seeming relish, sometimes looking like a smiling gourd, I know—but I found the cloistered pace, the free-time exchanged for lack of power, more to my liking than walking the silent streets and looking for a quasi- revolution that smelled of brimstone—or of incense.

I also found I like to teach.

I am not going to Heaven or to Hell; the first is just a bunch of trumped-up exhortations—and the second so much an evocation of here-on-earth that creating another such—is redundent.

If someone were to ask me—before I lose my mortal marbles—what (despite disbelief) is my preference in-extremis, I would answer in this way: I choose to go to Limbo (not the dance, but the holding-place for in-betweens). There, I could engage in disputation and ribaldry for all eternity—with the unbaptized babes and the hairy heathen, with old opinionated philosophers, and pre-baptismal souls that die and stay forever young—I could make friends there.

But if Limbo is closed before I die, my choice would not be to wait around in Purgatory—but go straight to Hell. Peace, my friends: Don't laugh, fulminate, or castigate—that won't get you out of it—just read on: If I must, I would be willing to go to Hell and suffer the inversion—the up-ended recapitulations—of my favorite pleasures.

Here is an example: I can see myself as one of those adulterous souls consigned to the upper limits of that demonic place, buck-naked to be sure, blown about like a fat feather in the winds, grasping at but never touching the fingertips of my beloved. Is this the way we can finally be together? Is this what you and I deserve? We'll show them, you and I. We'll masturbate upon the torrid currents for all eternity, our strokings encouraged by momentary glimpses of other sinners' talents flashing by.

But stroking and watching (even for all eternity) are not enough, really, finally, to get us there. Some say that Hell is about "too much." But I suggest that Hell, more so than living—is about "never enough." To follow upon my example: Unrequited sex for all eternity, even when suffused by "never enough," becomes "too much." The absence of earthly measure eventually becomes boring, and torment ceases being effective—change is then required. What? Change in Hell? Why, yes, Variety: Some editing, and switching partners after a century or two—or obdurate interest in a show of later chastity—might help.

Too folksy? Here is another scenario: I could petition to join (just visit with) the Devil on his block of ice. We would sit awhile (Lucifer and I—imagine!) before I try to break his sullen silence—get some conversation going. (Too much introspection is bad—even for the Devil). I would greet him with proper ceremony, then—as with you (if you were there instead of me) I would ask him some questions:

First, I'd ask him to enlarge on what he tried to do back then (the insurrection in Heaven)—what was more important for him to achieve than Heavenly bliss—and why, with all his smarts—he failed. We would sit for a longer while. Then (if the script holds) he would turn to me (eyes blazing, talons bared, and all that) and break the primordial dam—the eons of pent-up silence—by spewing forth that (uniquely) Devilish torrent of hates and frustrations: Bad counsel; mislaid plans; the grievous loss of his once-gorgeous self; confessions that he is lonely (Hell is no place for friends)—and the admission that he still fears God.

After that, the Devil would become silent again, and then he would look at me and say: "Hell could be worse than it is. What if God were to send all of you up there to Hell?"

ABOUT DESERVING

Deserving needs a maker whose plans can best be thwarted
by ungrateful undeserving ones like you and me.
But, if you read the books a-right, we all are poor performers—
spiteful too, having been made to prove ourselves
day by dreary day, but especially at night—
when the rules of deservation are most confusing
and difficult to obey.

In public we are all deservers—payback from those many
sins of others we have appropriately hidden or forgiven.
But sometimes cover-ups fall off like smelly blankets,
and then (the abstemious say) we will surely go to Hell.

There (they tell us) we will twist in fire and freeze on ice,
and listen to the Devil rave, and justify himself through vice.
We together will excoriate the Maker whose idea this was,
before He made us so ungrateful for His beneficence
that we had to fashion other rules,
which afterward we broke of course—
and blamed Him for all the grief this caused.

Is creation, then, a mere misunderstanding—
one held to despite all earthly agony—
because of some logical necessity for both
devilish and celestial pomposity?

WHAT I DESERVE

The following, for starters, is a list of what I deserve: I deserve to leave behind where-ever it is I am, namely, in this oasis of small talk and bloated supermarkets where I neither know nor want to know anyone. But really, they are all so nice. Nice! Nice! A pox on "nice." The coming generation would say "fuck nice," but I find "fucking nice" to be too trendy. Better to revert to the old—however eradicated—" pox."

In contrast to niceties, I deserve (now, not later) a hostile, or incredulous, or garrulous, or lugubrious, or lascivious, response to my efforts. I want to be an accomplice or a mark, not taken as a patsy or a plant, but regarded as foul-mouthed and dark-souled. In return, I can be encouraged to tell my tales as long as breath and wine hold out—for, you know, I was tested for endurance upon the mountain, and for willingness in the sack—and I did well, oh, fairly well—at both.

But I can't rest with that—for "fairly" doesn't get to "very." So I further say that I deserve to be probed, put down, taken up, pulled apart and stitched together, told to find another place to live, or invited back when traveling through. I deserve to be loved—not for what I am, but for what I used to want to be. I have not tried enough, true, but I deserve a few more chances—beginning with a new big bang, or more happily, a few small whimpers. But I must pull back: No persuasion I now can muster will do the skippy trick that I have always thought I wanted.

Looking back, I say I deserve
to be looked at:
Hey, look at that crazy man —
scribbling still and painting too.
Then the child said:
If he really wanted us to look,
he'd show us what he's doing in his head.

I sometimes think of returning to New York and living in two small rooms near Carnegie Hall—that place of all races and religions. My scenario goes like this: Most days, I venture out with my now small steps, perhaps for a pastrami at the Carnegie Deli—too large and greasy for one, but I doggedly eat it all, abandoning the extra bread and pickles mid-way. Then, feeling close to death, I walk into Central park and point myself northeast, toward the Metropolitan Museum, stopping at all the water fountains. Pastrami, you know, gives a killer thirst! I then walk the winding path that leads to the public toilet, where I donate pastrami's completion to the collection. Happily reduced, I continue to the Zoo, eat pop-corn to soothe my gut, talk silently to the animals, and look at girls.

But sometimes, on hot and smelly days, I leave the path and move across the grasses where I can watch others watching me with the interest that poets and predators use to meet and greet each other. This is a formal, but seldom actual interest—one that would not interfere, if such were to happen, with a mugging, a flirtation, or an epiphany. The only requirement for such interest—to receive and return—is a certain style of snort and shuffle, a show (a fleeting glimpse will do) of the transcendent eternal—the shining of deservation that still (however dim and rare) illuminates (and celebrates) the sags and wrinkles and the gimpy gait.

The Met is a great leveler, for we all have come to see great art—yards tons acres of it, all great and all together, waiting to redeem and thereby undermine us. Earlier, when I actually lived downtown, I would do the museum in a day (strange, such a sex-for-hire expression as "do" standing for appreciation). But now, as I seldom visit New York, I spend more time looking at fewer works: I view (a less offensive word than "do") the bounty in small servings—perhaps just two or three paintings in an afternoon, maybe a Greek warrior, some armor, period furniture, or Heifetz's Stradivarius. Few people visit Rockefeller's New Guinea gallery, although it's a good place to rest when one's feet begin to ache—and to mull the mix presented there of beauty and savagery.

But sometimes, wanting more company, I join the crowds in the traveling exhibitions: The best of Velasquez; masterpieces from the Hermitage; rare carpets of the world —plenty of people to watch and nods of approval (like Frisbees) to catch and return.

But great art is like anchovies or chocolate mousse—one cannot eat too much too often. So on other days I turn south, to visit my old haunts downtown. I travel by subway or bus—imagine, taking the subway any time you like—and I get off at 14th street, as I used to years ago, and walk down to the Village. There are more shoe stores and pizza parlors now, and many more people than there were before. The Waldorf Cafeteria on sixth avenue is long gone as are Maxwell Bodenheim and Joe Gould, and all those lovely scruffy others. But I am no longer looking for that secret salon of wit and heavy-lidded eyes. I never found it then—so why look now?

Now I am content to wander, try to fit my memories into these altered places, and watch the checkers and the skateboard contests in the park. On occasion, I might buy an Italian ice and continue on to Soho—where the elite dealers meet to plot their marketing strategies, and where old artists come to be repelled by the bizarre goings-on—"nothing I would ever do, you understand!"—that pass for art these days.

And is this what your life will be, your rescued time that you retired for? Tomorrow and the next day and all the weeks to come, walking slowly through the crowded streets, looking at the carrion of old dreams while the fast young ones move past, impatiently, rudely, unknowingly? Lucian, it may be the standard stuff of poetry, but do you call it living?

Well no—just remembering—a song I sometimes sing when I am sad.

INSIDE AND OUT

You are:
A gibbering mass of post-conceptual jelly —
what a travesty. Such protoplasmic quivering is
a cosmic affront because shaking is mere process,
while the cosmos, taken rationally—is stationary.
Penitentials can be fat, even when
they contemplate Pure Form.
It's the Will that, once aroused,
will bite their saggy asses to the quick —
and try to make them skinny.
Willing in itself is filling—it sometimes can be thrilling.
Best to watch it, though, before it overflows,
and grows the grass around your rotund ass
so green—it must be mowed.

Forms are not like grass—no need to feed them
or to worry about how fast they grow.
They are abstemious in practice and intransigent in principle.
Every Form goes nowhere—it is just where it is.
The world outside of Forms, however, is what-you-will.
But formally speaking—without a a Form there is no anywhere—
not even the there where I once was headed.

Materialists say a "where"—should always be somewhere.
Formalists reply: "Twinkle-twonkle didley oncle,
swizzle-sticks in hez carbuncle." Twaddle? Oh yes!
Materialists can be dumb— but Formalists are more remiss.
I say—no matter when or whether there's a where,
I love language less than a woman's fair caress.

Contra-posto is the Hellenes' answer to Archaic stiffness. In summer, trees sway their parts in the many ways the wind provides. In winter, some trees turn frigid and stand in place. When the winds blow, they tend to break. Pharaohs, too, are stiff and stand sideways—sometimes they also break. But when erect in the dynastic middle, no one would dare look a pharaoh in the face. Venuses (Venus is one—her pictures many) are not like that: They, like summer trees, weave themselves into the different ways they can be looked at—sometimes, they bend and sway, other times they run past trees. Catch her if you can—but please don't touch! No-one should touch (a) Venus.

Squares are sometimes like stiff Pharaohs, other times like Venuses. When opaque, squares present themselves as essences—pure form—although sometimes (quite often, actually) they are merely decorations. When, however, they perform as windows, squares can contain a Venus and many other stories. At times, such stories are beguiling, shocking, or telling—at other times they can be simpering, dull, or just mis-leading. Van Eyck's windows are a measure of the former.

Stiffness is the narrative of types; contra-posto is the narrative of tokens (of a type). Types stand stiff and still—like Pharaohs. Tokens, like trees and Venuses, are always taking different poses.

Square, the way you look when you are flat, is boring —
even though you claim to be essential—pure form—
especially when pictured without nudes or trees or
the bloody gore of crucifixions.

But such opacity mimics the theology that encourages
blank faces to substitute proprieties of dogma and décor
for the terrors of birth and death and insurrection.
Who can blame them, though?
Terror is uncomfortable—gnawing as it does
at insides unwilling (still) to show their inner side.
Dogma always is afraid, and wants to be correct outside.

I disagree.

You, my friend—my sometime self—are wrong in this.

Consider:

Different tokens all belong to different types.
There anyway may be as many types as there are tokens.
Take the bus—you'll see.
But we-all need to find us out—to find,
however much it hurts—what it is we fear we are.
Whether in fact or fiction—for which type are we its tokens.

Never fear:

Such telling will only annotate and celebrate
our moment of first glazing—
the taking on of shining skins that mirror
what we hope we are.

JACOB

My daughter brought me Jacob when I was sick. She made it when she first heard, and worked to give it the powers to make the future right and bright and bring the old man back to where he still belongs. It did just that. But considering all, I think it proper—and not just because Jacob's mission was such a great success—that I should recognize the way we were, and use the pronoun "he"—not "she" or "it" when I refer to him.

Somewhere in this protocol, Jacob achieved emancipation from his artistic designation. He is not "The Jacob," like "The Mona Lisa," nor is he "Samantha's Jacob"—although he is that too. More precisely, he is a piece Samantha made as my defence—and I discovered that his name is Jacob. That's right; I discovered it. He was unnamed before we met and I found his name in a dream just before the dawn of waking from the ether. It was the sort of dream that spills across the edge of sleep because of its urgency for the later time of life. I heard myself say when I awoke: "Of course, he's Jacob."

We can conjecture all we want about the origins of the name—its origins outside of me. But I don't really want to, because accounts of naming sometimes violate the named; they put them into a thrall of begats—as happened to poor Aloysius the Third who, until the day he died, had to tell the folks about the other two. So my benefactor's name is Jacob—plain. It suits him well; he was not chosen from a book—but found in a dream. And yet the naming helps connect him to the sources of his power—in song and ancient ritual.

Let me tell you a bit about him: He is all ceramic head, more mask-like than in the round, and resembles nothing so much as a boar, a wild boar with a long protruding wrinkled snout which ends in a curve of tusks. But his forehead is broad and scholarly, with wide-set serious eyes—not the all-knowing kind, but serious nonetheless and wary—for there are always enemies of the faith or in the bush that must be spotted early.

The top of Jacob's head parts company with the anatomy of boars, for it has two horns, one on either side. To be precise, only one is the standard horn of the kind that impales young Spaniards in the running of the bulls.

The other horn is more like a lizard—a small dragon—an ancient reptile who through the centuries has crawled from left to right across the bumpy brow. Samantha has equipped him well, don't you think?

Jacob is not small—he is an armful—which my strong daughter had brought to me, wrapped in a towel, the night before the day they planned to give old Lucian some grown-up scars. Her eyes were wide as Mars' twin moons when she came, for she did not know Jacob's name, or if he had the powers she had built him for, or if her world of the large man fronting for her wills-of-wisp was going to end. But she up and made him, she did, instead of sitting in a corner, waiting.

Jacob stayed in one place, propped against the chair by the far side of my bed, not the place where the nurses stand when they tend to me. We—Jacob and I—could see each other clearly. No one touched him. Actually, most people didn't see him—not because he made himself invisible, but because he didn't belong there, shouldn't have been allowed in. Something to that: What would hospitals be like if everyone could bring a Jacob? One woman, though, did see him—saw right through him; she had the trash-collecting round, and she looked at him approvingly. She said: "He's taking care of you." Nothing else, no need. Jacob's eyes glistened as he watched her; his glaze was the color of her skin. My eyes would have glistened too, but I was weak and white and smelled of hospital-bed; it was his time to look.

Another woman saw him differently, but said nothing —not to him nor me. She was the head nurse, one of the minor angels, marvelously skilled and fully starched. She may have had a molten core somewhere, reachable by invading her propriety through a secret opening in her tied-up soul—but what I saw (Jacob didn't care to look) was at all times crisp and clean. She could draw arterial blood (the hard-draw) best; the others made my arm look like dry holes in a Western oil-field. But when the others failed (when nothing came, or I made too much noise) she would tap my skin with a transparent finger, then—faster than a Russell's Viper—put the needle in, and without a word would watch the redness well up through the tube. At one such time she did glance at Jacob and I could see her nostrils twitch as if she had caught a whiff, just a trace, of the original parfumeur—of Old Nick's mix of spoor and semen that in bygone days came wafting, even over the convent walls.

Jacob lives with me now. He shares my room with Esmerelda, another of Sam's potent spirits, a girlish mix of horse and dragon whom I have draped with hand-made pendants, and pat her head from time to time. There also is a third small fellow, as yet without a name or function, who is kept in reserve. Sometimes, when my daughter faces a particularly onerous task, or has a particularly vexing boyfriend, I ask my guardians to visit with her for a while. So far, it seems to work.

PERFECTION

Tell me friend:
Are you happy walking between places, searching,
as I'm sure you do, for a sign that says:
"Remain in line until your number's called."

Will you wait for number seven or eleven—
for that bus or train or plane that
takes you to another place—to where
your searching must begin again?
I ask you: Will you find her there?

I must ask again, my friend:
What kind of girl would be so perfect that
you could love her unabashedly and dispassionately?
Will you find her in some other place, another day,
through your searching, calling, and comparing?

I will tell you, friend:
You can do it only if you make her up yourself.
Put everything you've learned into the mix.
Anything lacking can then be fixed
by further ordering from your manuscript.

What? Perfection makes you frightened?
And sends you back to walking straight
to where each soul that greets you has a flaw?
So you can heavy-pet them in their places
while they lie quietly—waiting for the fall?

ESSENCES

One always looks for essences in things, but what can ordinarily be perceived in things are not essences, but sensibilia—so finding essences must take another kind of looking. Well, one can close one's eyes and meditate on the "in-itself." Those who look that way are concerned with finding an image beyond appearance—one that reveals only what cannot be removed without loss of identity—that which makes a something (necessarily) what it is—the essential as opposed to the accidental—a face without its freckles.

The search for essences is not to be undertaken by distinguishing beween qualities that ordinarily describe a thing—qualities that are given it through other sources, such as practical additions, limits of perception, or the whims of other powers. Some philosophers (as I said the last time I talked this way) do ascertain differences between "primary" and "secondary" qualities of things, which—if one is comfortably speculative—can be mapped onto the distinction between "essential" and "accidental" qualities. But this is a mistake. I think that essences are not sensate qualities, but rather, definitions. The term is a linguistic stipulation that permits us to distinguish between things-in-the-world and things-in-themselves—the distinction between enduring and transient—the unseen identity underlying differences. All this seems harmless enough for now.

But the search for essences will at times take on a different character. It can seek a distinction between "real" and "apparent," "empirically true" and "undeniably true." In the latter usage, the term 'essence' takes on a religious and mystical tone—an admonition to search for an underlying reality by rejecting all that is transient and ephemoral. This, of course, requires (demands) deep belief—a judgment somehow (don't ask further) "given." Essences so discovered are eternal—but they guard themselves from being vulnerable, as we are, to time and change—especially when we cease believing in eternity.

The essences that figure in this story are not so much about the identities that underly appearances (the story is out of memory and fantasy—not philosophy). Instead, they are about an iconic—singular—occurrence which revealed a world where identity and value were deeply transformed. The story is of my experience, through the medium of a (sacred) drug, in which my usual world was replaced by one composed of essences—some revelatory, others hostile, but all vital—and necessary—for the demands of my newly found ecstatic world. These essences, whether in the guise of trees, stones, shadows, wind-gusts, apparitions, were em-personed through the role that I, as conduit between the natural and spiritual realms, had given them.

These things-turned-personages became the inhabitants of my life: They instructed, scolded, pleasured, frightened me. Trees listened to me talk and then replied; I was as one with the larger rocks; the wind sang along; the chirps of insects provided counterpoint to the louder voices in my head; the forest and the sky became my home. All were eternal, sometimes fierce—free to change and be the same.

To discover that one's world is (now) composed of essences, gives rise to the vision (more than mere belief) that one has penetrated to that "core of being"—of which the artifacts encountered in the relinquished outer world are only imperfect and often misleading facsimiles.

Such a vision—although, as in my case, physically induced—has a religious and mystical aura. It separates modes of cognition, and it offers—as a consequence—unique insights into "being-as-the-world" (not "being-in-the world") that are critical for understanding the meaning that the confluence of essences provides—all of art, love, duty, hope, happiness, sorrow, anger, hatred, resignation—all brought together within a "singularity" of understanding.

The quotation marks I use here emphasize the theoretical largesse needed to accept my tale —not as plausible, but as evocative—and further, to suggest (now that I am back) that the search for essences is indeed a strange, sometimes other-worldly, pursuit—one more cogently couched in poetic form than presented in argument.

The experience of essences is not divisible; it locates knowing in a contemplation that arrives at something being what it is. To find an essence through contemplation is not a matter of thinking things through, but of thinking through a thing—to the irreducible place where it is just—and only—what it is. For this, the perception of sense-data is not crucial; indeed, it can confuse transient things with their essences.

In Academe, the topic of essences often results in friendly argument—not a big deal, but a testing to see—in the light of historical change, new psychological findings and linguistic evolution—where different ways of cognizing will get us.

I bring up the issue here for a self-serving reason—because once (it might have been "once upon a time") I (myself) discovered a world of essences—although, then, I didn't think of it that way.

I once made (drew) a green line (the circumstances, as I tell you, were extraordinary). That line was everything—everything that, after all the rest had been discounted, remained essential. It was pure, my line, perfect—the essence of both "green" and "line." It both divided and created the page. It had only one dimension, but was as large as the world. Its green was the gathering place of all color—thick and thin, on the paper and in the sky, seen and unseen.

Later, after I had slept awhile—the line was still there, still green, although it—as an essence—was gone, vanished, no longer anywhere.

Oh, there was something there—to be seen—when I looked again the morning after. There was a pastel stripe drawn on a sheet of news-print tacked to a board in a rented room above a bar on highway 17 in North Carolina in 1953. It was not (no longer) an essence; it was just a stripe. But what I had drawn earlier—in that potent night—must have been an essence (as I still believe). This is because—having vanished so completely—it could not have merely been a thing.

The following is a warning to those
who only kiss directly and intensely
when
underneath the mistletoe.
In so doing, they too much
toe the line of proper color.

You callow fellow yellow had best
put a glaze-on before you are
set-upon by Indigo, and
get diluted into the neutral brown
that is a color of indifference.

Crimson lake will give,
to any sunset, its due sake.
But when ingested (never lick your fingers

or suck upon your brush)
it is more
deadly than a coral snake.

Emerald green is fine for foliage—
but too much grass will
still your heart before you can
plan ahead to show your garden
and so express your smarts.

To bring all this together, I move back along my special set of strings:

I was drafted during the Korean war. After boot camp, I obtained a weekend pass back to New York where I sat with other strangers at a table in the Waldorf Cafeteria in the Village—talking to Mickey the Merchant Seaman. He was an old salty dog, with a friendly round face and eyes that had stopped recording much of what they saw. After a while, my complaints about the military and how much time I had left to serve—must have bored him; so he said: "I gotta go, but meet me here tomorrow morning before you leave—I want to give you something."

The next morning he showed up with a brown paper bag and told me that it was a gift, freely offered, which would help me. "There are special cacti inside, that the Indians call Peyote. They worship this cactus as a God, and eat it in the ceremonies they hold when they sense a coming separation from their land, or when the game is scarce, when there is too little rain, when disease kills too many, when an old chief dies, or when a new enemy appears. After eating they hold it down until they throw it up—the wisest can hold it down for many hours. Then they wander off alone into the forest or across the plains. There they dance, ask questions of the trees, see visions that show them what they need to know. They wait for the visions that will frighten them—with apparitions no one but they should see. In a few days, most come back—but some follow the figures that had earlier frightened them, and these do not come back.

The ceremony then continues, and those who have returned tell some—but not all—of what they have learned. From this talking—which can last for many days—each learns separately about the center everyone uniquely has—and what part of it can be shared. Some of what is learned this way no other person, however close, can understand. What is right for all to know is for the elders of the tribe to say. Sometimes their sayings help the tribe's understanding of what to listen to—sometimes not. The God Peyote is opaque. The cactus never tells anyone everything they need to know—however much of it you eat."

Mickey then slid the bag to me and said that I should eat them all—as fast or slow as is right for me. Do it through, he said—don't back down. But be sure to give yourself a day or two on the far side of eating—otherwise old Peyote will leave you in the dusty road—manna for the M.P.'s.

When I got back to the base, I showed the cacti to a friend named Pete, also a draftee, who lived with his wife in a settlement of quonset huts outside the base, and who was deeply concerned about the scurrilous treatment by our government of American Indians. He also smoked a lot of pot. Pete approved of the cacti on political grounds—although he had never eaten any—and we agreed that, come next weekend, we would ceremonially eat them at his place; I, having no wife, had no "place"—except for the barracks. Pete's wife Trisha didn't approve but said nothing—she had been there before.

So we settled down—to get high and to make solidarity with the Indians. Close-up, the cacti looked like old teeth, with a mossy crown, dark brown roots, and a fibrous shell. Evidently, we couldn't eat them that way, so we thought to peel and slice them like potatoes. They tasted like raw earthworm dirt—which we first saw as a test of conviction—an obstacle to be overcome. We tried to mask the taste in various ways—with chocolate, swigs of ginger ale—then we settled on Fig-Newtons because we could insert the slices in the gooey center and gulp them down without chewing. Neither of us knew what to expect. Time passed and nothing happened—no buzz, no blur, no heightened chatter. Pete's wife had lost all patience; and the taste was vile no matter what we did. We had stopped talking; and at some point, I don't remember when, I left.

Fortunately, it was summer—because I walked the woods for hours, maybe days. As I had become enchanted, I did not alarm the snakes who would simply watch me pass.

I met many friends that I did not know I had—trees who said they knew me and wanted to talk with me. And we did talk, in the darkness that we shared. But our talking was not idle chatter about wind and water—for they were not casual friends, these trees, but relatives, blood of my blood, who were concerned with how much I had closed myself outside myself in recent years. I admitted to them, weeping now, that I needed forgiveness.

For what, I do not remember, but certainly, for all the things I did or did not do that made me feel that awful way—all that had separated me from the inside of what I am.

"Bless me pine-tree for I have sinned; in thought word deed, body and soul, from crooked toe to nasal hair—right through the middle of my brain, and past the input of my mouth and outpouring of my ass." Centuries passed and then they (my ancient friends) told me there was nothing to forgive—that that's what people do, trees too, all of us out here. The pines and I, we sat and cried together, and we sang. Our song followed the cadences of rustling leaves. The frogs sang its chorus with us too—until slowly, very slowly, their song turned into a blame-filled croaking.

"You too, Gramps?—they intoned. With your baggy branches and scabrous roots, what with that hairy wen sitting on your nose? You did and do such things? Disgusting! We've seen your bulbous bouncing on a young birch tree stretched across the back limbs of a dying oak! Now we know you! You are not a gentle forest-murmor like those who are my friends. You are the predatory city-vine that lurks at forest's edge and hides the straight-a-way from the pilgrims who seek the true-brick-road. You are not our friend a'tall, a'tall.

I ran to escape the arms that clutched and scratched at me, and found a pool-room in the middle of the forest, empty except for the proprietor who let me play alone for a while and then suggested that we play the game together. I had been making marvelous shots—the vectors of the table were illuminated, force fields perhaps, and they carried my balls straight to their appointed pockets. But when he joined me, I could not sink another ball; the table tilted, my cue was crooked, and he began to shrink—a squat Tonto with a pointy face—so I went out into the woods again.

How much time passed—where I went, I do not know. Perhaps to make my peace with the trees—my gnarly kin—that I had so maligned, and to forgive the frogs for bad-mouthing me. But that space in my memory is empty. In the next remembered time, I was in the tiny room that I had rented—cheap and buggy and meant for transients, but a place where, most nights, I could escape the barracks, set up an easel and unwrap my dreams. It was there that I came to make (what is nowhere, still) the essence of green and line.

The nature of an essence specifies that it should be out of time, so I couldn't know how long it took to make mine. The paper was already pinned up on the board, and the chalks were scattered on the table. Green was but one of the many colors.

My essence, as I describe it, is centered by (and in) a green line. Why green? Because this green is the green of Green-ness, not the changing green of ordinary greens.

Sight sound smell taste touch are all particulars (fleeting tokens) confronted with this essential green. It could have been another color, true, but with essences there are no regrets—not any "I think it would have looked better if "—none of that. My green was the most beautiful green I had ever found—a conceptual beauty of course, sufficient unto itself, like a found stone—only I had made it. Think of that!

"Je suis le Dieu" I cried—I remembered Picasso had also said that. The line responded smiling with a full-frontal face. I looked at this line of lines for a long time, and it did what essences do, it presented itself in unchanging terms—a perfect division of its page, beyond time—the essential model for transcending the schism it itself had made. As a point can be a speck or a juncture, so a line can be a separation or a path. My line was both; it had become the catechism for all things that need returning —for coming back together into one.

Time outside the green-line did not, however, hold still for me. Unlike my essence, I was changing. The cactus chemistry was calling up my Hyde, and I began to see the Lightning Gods, like those that appear inside when your fingers press down hard upon your eyeballs. My eyes were open, and yet I saw them standing all around and more to come from every corner—jagged moving Ziggurats with skins a checkerboard of black and white—not threatening me particularly, they were too ancient too indifferent—but they crowded all the same into the spaces of my little room. They did not look at my green line—it had lost its nature and its power. The only place left vacant was my bed—so I went to sleep.

ROACHES

The troubador Reinhardt Mey once sang: "Alles was Ich habe ist meine
Kuchenschabe."
They crawl, they fly (especially down south) in and out of cracks and other
spaces.
And they bear the hatred of the world (especially up north) upon their
flimsy carapaces.

But cockroaches have long-gotten a bad shake:
They do not bite, carry fewer germs than flies, propogate through necessity,
eat just enough to live and make their tidy places.
But I am like the others of my tribe—I want to spray them, squish them,
kill them all!
Such a fool am I.
What is worse—I ask you now—roaches crawlng over you at night—
or a rattler coming down the parlor stairs—to bite you just in time for tea?

Once, beneath a kitchen sink in Brooklyn, I found a paper bag with old
potatos.
The roaches had long been eating quietly—but I disturbed them with my
probing.
Out they came: Platoons, battalions, divisions—the world was full of
roaches.
Although interrupted at their eating by my petulence, they showed no
malice—
but they did cover the floor, and without fear, crawled over my naked foot.
So I sprayed and sprayed—to get them off my feet and also off the floor.
But roach-spray wasn't very poisonous in those early days,
so many survived—to leave my foot and run across the floor—outside—
to where the birds and spiders wait for wayward bugs.

I have some roaches still—not so many as before.
They are the children of those that stayed inside the door.
But they show me no malice and have no memory of the poison.
So I leave them pieces of potatos in alloted places.

In return, they don't presume to share my bed
or crawl into my shoes—which I still keep on the floor.

ANGELS

Angels are mostly of two kinds: Some of them—the older angels, are of the higher kind—and they weep. Others, the lesser angels, dry-eyed, only do their duty. Why is this division necessary? Does it hold in heaven too?
We can suppose that, for God, human history is but a minor configuration of Being—there is much beside us to attend to. So in the short term we humans are on our own.

But we must also keep in touch—by prayer, supplication, and crazy dancing—with the ineffable Real-of-Reals. It is all one universe, I know, so we're lucky to have the angelic go-betweens—whose main functions, as regards us, are two: The first and most important of angelic tasks is to ensure that small mistakes don't add up to changes in the large direction; and the second task is to show that God cares, although it may not always be evident.

The nurse who so adroitly took my blood just after Jacob came, is an angel of the second kind, doing her duty as she was created to see it, and alert to every sign of chaos setting in—like Jacob's randy smell. Her focus is on things that need to be set aright. She derives no pleasure from this—oh maybe a satisfaction of some austere sort. Like Kant's moral person, she does good not out of inclination—not because she likes it—but because it is her duty. And, as you know: "Duty, duty must be done; the rule applies to everyone."

If I were an angel, I would not want to be like her; I would prefer to weep.

Bawling and sobbing, see me cry—
sluicing high above the morning coffee—
dripping droplets into foamy beer —
making wet the proffered nape—
offered in sympathy, but not real fate.

All these are signs of weakness, I know—excuses for putting-off what needs to be done. But the bumblers among us cannot be abandoned entirely—God knows—so we have the angels who share His optimism and our dismal outlook—and worry about our our fate. Some angels cry.

Tears are, in fact, a potent testimonial: Achilles' tears splashing down on Hector after he dragged the body through the town; I, weeping my mother's demise onto my maiden cousin's neck while the tribe looked on approvingly; the imported claque blowing their long and saturated noses into red bandanna handkerchiefs during the intermission of Tagliavini's Met debut—"better than Caruso," they said.

There are tears that accompany protestations of love, or try to palliate the reasons for breaking-up so soon. And there are those other tears that trickle down one's nose for no reason at all—quiet tears that come when looking at the residue of last-night's supper; the inside of your slipper; or the face showing in the morning mirror.

Tears are the printed t-shirts of humanity—our promise that we will be as good to others as we are to ourselves. But, inevitably, we delude each other—for we weep to mask the fact (to others and ourselves) that we would be doing exactly as we wish—if we were better at wishing than we are.

Angels weep in other ways—to let us know that Hegel's slaughter-bench of history is very much on all their minds, and they are doing everything they can. And angels let us (in painting and poetry, and our replication of their voices) represent their weeping, so that we may forgive them for not doing more than can be done by anyone—even as they forgive us, when we weep, for not doing as much as we ourselves could do.

THE NEED TO PEE HURTS POETRY

I once stood on a check-out line
poe-tasting with my grocery cart—which was
brimming with rewards for the poe-tizing
of a previous week.
First I bought a case of wine, then some sirloin steaks,
ripe mangos, red peppers, and a chocolate cake.

Why not eat well, I said to others waiting there—
those citizens speculating on their dis-satisfaction
with having only brats and chips and beer.

I said I might as well stay here—
instead of buying air-line tickets to far places
full of bronzit-baked bikini-babes,
and basted bankers reddened by the tropic sun.
You know the babes are pricy, the bankers nasty,
and the food is spicy and not tasty.

Then all at once I felt a drizzle.
My pee was trickling from my pizzle.
My sweat-pants couldn't catch it any more.
It went all down my inside leg to make
a puddle on the market floor.

There was a silence, then the bagger-boy
looked at me and said: You'ld better wipe your shoe
— it's wet.

ART AND PLACE

Artworks have no settled place to be, no more than they have a common look that circumscribes the particulars of their ambitions. The marble carvings and the welded beams, with their privileged sites, are not any more in an eternal place than are buildings designed for section-eights, or printed versions of excessive poems.

Think of the Elgin Marbles—named after an English lord, sculpted by ancient Greeks, scrutinized in passing by the Romans, and later recognized as prime pillage by the Western powers. Those friezes gave neo-classic raptures to Victorian Englishmen, and more recently, in facsimile, have adorned university stairwells—reminders for undergraduates of the relevance of higher education.

Where then, among all these, is the proper place for the Elgin Marbles—that place in which their meaning can be most clearly ascertained, their qualities best enjoyed, and their influence on the future of art and life most cogently assessed?

Evidently, there is no such place—and no-one now much cares about originals. Instead, there is a going narrative of the better places, which continually renews itself—as do the histories of the much travelled objects that are its subjects.

Physicality does not confer identity on art. I wonder, in passing, whether anything—or anyone—any longer achieves identity through a material place. Maybe in the countryside. But even there—among the corn stalks—the old familiars die, the young permit the weeds to grow, their offspring curse the need for mowing—and sell the place to large conglomerates.

So too with the relics in Grandma's attic—sold upon her death to the wily antique-dealer, and now cohabiting with Kwakiutl carvings in a penthouse condominium.

Painters made portraits of significant others in all the ways art-history and propriety would allow. One must note, however, that it is a mark of exceptional talent (like Velasquez) for a painter to paint an ugly king as ugly—and get away with it. Van Gogh painted his ugly self, but the paintings let you know that he-himself—as he thought himself—would not want to match their beauty. Rembrandt looks sadly out from behind his magic glazes at bourgeois frolics—while Saskia encouraged him, even with his bulbous nose, to find the older beauty in her naked plainness.

Cezanne modelled himself after that mountain in which geometry clarifies the form but lets no sentiments intrude—he painted his wife as massive as a rock. But his late bathers retreat from all the heaviness. They are wisps that open us to nature's benign instruction—but they themselves, while naked, are without substantial flesh.

Picasso's self-portraits tell us nothing about himself—only his skill at painting most everything while concealing what importantly remains. DeKooning avoids himself except by giving painful evidence, through his "Women," of having once been there—while Chuck Close makes everyone look fashionably good.

The Sardonapalus of Delacroix reclines in terminal musing while his retainers dutifully kill his naked concubines —of which he had so often made public use, and which his thugs could not but have desired, had they not been dulled by a life-time of sadism and servitude.

Just think script—you modern movie-makers: Those brutes, rather than emptying themselves in obedient killing, could have fled together with living grateful girls—despite the tyrant's roars (after all, his enemies were at the gate). Then they could have found—however little more the men were than lesser beasts, and the girls not more than much-used beasties—more in life than in death. With a glimmer of freedom, they could have crept past the carnage on the road—and into a longer life of fucking, foraging, planting and birthing, in the wilderness. Far better this than the assigned roles Delacroix gave them in his "Fall Of Empire" antique theatre.

But Delacroix did not appreciate naked women as did his rival, Ingres. For Delacroix, they were the accoutrements of male power—viewed and used as the priorities of occasion required. For Ingres, women were inhabitants of an ideal harem—captive, bathed and well fed, required to perform learned services, yet able to control, through the opulence of their flesh, the possibilities that could neutralize their lack of power.

Ingres' Odalisques are well-served—whether actual or fictional—in having their depictions conceived by one who saw them clearly, deeply wanted to be there with them in his painted place—but could not.

Rubens was the most fortunate of the greats. He had the most of beautiful women—whose likenesses he presented directly to his patrons—and other times put these women, enhanced as only he could do, into the most elaborate tableaus that the Pagan Gods could devise for the pleasuring of their immortality.

To paint so well, and love so fully, and live so long, is well-nigh incomprehensible to the modern mind.

OTHER SENSES AND OTHER ARTS

Revolutionaries don't provoke—as Tamirov said to Gary C. when Stukas bombed and Spain was burning. Both painters and writers sit on rocks and look at bombs bursting—the better to use them afterwards. But writers—after the bombing is over—peep out quietly at the carnage— not wanting to miss a thing—before they stuff the gore back inside their covers. Painters who look at scary things will paint them later when they have found a form into which the memories fit. This can take a lot of drawing which is out of ordinary time. Time-passing is more compatible for writers. They, after all, write in time—and you, reader, also read in time. These times are not the same—but because they both move, they are like strangers meeting on a train. Soon enough, the distance between upper and lower berths succumbs to a joining of shared interests. This can be called a "reading." Consider—in contrast—the exposed act of looking at paintings. The need for privacy in appreciation differs as regards visual and verbal art: One can truly have the great masterpieces of the written word in one's own home, even beneath the covers—while one must seek a public space—a gallery or museum—to see and appreciate the great works of visual art.

But times change: Reproductions (2D and 3D) are getting larger and better—while one can listen to recited literature while driving or shopping.

Painters who paint self-portraits do not do as well as writers when both go to war. Wounded painters carp about the pain of art because they dislike showing scars to models —who of course, in their own lives, lose their glamour and become as unsightly as old scarred painters. Hurt writers, however, can hide behind the dissemination of their works—where wounds and scars are anything that language will make of them. They need not show much of themselves—except at occasional readings.

However—painters and writers are both artists—don't you know. They both eat the tasty grease of promiscuous evenings, and both are faced when they wake—together with their consorts or alone, with the unsightliness of morning and the acidity of bad after-taste—whatever the destinations of their makings.

In the Romantic days, the solitary artist endured the tension between the highs of accomplishment and the lows of expression—the downward swoop from mastery to misery. This required the uses of cheap wine and contructive introspection to mask the smelly end of a sweaty day that, despite the leaping and the diving, may not have gone too well. Today, in contrast, the art of film employs a lot of people, and so the smell is more communal; if not as well aestheticized. This may be because of the commonplace of sweat—no one is immune from funk at end of day—so the aesthetic possibilities of orchestrating body-odors into film remain ignored as being too vaporous, vacuous, and plebian—to be art.

This is a pity. Film has been particularly good at portraying the fictional disconnect between stale odors and lusty sex: Think "Barbary pirates and captive English maidens—gunpowder and cologne on the high seas;" or "a chance meeting, after all these years, on the midnight train—in a shared compartment—with a long-lost love." But can you imagine how Marilyn, or Clark, or Ingrid, or Humphrey—smelled in the flesh at the end of an all-day shoot?

There once was an attempt (called the "Feelies" as I remember)—to electronically introduce distaff bodily sensations into the central visual meat of movies—a communion between all the senses that would evoke the experience, say, of bedding-down with Clark or Marilyn. But it got nowhere—last I heard. A good thing, actually. What would you do, you ordinary creature, with the suffocative power of the smell of greatness?

So the art of "Smellies" (a co-conspirator with "Feelies") will not either bridge the aesthetic gap. Rancid greatness does not have the crowd appeal of a perfumed trivial provocation. Profoundly rich and deviant odors, except for connoisseurs, are not yet part of the history of style—however much they are part of living.

There are many places where art can hide and so avoid bringing its makers into early prominence, while giving hope to both old and young by the very fecundity and breadth of art's history—which has alternated between sweet and sour through some thousand years.

It gets curious and curioser to consider
the virgin blushing at the caudal kiss.
But who can know for sure,
the ingredients of the Devil's spoor?

Art's odor has many flavors—some of which should be welcomed by the young-and-hungry, and then remembered through the traces that remain when the elders leave the table. Old art is a vampire that demands a string of progeny, with ancient perpetrators biting young and willing necks—so as to ensure that the originary line, while closed to outsiders, is yet continuous in its familial derivation. But young art, unless it dumbly succumbs to the toys and joys of ancients, has no mandate to be kind to those old scribbler-schmearers of the discontinued. They, the venerables—now limp and sclerotic last-ditch divers into the core of (decreasingly available) novelty—still dream (and why not?) of their places in the exclusive theory of what remains—after all is said-and-done.

Titian's nudes never smell; Rembrandt's sometimes do. The Deities, as in Rubens' painting of "The Union of Earth and Water," have their separate musks—each fragrant in its own way. Bringing them together shows an ideal communion between the aggressive lust of storms and the open needs of drought. The allure of its principals is clarified when one imagines the wet-odiferous and dry and gritty nature of their mingling.

With Cezanne's bathers, though, nobody wants to know whether the local girls smelled or not, because—so painted—they have lost their odor together with their ardor. They have (how did it happen?) become abstract—substituting intersecting lines for quivering limbs.

An exception is found in some old-age Picassos, where he winds his dark-green brush up the cleft in the backside of a surprised Cubist nude. In the main, however, abstraction is bad for smell and indifferent to taste—although it translates well into sound (think of Pollock and Steve Reich). But I am for the reintroduction of smell into painting (not the smell of paint but of people—George Grosz and Lucian Freud sometimes do this well—Balthus and Breugel too).

Smell is a good authenticator of place—you cannot indifferently walk past a place when it presents a smell you recognize. Brothels once perfumed their doorways as beacons for our raunchy forbears; and the latest salons of fashion now insist we cannot know the difference between scent and stink unless we come inside, have a glass of wine, and pay the price of fashionable sniffing.

Most places are connected, like most lovers, with their smells, and the interpretations of artworks should include the smells of places they have passed through. Van Gogh, Gauguin, and friends did not smell the same in the café Momus as they do hanging in the latest hallowed halls. The smell of art changes with its places; even the most enduring of our loves smell different as the years go by. Does not a Titian Venus attain a sharper edge of funk after we have looked our fill at Schiele's women?

Wagner and Kandinsky wanted, in their ways, to bring the senses together within an aesthetic place and time. Wagner strove to establish his works as the foundation for what would be the (historically inevitable) synthesis of all art forms: The Gesamtkunstwerk—music, drama, dance, poetry and metaphysics—all together in one bewitching brew. Kandinsky was less political and wanted only to affirm, through his own work, the elements common to all the arts—namely, art as a (the) sensual source for attaining the trans-sensual unity of spirit.

John Cage permitted random sound to join with whatever noises his compositions make—an experience we can also have while listening to Bach by an open window.

It depends, as Cage implies (and Bach—who knows?) on what we listen for—and who's cooking what on the floor below.

Then there is the sensation of taste—which needs to distinguish itself, all the more these days, from taste as value: "Good-taste" is not the same as "tasting good."

Taste is intimately involved with smell. If the receptors in either smell or taste are compromised, the other does not function well. We can smell at great distances—as in the acrid smell of forest fires, or the upbeat smell when crossing Brooklyn Bridge, of the coffee-roasting plant. Taste does not have this distance—you put your tongue and mouth to the eating business, and wipe your chin, or smack your lips when it ends.

But taste and smell do have first claim on place in early memory, and both can marinate our older years with wafts of once upon the time. We then shake our heads and try to stand erect, to be proud of what we have become—although we are less straight-forward now than we were back then. But even now, when tasting is no longer as intense, we fasten (old-age-trading) onto nearby sights and distant sounds as our protection against what, despite our progressive drying, we still remember in that long some time ago.

The enjoyment of how things smell and taste is a young pursuit, fitted to the feral forests of prey and love. Remembering is more for older ones, who cannot any longer run down a deer, nor have the temerity to compete in the rip and slurp of prey when something gamy passes by the entrance to the cave.

Nowadays, the old ones concentrate on slow-low-cooking—they no-longer slap at hungry flies, and cooking slowly gives the extra time they need before the end of eating—a important interlude before it is time to leave.

"Good Taste," in these late days, is not much about tasting. It has left its incestuous relationship with body-juices and now sniffs around for more distant partners.

Taste—so adjudicated and found wanting—abdicates its youthful role as enabler of prurience, gluttony, and other life-enhancing functions, and becomes an apologist of aesthetic and cultural novelty. So construed, it enters into a normative mode, as the arbitrator between practices and preferences—between high and low, rich or poor, relevant or dated taste. Within our social scheme of anxiety and acclaim, such critical directives mold our most important choices—those through which we hope to justify privilege and success by acquiring valuable artifacts, a distinguished home, and admiring friends.

But many strategies are available—taste is profligate: Choosing while knowing that your choice does not fit the tastes of others, can sometime affirm your sensibility as one who exhibits superior—even novel taste—a lesson for serious consideration in the new salons. On the other hand, novel, yet aberrant, taste can also be likened to baring the plebian backside of your tenement past—where the origins of untutored appetites can still be found. Why then, young hopeful, should you risk a venture into post-taste-taste—which can reveal occasions not-yet forgotten, for the titillation of those who do not want you anyway.

But now,
even when it seems impossible,
you, my lovelies, should abandon
up-town stuffies and their nasty snifflings,
and come join me in my
almost-purified remaining place.
The fare will be cheaper
and tasting so much sweeter,
when you and yours get there.

I don't do taking risks these days—and you shouldn't either—because there really aren't any, any-more—due to the inflated price of trying—worth taking . It may once have been that risk-taking was necessary—but now our memories join our still-sharp smarts to show us the swift demise of outdated proclamations and the gestures they require.

Now, I can look up my creased and bumpy nose at you as scathingly as you look down your smooth-slick nose at me. That's progress—that also is my life, and should be yours as well.

I once had chances to go places where I could have been more myself—had I not been me—but that's how I turned out.

THE LEAN AND THE FAT

Willing is required for eating. Anything edible
is permissible for gaining entry to where the Will abides—
that curator of what goes in and what comes out.

Even so, Will must rest awhile between recurrent
dashes to fill the space between a glottis and its anus.
Resting before biting or after chewing is merely palliative.
It brings a passive tranquility to necessary travel
beyond the door of mastication and past the chute of gulp.

This is the ancient way that opens the outer zig-zag to inside living—
By tracing byways of digestion, the trickling drip-drop of absorption,
and proper access to the trusty portal of elimination.
The Will itself is seldom needed for moves beyond the gullet.
It is the prime—not the efficient—mover.
After its first imput, the lesser causes will take over.

Those who opt for Form, in contrast,
barely nibble at the wafer of nutrition.
This gesture is not obeisance—more like solidarity between
anorexic supplicants whose knees become more bulbous
as their flaccid shanks grow sorely skinny.
Yet, they are offered as testimonials of submissive faith
that give a martyr's glow to the pain of all that kneeling.

Feet, when forced to dance on toes, get crooked.
Not as bad as in the Orient when they're bound—certainly
better than lip-extenders and clitoral cuttings. Not yet death.
Skinny shanks, even bare, are less distinct
than naked collar bones which, in special circumstances,
show themselves along the runway or on the beaches—
cutting horizontally across the vertical path beween
Mascara and barely budding breasts.

The formal function here is clear. It shows the transparency of Will
in acting to rid the body of all excess and so help it acquiesce to Soul.
The runway is a practice way between acclaim and the skinny-end of death.
Beaches, though, are full of fatter life—potato-chips and blowing sand.
Containment is to sand as abnegation is to flesh.
Both reveal the dry, bare, bones of Form.

Too much Form ends in emaciation—too little gives us constipation.
Both make travelling to a place where we would like to go,
more difficult. Jiggly fat hides Form—skinny mannequins
show all too much of it. Gnawing on a meatless bone may be
food enough for some—but I prefer the Will's demand that
mastication should exceed one's capacity for moderation.

I cannot do with deprivation. I will not heed bad-mouthing
gluttony and its boon companion—the slowly felt,
yet much anticipated, striving for a flatulent conclusion.
Excess, as I have come to know it, is the harbinger of
a deeply-willed, however indecorous, redemption—
a recapitulation of the primal urge to always be becoming.

ART AND LIFE

This is a rumination on the interplay between art and life. It also is a poem, and it often turns into polemics—which I present indifferently as poetry or prose. It is not necessary for you to distinguish between the sensory varieties of symbol-types—for here it's all (in) words. The visual and auditory arts (e.g., paintings or song-cycles) have to trust their essences to their discursive kin (as employed here)—to give them all a fair accounting.

All art has the broad features of accrued value and indeterminate duration, while life is characterized by indeterminate value and finite duration. Despite these formal distinctions, each realm has historically contested with the other for its own ends—art to confirm its completeness, and life to achieve fulfillment.

From time to time, the arts have taken on the several tasks—denied them by Plato—of offering both critical and celebratory ways of representing the world. Plato, famously, considered the arts as imitations of imitations, and thus having no power to represent—or argue for the nature of the world— much less to shed light on the abiding reality of the Forms. For a time, however, Western art—particularly in the tropes modelled on neo-classic values- had tried to represent, through the flow of refined and informed imagination, those perfections that approximate the essential and timeless nature of underlying reality. This was "high art"—the art of Bach and Michaelangelo. Its achievements required a system of ataliers—a master-apprentice relationship, controlled by the accumulating certainties of excellence—measures that would insure the continuity of aesthetic value through the vagaries of social change.

After that we reverted to Plato's view. The later movements in art, those based more on personal expression and a relish for historical discord, (art conceived as existentially, formally and politically radical) found continuity, in style and outlook, with the revolutionary (post-enlightenment) task—given the weakening of religious belief—"of what must now be done." This "now" is not a deductive extraction from history, nor an express emblem of wealth and power—rather, it is a response to individual experience and present situations—often to subjective pleas for communal authenticity. In this (modern) context, the artist ceases being a professional and becomes, instead, a sort of shaman—possessing insights into the secrets that, for reasons of public danger and the onus of class restrictions, are individually recognized but socially suppressed.

Rembrandt, in his portraits, gives us a pictorial revelation of the scars of inner life—and shows the look of private "empathy"—a concretion of public "sympathy."

Manet, in hs "Dejeunaire," presents a person—a woman—publically naked, looking directly out—past her picture—as an accusation against those of us who fear the taint of repression and the power of exposure.

Alban Berg, in his "Wozzeck," exposes the public cruelty that can turn ordinary life into a private nightmare—and then, at the end, has the child sing a little ditty—hip-hop—to continue the audience's consternation.

The modern artist works within the waiting game of artistic fame. This game is rarely suited to those who anticipate an outcome favorable to them and to the art they make.

During the demise of salon-culture, the modern artist was faced with developing new ways of winning or losing, that would give the waiting experience some effect on the way things actually go. But as such strategies had little precedent, their adoption required a new introspection—a deep-diving to find an equilibrium beteween the now-unfettered—but transient self of the artist—and the equally unstable (but deeply controlling) world of social life.

This historical happening called for an a-historical stance, one obsessively personal—often angry, sometines despairing—where artistic value is derived more from present experience than from historical examples. Art becomes free by forsaking tradition and by assuming critical—or escapist—images in its presentations of life.

But this poses categorical problems—which impinge on the formal freedom required for novelty in art. The ways of art-as-criticism, or art-as-therapy, become closer to "forms of life" rather than to "forms of art." And it is here that the dilemma emerges: At what point do these forms of life so converge on what they want of art, that the older distinctions of formal excellence are lost to the actual practices of art?

It is is now a commonplace to say that art so resembles life (the artifacture of actual living) that one cannot—or need not—look for durable distinctions between the two.

But this reveals the spoiler: If art is life variously configured, then life must be art let loose—decategorized—for reasons of a disenchantment with the belief in, or a need for, a stable distinction between the two. The formal meets the actual in the controversy over where aesthetic value is found. It can be found, as indicated, in the physical (sometimes emotional) detritus of our living. But more to the contemporary point, it can be found in the other direction—in the individual's self-perception as being an art-work—a fiction, masquerading as a person that, in various ways, represents itself. The acceptance of this ambivalence as the (true) nature of living, is tantamount to a new historical moment of self-discovery—the realization that our actions are all performances—by a subject (character) devised (by us) in order to portray the various fictions through which we accommodate (control) the world.

It is not discomfiting, these days, to view both ourselves and the world as fictions, created (by us) to construct a reality that requires both in order to be perceived (by us) as real. But where and what is this "us?" Our projections of self again ask for two separate beliefs—that other selves believe it is truly us that they are engaged with—and the second, a more risky one, is that we believe that we truly are the person we are representing.

What happens when we have grown accustomed to this strategy of categorical shifting? To maintain art and life within their separate categories—however necessary that may once have seemed—needs painful divestiture of what is now valued, and scary speculation about what may take its place. This becomes a question not only of categorical change, but of categorical dissolution—ways of abandoning the distinction between art and life once historically entertained—for often trivial reasons. Perhaps the growing uncertainties will soon become so frequent (and useful) that the very distinction will cease to matter. Remember: Plato thought art to be inferior to reality—yet now most everyone you meet is an artist.

But then, where are we? The extreme answer is that art, has indeed, become a form of life: Anywhere one looks, there is something that appears to be appropriable as art. And in anyone one meets, there are presented fictional simulacra of themselves—awaiting our multi-valent responses. To enter into an engagement—to find an intersection of (aesthetic) "appreciations" with another self—to treat another as an art-work—is to self-make one's (own) self into art.

The thesis now is that Art and Life have taken on the characteristics of art/life-life/art. The earlier task was to distinguish between them; the present task is to understand their intersection; the future task will be to cope with their convergence—or disappearance.

The critical work to be done is here—and we are only at the beginning. We should avoid a philosophically reductive language—one fashioned to be impervious to the blandishments of sense, the distortions of desire, the conflicting imperatives of neighborhood and history. After having been repeatedly subject to such cleansings, there may be little left to do for a philosophy of art—except to seek other, more formally vulnerable (yet socially responsive) languages for "saying-about" its subject.

At times, artists, even when not regarded as truth-bearers, have been esteemed for their projection of other virtues—beauty, expression, and the like. These virtues, on some philosophical accounts, overlap with, or give material support to, the logical functions of truth. But such virtues, even when gainfully employed in philosophical matters, do not consistently contribute to them: Philosophy changes and takes truth along with it.

Art, today, is anti-formal and anti-systematic. It ignores alliances with classical canons of belief and academic practice, and instead presents itself as the public representation of individual and communal preferences. The present persuasiveness of art derives from open-society conditions of what the general "we" would like to enjoy and emulate. The terms 'art' and 'fun' become synonymous. So re-categorized, art now represents a variety of beliefs—indeed, brimming baskets of competing styles and activities—each centered in its own, however disingenuous, neighborhood.

All neighborhoods, whether shoddy or pricey, provide content for the images of the life caught in their art—the images that portray the local needs of those still interested in the patina of believing something. As social markers, these images are offered through cadences of speech, whose variations (often within the same language) evoke different identities—how one wants to sound or look, or be taken for. In the growing irrelevance of canonical guides (museums, manuals) preference becomes a matter of noticing—paying attention to something—and of being noticed noticing.

Modern forms of thought are tailored for ths mode of noticing—politics, e.g., is now less a matter of free choice than of solicited emulation. But difficulties remain in the adjustment of private feelings to public images—often seen as insincere and manipulative. Feelings, then—more so than thoughts—seem closer to being the locus of our "true-selves." Feelings are private, hidden—and yet we can reveal them. We can also dissimulate—to our most intimate loves, even to our (divided) selves—about how we feel.

Our shows of feelings become "styles"—learned from the shows of others, and so can be revised—even to where we accept the changes in our showings as truthful indications of who we (really) are: "I don't feel (about. . .) the way I once did!" An unassailable truth—before and after!

To dig down beneath the layers of influence to what we really feel, can be therapeutic—or a fool's gambit—depending on how we value "really." This can be difficult, even painful—for the self. It can also be a basis for the criticism (made, inter-alia, by old curmudgeons) that today's art is insincere—because no longer truly felt.

But a historical process is evident here: Just as academic tutelage was once the enemy of Modernism, so personal feeling is often seen as the unwanted residue of the new, collective, art: If the way we "really feel" changes through times, so may the affects that supervene on art-works.

To push this further: What if, for argument's sake, there is no underlying, self-reflecting, constructed base of our affective life. Its absence would then indicate that the multiple public-selves we present to others are not undergirded by a private and singular inner-self that we can retreat to—in order to find out (attend-to, reinforce, take refuge in, appreciate, create out of) who we really are. What is it, then, that determines the finder—the "Who" who pays attention—and to what is the (often reciprocal) attention paid? Further: If art-works do not express an artist's feelings, what then is it that we respond to? Does this augur a return to academic verities? Who, anyway, is this "we?"

BEING AND SHOWING

Perhaps Plato was right in keeping artists underground—
where they could do the Gods no wrong by making untrue images
of how people are when no-one's looking.

The Romans didn't see it that way—so they made mysteries
that would heat the walls of Pompey. They watched the lovely living
wiggle while they performed in public places—and mounted
darker spectaculars to divert attention from the appetites of Nero
- also to gainsay the second coming of the Gallic hordes.

Then copulation went private—driven inward by Angel Michael's
baleful stare, and the practiced methods of inquisitors
for delivering more torment than the Romans could devise.
All this to keep the proles from favoring body flavors
over sacred emanations from the soul.

Artists took these prohibitions in their stride, for
their wantons were not Christians, but the old Greek Gods—
priapic fellows who would pluck the down off prescient maidens,
or bugger an apprentice youth, and think these all fine ways
to take the waters of a pre-baptismal afternoon.

Writers had it harder. Their languages were also used by priests
and pedants—not to say those others who would kill you for a word.
But there were dissidents through the ages—Rabelais, De Sade—
all striving to shake cob-webs off your pent-up testicles,
and shape your lips to words that will describe the sigh of streams
when engorged by waters of an impatient spring.
My battle with my soul takes precedence
over the notion that all of me is one.
I am two at least—but I or they or we
have been refigured many times
according to the demands
that difference makes upon a body—

at other times and special places.

That she still chews on your pale tumescence
while you view her dark and moisty offerings
well past dinner-time—is not unusual.
What is—is that the few steps taken then
before we came back later
to do the basics with the best intentions—
had been done by others who keep
their un-published tricks a secret.

Shall we dance, then, together with those others—
whirling fast while smiling all too brightly?
They do not care—they listen for the sound
of moans from distant rooms—
which we know comes straight from pleasure—
while they hope it signals caring pain.

THE DANCING TIME

A lot of time and too little time are much the same. The best place to have a long life is where there is time to spare for staying alive. This is the common wisdom, and one can go through happy days just thinking about being alive and glad of it by moving to a beat one can control. This is often called a dance.

One way to do this, for example, is dancing in the ongoing past-and-present. Such a dance is called a "Two-Step," a hippety-hop directed straight ahead, chin up—look past your partner's ear and maybe catch your pretty neighbor's eye.

It's a clean and open dance, though, nothing rotting in old drawers and nothing new to hide. This dance will not permit despair, for we have all been chosen—especially if we're good at smiling—to be partners. No-one wants a scold on such a floor.

The common rituals for pain and pleasure, birth and death, are all included in the steps. Ladies, mark the time that fits his feet and your's—one-and-two and curtsey when you're told.

But time can be marked in other ways, through dances that keep one busy by dissimulation, with elliptical partners and their twisty-turns, all too moist and hidden to be right or wrong. Don't worry, there's a velvet rope to separate the dancers from the walking world.

One such dance is the illusionary waltz, and another is the exclusive minuet. The first is a dance that circles faster than breath, a solitary dance, with incidental partners brought on board by veils, darkened eyes, and mirrored souls. To dance the waltz is to be ahead of time, for it is a dance of yearning, a race against mere dying—although it often leads to a noble death by sword. If unlucky in your choice, keep your distance from your pudgy partner with her yearnings and her winey breath. It is neither you nor I, my borrowed friend, who will poke each other from below tonight. Look instead at the moustached cavalier and Cinderella's daughter twining in three-quarter time across (she thought it was to be) the nuptial bed.

The second dance, the minuet, is more sedate, performed in a larger circle somewhat squared, with many partners who move predictably past, whose blemishes have been covered over by the powdered wigs and blendings of old power and rich perfume. They are all together, lord and lady, but they shall tonight sleep as separate pairs—two-somes formed by quick meetings of impassioned eye and arched brow (Is this to be our last night of love, my love?) as they circle round again to repeat the pretty-prances of propriety.

None seem wanting yet all are waiting, but it's the very devil to tell who's who, and a dreadful bore to peel off all that wet and smelly gear from one who is other than the one you wanted. Nevertheless, there is solid value in these dances. Both eventually will bring us back around—as many times as is remembered —to those others we once danced with naked in the spring-time rain.

There is ample chance to dwell on impredictabilty. Each minuet is taken at a different pace—this to permit unhurried dwelling on the mix of past indulgences and future fears we have been gathering to mark the passage of our lives. The actual mixing is uncertain— but the minuet provides advice: Seek a mix, it says, that is a bit above your station, but provides nourishment for the soul-mate of your present. It will not last for all eternity—but is good for (at least) some few days in the country.

Though the glint in his eye
kindles a tick in your quick,
t'is the tilt of his kilt that measures
your need for embellishment.

The waltz and the minuet come from Europe, from the land of the long-dead-whites.

Using either dance as a model for the movement of one's later life is really—sheer nostalgia—a doting on pleasures whose unpaid accounts go back years to when we knew only the tranquility and rhythm of a teat. But there are many stories we since have read—beneath the sheets when young, or now propped in an easy-chair—squinting to re-read the parts that tell us what next to do.

Duly noted in the chronicles of those glorious days is the pleasure of undoing the many strings of a whale-bone corset to see the flesh slowly bubble to the surface. Oh! It took so long—so much bubbling—but time was slower then.

Our newer loves wear jeans—and are too skinny to bubble anywhere unless blown there—inflated by the wind. Now we have come to know our preferences better: Bubbling shows a fattening! Fat is bad! Anyway—our fingers are no longer so nimble as to undo laces; we cannot stoop so low as to follow the most southern marks that corsets make; we have become too slow to race against the wind—and too stiff to bend and make the red welts go away.

Yet, such period pieces, when carefully constructed, can be fun. So we whirl Marlena through a scratchy Wienerwald, and pirouette blond Juliette across a second rondo. Then into the winey night we go—still prancing—toward our bedtime chores. What we have promised will not, in all fairness, wait until tomorrow—but the nights in winter cover all that we can do.

For those in good shape, the ones who frequent the gym past the point when gaping at the lissome young passes for fitness-training—for them there are other dances to consider.

Here are two I much admire: the Mambo and the Lindy-Hop.

I know little about the first but I have danced it some. It comes from the lower center of the earth, and while there is nothing as sensual in all creation as a woman with good calves who dances the Mambo well—it is a dance for men—more precisely—for the liberation of men. We western whities like to get straight to the point; we do not undulate, or shimmy, or tease with an offered hip, a reluctant shoulder; we do not laugh when we demur, or pout when the other's hip is taken back. No—doing such things would be un-manly, not the sort of stuff that wins a war or knows the time to buy and sell. We do not really like to watch our naked movements when we love.

So shall we try this dance a different way, at a time when we can be nothing but amusing—a funny still-flaunting hippety-hop old man? It takes two to Mambo; it is not a lonely dance, so we must be sure to share the movements with a younger someone from the center of the earth—dark, fecund, impatient with introspection, and while used to faster turns than you can muster, will, for the moment, laugh—and stay with you awhile and watch you creak and flutter.

Then there is the Lindy-hop:

Step-it, stomp-it, kick-it, bump-it.
All you need is Louis' trumpet.
But if your ass gets out of kilter,
the Bird will soothe you with his whisper.
And if your mind rejects the muddle,
Monk is there to give you trouble.

The Lindy-hop is a higher dance than is the Mambo. It is a mid-air mating of birds, quick thrusts between the cartwheels, wide splits, and flying fish. Only the young can dance it through the night—but go ahead, go out there and jump around a bit. Think of the early times at Birdland—when you stored up the applause you received upon returning to the table all sweaty, out-of-breath, holding someone's younger sister triumphant by the hand. This dance did not last you long—and your partner did not stay. Flying birds have poor memories; they learn their skills alone, singing a solitary song while learning to fly, and they take their lovers on the wing.

If you are brave—come out and try this: Ask the bird at the next table—the one with bright red wings—whether she would fly with you more slowly for a bit. Follow her until you can no longer see her in the dimming light. Then—don't say anything cute or smart—just thank her, try to kiss her hand, and return her to her table—then go back to yours—before you get carried out.

PORNOGRAPHY AND EROTICISM

There are circumstances when, despite our lapses and evasions, we directly experience our singular self. These are the moments of extreme pain or pleasure where (we know that) we are the one having the sensation we feel. This presents a dilemma for that art-life distinction—the one which serves to separate the actual from the fictional in works (or selves) that purport to show reality. Both life and art have exemplified the truth with separate images—but these arguably are different forms of truth. The difference lies between the truth of being and the truth of portraying—although each requires belief from the audience—even if it is an audience of one. Art gives a simulation, life is an instantiation—but both present a private reality that can be publically interpreted (by those who pay attention) as being true.

This dilemma is standard fare in theatre and film where actors present semblances of life for audiences to incorporate as virtual occurences for their enjoyment. In this familiar version, both actor and audience enter into a tacit agreement that the life portrayed will be sufficiently credible to satisfy the narrative offering that the audience has contracted for. There are the various genre-levels—each of which has its own requirements for believability: "Billy and Tessi on the Farm" does not demand the same kind of believability as does "Hamlet." (Of course it could—if Tessi is scripted to become, say, Ophelia—or Hamlet's mother).

In all such cases, good actors convincingly simulate the lives they are given to portray: Think of the tuxedoed aand satin-gowned leads making reciprocal passes in opulent nightclubs—then off to the hotel where the doorman tips his hat. (Up-scale delicacies for us midd'lin folks). Other actors are charged with believably showing that they are in pain, or in mortal danger: Think of your favorite cowboy or monster movies: (other-world titillation for the lower folks).

Evocations of mayhem, pain, death, the big-bomb, Armageddon, are all subjects that have wide appeal—their technical elaboration into super-reality is welcome—whatever the levels of audience sophistication. Intergalactic battles speed things up, make a lot of noise, move faster than your eye-balls can, and usually—against overwhelning odds—let the good-guys win. Going back a bit in history: Wagon-trains surrounded by hostiles will kill a lot of no-name Indians before the cavalry shows up. Pain is good when it is right.

More problematic is the fictional portrayal of pleasure: Love and sex present particular difficulties for believable imagery. Their portrayals involve actors —people with their own concerns about who they—non-fictionally—are and do. It is easier, I suspect, to believably die a heroic death, than to convincingly portray the seducer of the player whose (actual) love interest may be waiting just outside the studio door. There are any number of latent contents operating here—all closed to the audience: "Won't you reciprocate—for just a moment—if I go a bit beyond the script, and play (become) the one-in-your-life?"—or—"Please don't move when you're on top of me—it's unnecessary; breathing hard (but not in my face) is quite enough for the part."

In recent films, there are increasingly many portrayals of exposed bodies, the degree and purpose of exposure based on the blend of seduction and assault—sex and pain—love or hate—written into the story of the script. The relevant characters correspondingly show any of—joyful, needful, ambivalent, comfortable, disdainful, hostile, fearful—masks.

The genre that, to my mind, most clearly reveals the issues and difficulties in the theatrics of sexual experience is eroticism—or as it is often called—pornography.

I do not particularly like the commonly held distinction offered by these terms—eroticism and pornography. It makes too facile the complex differences between depictions of sexuality as art or as prurience, sex as a personal completion of love or as commercial indifference to feelings. The distinction is rife with ambiguity, duplicity, censorship, and historical obscurantism. There are ancient traditions of erotic art in painting, sculpture and literature—some tied intimately in with religious or mythical beliefs. Attitudes about whether such art can be both moral and aesthetic vary in history. In some cultures, such values overlap—in others, moral prohibitions preclude the possibility of their co-existence. The ancient Greeks linked their Gods with exhibitions of nudity and sexual prowess—the later Christians did not.

In our culture, the "erotic-pornographic" distinction offers a solution of sorts: Sexuality that is "tastefully" or "subtly" or "indirectly" presented can be (included in) erotic art. If such presentation is seen as a necessary part of a larger narrative—so much the better.

But sex—whether in theatrical contexts or back at the ranch—is always performed. Is the above distinction, then, a matter of public exposure as such—or is it a matter of the specific context of exposure—the nature of the "audience?" Do the kind and number of participants matter—solitary, a couple, friends, ticket holders? Are such performances acceptable when limited to connoisseurs in privileged places? In each such case, where does the erotic —pornographic distinction appear? Such questions (evidently) do not have direct answers—so more circling is in order.

When depictions of sex are—sui generis—taken as morally reprehensible, there is the predictable censorship of pornography. Nevertheless, outside that category, remain specialized images, too vauable to be dismissed — rescued by the term 'erotic'—that by virtue of their historical, aesthetic and social qualities, are open to select appreciation. Within the totality of presentations, then, some sexual images are "redeemable" (and available for appreciation) others are not.

If so, pornography—identified as the debased variant of the genre—can be denied access because the works have no redeeming qualities. Considered aesthetically, they are either bad—or non-art. With such a charged subject, it seems evident that not only moral, but aesthetic criteria, are used to determine the appropriate social response: Meaningful sex, i.e., that can be (redeemed as) art, has value. Indifferent, crude, or vulgar sex does not.

But this sort of distinction has been challenged by the free spirits of other times: The superiority of the "beautiful" to the "ugly" was a measure that, by early Modernism, had became untenable. The criteria of "beauty" and "good-taste," when confronted by such other values as "personal expression" or "social relevance," were rejected as aesthetic criteria. There is a historical range of dissident values that has been used to rescue eroticism in art from its enemies. One argument here is that erotic art prortrays an authentic human activity—and is therefore aesthetically (and morally) valuable.

Authenticity" however, refers to "truth"—how close the representation is to the reality in context. Pursuing this is a matter of ascertaining how the subject is "realized" in the various ways it is presented. One such way—an important one for the subject of sexually explicit film—concerns the nature of the experience as revealed by the erotic image—how (sexually) real it is to the performers. Put less strongly—how important is the semblance of this reality to the audience. A critical question here is when, or whether, the actors cease being actors when they're acting—when theyre making love.

Classic Greek and Indian Gods sexually frolic and so (in passing) instruct humans in the varieties of good living. Renaissance art (notably, Venetian) used such "Pagan" images to bypass church strictures—and please their affluent patrons. Later Western artists (notably, French) produced works that brought together skill and erotic titillation into the secular world. Japanese woodcuts give us a treasure trove of erotic form and performance without much sign of political hindrance.

Modern art, especially when culturally sidelined, introduced social and psychological issues to its images of sexuality—works of Courbet, Manet, Lautrec, Degas, Picasso, were suffused with the erotic—however much they also challenged the extant notions of taste, class, and morality. But it is with the moving image that the question of performer (once "model") authenticity becomes critical.

I return to my question above: What versions of sexual imagery are acceptable in both the conditions of their making and the experiences of their viewing?

My primary concern here is with the tension between actual being and its representation—between having and showing. I focus on the art of film because it mirrors, as no other, the elusive boundry that forms this tension—between the "real-self" of the performer and the images offered, through performance, of a "fictional-self." This question is not limited to film; for it has a great deal to do with the more general tension between artistic identity and representation, e.g., the artist-model relationship of the "Pygmalion-Galatea" theme. But the action in films begins as "real"—however much it is edited for imagination.

There were the days (if you remember) when an 8mm. 20 minute "blue-movies" reel, could be gotten through a friend of a friend, then fitted to a borrowed projector which no-one (in that mix of adolescents) really knew how to operate. The tape would break, and then have to be re-spliced. The speed would be too fast or slow—the sound, if any, would respond accordingly—too loud or faint. Hours could be spent, after repeated catastrophe, rescuing that original 20 minutes. The experience (finally) of seeing the actual film was scarcely erotic—but it was liberating, instructive—and unusually topical: We commended each other for our non-conformity—and pitied the larger world for not joining with us. Few women were part of the group that watched—there are a few more now. But this difference in gender distribution between performers and audience in erotica runs deep, and needs study.

Literary and painterly erotica present a substantial contrast to film. The former have a long history of artistic expertise, elitist toleration and financial support. Accordingly, their enjoyment requires a degree of education and leisure—reading skills—and a circle of afficionados for critical conversation—which typically required irony as well as strategies for the acquisition (and social uses) of ever finer versions of the exquisite-prohibited.

When erotica became a staple of electronic media—film, video and the internet—it also became a widespread and profitable, public enterprise. It offered unscrutinized access—no more slinking to the "adults-only" corner of the video store, or to the movie-theatre in questionable neighborhoods. Erotica had become identified with the comfort of private viewing—in which there is little incentive for communal discussion or serious criticism. Yet, because the viewing experience is of "real-people"- in a fantasy-place where the viewer might also want to be—the experience of erotica through electronic sources provides different anxieties in its version of fantasy.

Then there is the other side: Notwithstanding the insularity of viewer participation, producing erotic film and video is a cooperative making of performances—a commercial undertaking which needs actors as well as scripts and a production complex. Many people are involved. The formal demand on the actors, in one sense, is the same as in the other genre categories—believability. But in erotica, there is this difference: Actors must show believability through a unique kind of mimesis not typically required in other kinds of film. Actors in erotica portray actions which display sexual sensations in the character—but which the actors also, ostensibly, themselves experience. The audience wants (in some sense) to believe that the displayed actions are real—that the actors feel (as we should) what they are doing—that they are actually making love.

The fictional core of erotica is the display of orgasm and the accumulating actions that lead to it. The display is theatrical, and the actors—who, as in other theatrical contexts, are portrayers and dissimulators—and not the actual characters they portray. But in this context, the wanted display can undermine this distinction between reality and it's portrayal.

One demand is physical—the actor is being asked to evidence a fact, not (only) perform a fiction. Orgasm, after all, is a physical stimulation and a firing of nerves; it somehow shows. What, then, is a "good" performance? One that, on this description, is not merely performed—or, if begun as performance, ends up as fact: The actors should experience actual orgasm—and it should show.

But this demand is somewhat naïve: "Showing" an orgasm—whether on the screen or in one's bed—can be an acquired skill. There are methods of showing that can be learned, and such methods can differ stylistically—much like the demand in other genres for a "gripping," "authentic," or even, "beautiful " performance. The difference wanted here, however, is ostensibly a non-performative one. It is a demand for the "real thing"—a document of an actual sexual act—however much the performance of the act may appear gross, monotonous, or full of flubs.

Toward this end, it would seem that the simpler the script the better: Few if any lines to memorize; little character development; a practical hedonism, and the safety of a happy ending. There are, of course, some basic technical requirements: Care that actions do not occlude the camera angle; that the exhibition of passion occurs on demand; that all show a willing participation in the work-at-hand; that those directly involved end up looking spent and satisfied.

Why, then, should an actor fake it (act a part) when the real thing is consonant with both script and nature—and, given the rudimentary demands of most scripts—should be easier to experience, if not always to (artistically) perform. Yet, the reality of sex goes deeper than its representation. The former, if we want to separate the two, may be difficult to achieve— the latter takes some acting skills.

In simple erotica—that which we agree to call "porn"—there is little, if any, change of character. Indeed, on this level, the actor's subject would preferably have no character at all—or if one—only as a generalized projection of the popular image of a beautiful body, one capable of perfect sex, and climaxing when it's time to do so.

The truth (actuality) here, is measured by stereotype (sex well done) and demonstration (how it looks when done well). These, of course, are not the same. Only the second of these virtues is the one that theatre, historically, has refused to relinquish to ordinary life.

But there seems also to be the (covert) demand from audiences of erotica for the first: Imagery that presents sex as theatrical but also actual—"true to life."

The "to" is interesting: It separates "true" and "life"—thus avoiding a redundancy —not "true as life"—an undecideable comparison, or "true of life"—which limits the scope of living. Rather, "true to life" indicates a direction, a closing onto a desired way of actuality—an actuality that we, the viewers, (want to) share with the performers.

The perfect orgasm is the contrary to the perfect storm: It is something wanted, but never completely achieved—although immolation (the all-engulfing wave) is its common goal. In the context of representation, orgasm is as true as showing can devise—as viewed through (what we accept as) its most believable representation. But this, as in other genres, is a matter of history and style.

In life, truth comes less from style than (as Dewey says) from doing-undergoing—as true as can be achieved through the experiences of living with one-self and others. But no account, whether introspective or theatrical, can show what you, the audience, would know as true —even if (mirabile dictu) you were there yourself. The erotic film, in principle, invites you to become part of the showing you are looking at—all of us knowing that you can't really make the scene just now. But even if you could, would you want to—given all the acting required?

Erotica contains the documentary promise of being "true to life," and that promise is sometimes fulfilled —although its "when" remains obscure. The lions covertly filmed in the Serenghetti have their own "when"—porn stars must share their "when" with others.

The counter to this considers the when of life to be just that shown on film—where the participants are also consciously performers (as those lions are not). This is a life regimented by fiction—by the "when" that seeks its nature—and the theatrical images that fulfill its seeking.

We are presented here with opposing descriptions —both of which are true: An erotic film is a documentary of actors emulating sex-acts until the performative gives way to an actuality—and the actors become people who are having sex. The camera, however, does not distinguish between these states, and the actors do not (ordinarily) include—in their performances—indications (symptoms) of a transition (possibly a transformation) between the fictional and the actual. This "bridging" is not yet a considered subject in erotic film—but quixotically, it appears frequently in the home-movie versions. The necessity evidenced in the change gives the narrative a new subject—of actuality intruding upon fiction.

Some of the pleasure in viewing erotica is found precisely in contrasting the difference between the actions on film, and private sexuality. Both may be true to life—but the belief wanted for their credibility is different. For the erotic genre, as described here, the viewer's expectation is that the performer (should) experience what he or she portray.

But this has its hidden aspects: An appreciation based on such expectations is somewhat paranoid—it has a component of sleuthing—of spotting fraudulence. It looks to recognize the dissimulations of the actor who, like a once-upon-a-time lover, has merely faked it. But faking here, might be, in other contexts—in the studio—a professional requirement —at home—a palliating subterfuge.

The "privacy of one's home," is a precarious venue for fantasy and representation—it is the place from which one strays in search for new experiences. Home is the center of stability and family. Enlightened analysts might say that—to save a relationship—home-sex should be informed by fantasy: But shared fantasy can overcome the monotony of daily living only if the participants are willing to project their shared sexual actions into their private fantasies. In this sense, orgasm, its approach, diversity, achievement—is an important ingredient for a happy sex-life. Sincere faking (the emulation of actual achievement) is another. This is easier (and quite acceptable) in film—the script provides the approach and signals the achievement.

The signs of orgasmic truth—indicators (clues) for the sleuth of pretense in erotica—are usually immediate and physical: Sweat, trembling, untheatrical awkwardness, unseemly expressions, uncontrolled sounds—that delightful interface between the ugly, the astonishing, and the moving.

Falsity, here, lies in the absence of these manifestations of actual sex—as corroborated, through reflecting on their own experiences, by individual audiences. This gives rise to the criticisms of bad erotica and its practices of cheap-shot substitution of numbingly repetitive, rote gestures of sexuality for actual sex. This is most common in so-called "soft-porn " where the strategies of concealment become the subject. Some of these strategies may turn out, in the rejected footage of a shoot, to be real for the actors—but are not available to the viewer.

In the "hard-core" versions, the filmed actions are not concealed, but nevertheless are bound by informal guides for the filmic manifestations of direct sex withot narrative complication. This avoids the need for "personal" communication between partners by focussing on close-up displays of organs grinding in unison. Whose organs? Who cares—that footage was probably jobbed out. No faces are needed—except for the occasionally flashed grimace of pleasure—and no dialogue—except for the standard gutterals (often dubbed) of sexual activity. The presumption is that the new porn audiences, now at home, can seek their satisfactions at the level of investment they choose. There is no need for a "story line."

We should note here, however, that the range of such offerings is constantly expanding, and the level (and kind) of films produced is a matter of financing and changing interests. The above description is a base line—but aesthetic distinctions between porn and erotica increase in importance as the audience becomes larger and more varied. If this is so, sexuality as an art-form will lose its problematics and become, simply, one of many subjects of film art —dependent for success on consumer-response and critical assessment.

But I must question some of the implications of my own findings. I reject the road to fiscally based distinctions in and between the arts—and I remain unhappy with the post-cultural view of personal preference as the primary measure of aesthetic value. But I remain torn: I am a (self-styled) elitist with, yet, an ecumenical interest; I want value-judgments that have historical authority and yet are untainted by easy money. So I propose the following as a way of understanding sexuality in film: Instead of coupling "embarrassment, titillation, sin" with "disparagement, containment, prohibition" as the bases for our judgments and actions, we should seek alliances between that subject and other ventures and considerations of high—but not necessarily aesthetic—quality. Where moral and political issues are concerned, erotica remains one of the most revelatory of artistic subjects. It can present a singular challenge to the decorative pleasantries of much contemporary art-making.

My distinction between sexual content and aesthetic value, comes to this: The better the art, the more valuably it deals with the content it takes on. Historical art amply demonstrates this. We shudder at depictions of martyrdoms and mayhem; we abhor revelations of corpse-strewn battlefields, torture, and summary executions; we look dubiously at the pomp in coronotions of Doges and Emperors: We regard the frolics of divinities and lesser nobles with weariness and envy. But these all tell us something important about ourselves, our heritage, and our present practices—and they are still good art. Further, while their styles may recede into the past, their coupling of content and aesthetic value remains present. This suggests that we can learn a lot about important contents of our own present by looking at their representations—descriptions, depictions etc. Sexuality is one—but a significant one—of these contents.

On a different note, however, there are other social and economic issues to be considered. The artifices portrayed by bad erotica—what I call porn—can be more exciting and satisfying to some than the complexities of good erotica —art with sexual content. Porn, in a strange sense, always succeeds; it does not complicate, or cloud its issue. No-one, whether performer or viewer, is ever rejected. Actual sex-life, to the contrary, is vulnerable to issues of rejection and complexity. One argument in favor of porn, then, is that real-life sex is often unhappy—and participants may sometimes need to become viewers—to withdraw into their solitary selves, offering themselves instead to an always-benevolent chimera for their satisfaction. The dependable conviviality of porn becomes welcome as an opening beyond the actual—or the aesthetic—even when it is patently implausible, untruthful, and formally inept.

For the more critical viewer, there are other concerns: Erotica can reject stylization in its mimesis (an evocation of traditional forms), and be directly concerned with convincing its audience that the experience is real, that the portrayed sexual life is actually occuring. This can be called "true—life" filming. The performers may, in fact, have actual orgasms—exhibited in yowls and ejaculation by the male, and attested to, through grimaces and howls, by the female. Because ejaculation is taken to be the achievement of male orgasm, it is hard to fake. But the absence of such physical signs makes orgasmic achievement in the female less apparent—and so more theatrical (more subtly representational).

The female response is of particular interest for the distinctions I am trying to make: The audience for erotica is still predominantly male. Their preferred subject is the female orgasm, which, like the notion of "intending," remains hidden.

To diverge a bit: "Intent" is a difficult criterion. There is "overt intent," where an ongoing course towards agreement between parties (actors, directors, writers) defines the circumstances of the act—this is in the nature of theatrical performance. There is "hidden intent," which one party knows but the other does not—this characterizes possible duplicity in personal encounters. Then there is "underlying intent," where the parties' motives are hidden from themselves and/or from each other—an intent which neither party (if we go deep enough into the roots of "underlying") may know. This approximates the layerings of fact and fiction in both life and love.

This schema of intention is not exhaustive—the layerings are multiple and subtle. Even so—that there are many levels indicates (for our discussion) that sexual satisfaction—whether in the theatre, at home, or elsewhere—whether depicted or experienced (or both)—remains a commingling of fact and fiction. So in erotica, anothers' fact may becomes my fiction—which I then turn (or dream of turning) into my fact. This is subject to the play of overt and hidden intentions, as well as to the realities of physical stimulation, the persistence of memory, the residues of guilt, and the hoverings of public attitudes.

It is an article of faith for (male) viewers of erotica that the abundently-endowed woman, who exhibits ample evidence—through her paroxisms—of having an orgasm, actually has one. Yet, as I indicate, this actuality is inferred (by males and sometimes females). The female orgasm remains a mystery that veils the wanted distinction between actuality and performance.

But the glazing over of a true-loves eyes at the consumate moment, should be good evidence for the coming of (even) a porn star. Surely we, sly mastadons that we are, must think we can discern whether our love is faking it or not. And can we not take that insight into a heightened fantasy of appreciation, and determine whether Princess Feather, whose actions seem so genuine on film, would not be equally transparent off-camera when nestled in her lover's (if not our) arms?

But one particular charm, and value, of erotica—is located precisely in its play between the physical compulsion and its performance. Does Princess Feather care how she looks when she is coming? Of course she does—especially when on camera—she's practiced it many times. Some of her "real-life" lovers she treats as cameras—others, she does not —the lovers never know—she herself might not remember between times. But that is how Apollo and Daphne, Heidi and Peter, Adam and Eve, Danae and Zeus, you and I, and other exemplary couples, experience their sex lives.

All of this is an ideal content for art. In the making of erotic films, the variability between living and acting goes beyond the level of the script which, in ambitious productions, will present Princess Feather as, say, the paragon of innocence ravaged by a priapic brute—or in another role, as a secret agent of unspeakable intentions and unappeasable appetites.

Does it matter (to her) that she is neither—but just an aspiring actress? Not if she wants to be a good actress—it is a truism that actors are not the characters they play. It is also true that actors must transform the scripted characters into the ones they can actually play. Sometimes, the script transforms the actor into someone more different than he or she could have previously imagined.

But what matters to us (the audience) is that Feather has the capacities to believably be the fiction she is playing—even if she must take on—"actually become"—her character. The physical demands of erotic film make this evasion difficult—especially if the plot is complex, showing passages of unexpected actions—and others that violate apparent intentions. Erotic film, unlike pornography, can end in discord.

These eventualities—the inclusion of discord and ambiguity in the script—have been some years in the making. They occur when filmed erotica is free to include complex characters and psychological changes in the story-line, and so can aspire—first to melodrama (high kitsch)—then art (believability)—then to good art (the profundities and pitfalls of new insights).

The audience for erotica remains varied, but in the last, say, fifty years, it has increased in number—especially in locations where prohibitions have diminished and a range of media presentations is available. Interwoven here are economic and social issues: Because the products become more readily accessible to internet consumers—what is looked for in the consumption of erotic art varies with the sophistication of viewers—insofar as these can be determined. This creates new pressures within the genre for financing and for the talents that different artistic levels of production require—namely, a greater range in acting capacities and story-lines, and more talented writers and directors.

A time ago, when the adolescent-adventuresome would gather around the 8mm projector, beer would flow and gasps would fill the silence while we looked at the silent pumpings and writhings which showed how bodies unconnected to any one we knew—did such things. This was an important lesson for us all. We realized that we had been too much connected with the catechisms of personal guilt and public propriety, to admit—even to ourselves—that we, watching the spectacle, could ever do such things. But it was strange to actually see such things being done —exotic and novel, sometimes indigestible, things. The experiences of those bizarre and unbelievable actions, flickering at uncertain speeds, redirected our young-lives, with their late-day dolors and inadequcies, into new imaginings.

When we went our separate ways, my first ambition was to sleep away the memories of dull days past—and dream of cavorting with Venus on a cloud. But I was disappointed in this—there was no Venus in my dreams—just scary stuff like gray bodies breaking together with the breaking tape, and no way to bring anything back together. But I kept trying because there was something—but what?—that needed fixing.

In these early times of disobedience, we watched foreign bodies that had no names, no reasons past or future to be doing what they, in the confines of their small and squalid beds, were doing. What was the point, then, of our watching what they—probably foreign and mostly dead by now—were doing?

I think now that these primitive scenarios that we saw, were actually quite advanced aesthetically—an early minimalism: Most often there was no sound; actions had no motive or background; the performers' neutrality was achieved through an impersonal mix of pattern and repetition; the actors represented nothing beyond the close-ups of their organs—but those delivered a timeless show of sexual prowess and sufficient proportion. There was no ambivalence or private pleading in these films—no person (no "character"), no story (no "plot"), no conclusion, (no "moral").

This indifference, I venture, is a difficult achievement worthy of a comparison (if only Quixotically) with more current developments in "high-art"—with, inter alia, the ongoing repetition of descriptions in novels of Robbe-Grillet; the serially color-coded representations of an image by Warhol; the consecutive repetitions of cadences in Phillip Glass's musical lines.

My aim is not to denigate the achievements of these artists, but to suggest that certain developments in artistic high style, particularly in the "late avant-garde"—such as repetition (non-development), impersonality (indifference), reduction (bareness), monotony (boredom)—have a source in primitive erotic film: The same characteristics of mechanical repetition that are to be found in such early films, also occur in the sophisticated modes of "consecutive sameness" in today's high art. These early forms of rudimentary sexual coupling can be seen as (unwittingly) exhibiting —for later ironic appropriation —their monotony and lack of sequential development—the admirable lack of organic tension between part and whole.

The above is a comparison of both aesthetic change and aesthetic value. It indicates one continuity in style that underlays (if one cares to look) various present ways of art-making. It is in the extremes of monotony and reduction in today's art, that suggest once-unlikely similarities with a discarded genre of the past. They also suggest that today's aesthetic attitudes of pure form, and impersonal attention have historical antecedents (however questionable on other grounds) that show evidence of similar concerns.

Both high minimalism and low porn prize boredom. There are, of course, difference reasons: For the former—images of chic aloofness evoke economic and social exclusiveness—as well as aesthetic (and emotional) "coolness." Feeling and empathy are sentimental—and can get wild. Boredom is a mechanism of social control which also generates good taste. In pornographic films, monotony soothes the fear of inadequacy by focussing not on people, but on sexual parts—which show only the repetitive comforts of continuity without personality. Parts without people do not threaten— neither do they show joy or despair.

In both scenarios, the obligatory boredom evokes indifference and disengagement—from self and from others through the non-cumulative nature of its imagery. These images are a denial that life will end—and suggest that our fear of our own mortality will be allayed by the very experience of monotony. This is a shrug of indifference—and smugness—toward the logic that says life must end. Sadly, it is also an aesthetic of loneliness—the loneliness that needs acquiescence to boredom to be endured.

But there is hope: With an increasingly sophisticated audience, no longer tranquilized by privation soporifics, and wealthy enough to be impatient with the poverty of porn, the sophistication and skills of erotic film have the impetus to increasingly match, and sometimes exceed, the offerings of the general film industry. Adventures into the badlands of sex and art are not only economically potent but interesting conceptually—their contents of perversity and exploitation are open for artistic invention. They can be socially quite radical—and suggest new form of narrative.

I offer some examples —old and new: The breakout film, "Behind the Green Door," is about interracial sex—black male and white female—the most feared coupling for proponents of institutional racism. "The Devil and Ms. Jones" shows the clash between the pain of orgasmic incompleteness and the desire for fullfillment—even in Hell—thereby suggesting that the Devil's domain is porous, and good and evil are transitive values. "Deep Throat" identifies the clitoris (not the "womb") as the central location of female pleasure—and so extends sexual activity (admittedly by an outlandish conceit) beyond the "missionary position"—thus decoupling sexual enjoyment from the task of pro-creation. The recent film "Fashionistas" shows the interplay of high fashion and SM practices in an affluent world—a model framed for would-be achievers—where good taste is a catalyst for exploring the rewards of the interplay between aggression, pleasure-pain, and worldly success.

The popularity of these—still clandestine and checkered offerings—have helped make possible the production of films with extensive erotic content that are shown in main-stream theatres—in which the erotic content is presented as consequences of broader themes. The films I note here all have intriguing references to color in their titles: "A Clockwork Orange;" "I Am Curious, Yellow;" "Blue is the Warmest Color." The reference to color may be an appeal to a larger form of sensibility for the battle of appreciations. The (cold) "blue" of old movies changes to the (hot) red of present offerings, then into the transcendent yellow and the inviting blue (sun and sky) of future possibilities.

The specific contributions of such films to "Art" is a matter for criticism to address—whether overt sexuality in a film is to be considered simply as a mark of an always peripheral genre, or whether the desiderata of criticism can expand (as they easily do for the most horrific shoot-em-ups) so as to treat sexual imagery as a constitutive subject (a more desirable one, hopefully, than killing) for our imaginative lives.

The present audience for erotic film—(mostly mixed gender by now) —may find enjoyment in the tension between the interplay of actuality and performance, truth and illusion, in the representation of sexuality.

Consider this dialogue—instanced by Princess Feather—of the (as-yet hypothetical) film: "Priscilla's Predilictions." "Did you see me come?"—the character (Priscilla) cries-out in the last scene. "It looked good!" says her co-worker (not listed in the major credits). "Did she really come?"—the viewers (regionally scattered) argue after viewing time: "Her eyelids fluttered a lot at the crossing," said one. "But did you look at her toes—they didn't move at all," said another.

One more variable: "Did I come?" Feather asks. "Does it matter," her manager responds "to anyone important besides your husband?"

When, then, does it matter? At times of: "Love?" "Lust?" "Attraction?" "Exaltation?" "Degredation?" "Indifference?" "Submission?" And In which modes? "Non-representation" (only participants allowed)? "Voyeurism" (hot-breath of the audience)? "Significant content" (mirror of a troubled soul)?

The appreciative stance for erotica may be unique in still other respects: Part of its increasing subtlety, as I have said, entails getting past the artistic fiction to the performers' actual state—and then back into the fictional character. This is the age-old ambition in art to dissolve fiction into reality and then make reality into a new fiction—so as to keep the audience wondering about themselves, and coming back for sequels to separate the wanted fiction from the familiar kind—the one experienced as reality.

Or is this ambition too manipulative—too coercive—for the task of making art? Is it not a form of economic (not to say, psychological) coercion to insist on a proof (convincing semblance) of orgasm (or any other affective state) from both players and their characters—in order to to sell the up-scale film?

Yet, there is this truism: Technology can make honesty obsolete—when the fiction is better (more true, good, and beautiful—or more false, bad, and ugly) than the life it represents.

Young love is always suspicious of—if not falsity, then deception: "I don't really know how it's done—and you shouldn't either. We're too young to know. But no one will tell me when it's time for us to know what we should know."

Later on, when young love ages, secrets of knowing are revealed to ones by others. These not fix what needs fixing—even when we're all in it together. The strangeness of it all may be exacerbated (careful now, kid!) by the subsequent call to even stranger practices—that still elude knowing.

The coital scream is open to many interpretations: Is it a cry of pain? A fear of death? A glandular disturbance? Pure ecstasy? Suppressed flatulance? An interest in making art with your own noise?

Perhaps erotic noise is of the kind that begs the issue of identity. Screams without a source or reason need pictures—of the doing and being done to. Aesthetic reasons for a scream require representations; they don't convince without the posit of a self or selves—each with a special intonation and separate pleadings.

No solitary screamer in the wilderness can make art—the hermit usually does not scream—just thinks about its necessity. In both Hell and Heaven—for a meaningful sound, an immediate chorus is required—from a distance, the sounds of adulation and despair sound much the same.

The male lion can have fifty orgasms in an afternoon—I don't know what he's thinking. The female lion, they say, is programmed to wait it out—I don't know what she's thinking either. Humans (if they're truly human) make up stories that keep them going—in chapter after chapter—into the twilight of mimesis and memory. (Think Boccaccio and Sheherazade or Proust). The best enjoyment is found in reflecting on the stretched-out time (actual, historical, neurotical, fantastical) it has taken—in the times of getting there.

HERE AND THERE

Strictures are not native to the Bohemian soul,
whose experience is never complete without a rise or fall.
Whether a rise through grace or a fall into perdition,
it's the extremity in the way of both that matters.
You know you've reached it when it hurts —
and you then can chant and wail. or say the word.

But here, in our community of grace and land-estate,
the give-and-take between punishment and reward
must be carefully maintained—for the good of all.
Give in if there's no way out, enjoy as best you can,
and weep in the morning if you're hurting bad.
But don't cry-out for others' help unless you must.
Everyone will know of course—the times you rise or fall.
The oak panel, needing oil, sees and tells the oiler all.

But neither players nor voyeurs will say a word until the leaves
are finished falling, and night shadows down the shortening days.
Then, it's time for winter frolics flush with hearty dinners,
red-rimed eyes, and the fireplace smoke that accents the smells
of willing flesh. The stories of last-year's summer can now be told.

To spite the outside cold, the hottest escapills will be recounted
with on-site commentary, relevant asides, and historical support—
all told by local experts in the cadence of debauchery.
Some such tales, believe-me, are told in the first person voice:

"There was a partly open door, you see, and I just had to follow
the noises to their source, and then I saw the most unlikely couple
doing the loveliest of unspeakables—while all the time they cooed
and roared. We-all heard the sounds—but didn't say a word."

The sly old fox had installed a two-way mirror in the library
which overlooks the guest apartment abutting the garage.

We were told to show no light and make no further noise—
so we sat on steamy cushions in the dark, and watched the moist
yet awkward twistings of our just-invited guests. They came because
they were so anxious to belong. Good show—our host intoned.
I'll ask them to come again and sing a slower song.

The show was not, in fact, particularly raw—
more awkward and a-rhythmic then your standard flick.
I liked the couple better later, when they were dressed,
invited in to join the rest, and awkwardly sat at sipping wine.
Their expressions showed they knew they had been watched.
Perhaps they had auditioned for just this time and place.
But what they wanted most to know—they showed the strain—
was whether, having paid their dues, they now could sit and chat
with guests about the seemly and uncertain in the worlds of
finance and artistic interest—and whether, without old fear rising,
they could watch the moving mouths, once fastened on their bottoms,
that now smoked the flesh and spat the juices of those vile cigars.

PERFORMANCE PIECES

Erotic performances are usually watched by men. But at the night before, there were two women who insisted they had an equal right to watch. They—as everyone there knew—had often been at such viewings. But each said that it is a matter of principle which, even though all that had been settled long ago, needs bringing up again—each time—as a confirmation of female gender and its new power. The men put on the called-for faces of Victorian disapproval—but of course, listened silently, and did nothing further to dissuade the two—who then lounged separately on the softest cushions—which gave an excellent vantage from which to watch.

One woman was of unspecified Hapsburg origins. She had once been a great beauty—neo-classic proportions between shoulders and waist, long legs tapering into delicate ankles. But she was heavier now. The raven hair was mostly grey—but still well disheveled—flowing in counterpoint to her extravagant gestures. She smoked cigarettes incessantly, and her green eyes had long been reddened by the smoke and the Scotch whisky she sipped throughout the evening. Her nose was aquiline and her lips moved like serpents when she laughed, but they were countered by the covering flesh that made all her body—once a joy for the fortunate who had been privileged to touch—now sprawl in loose and overlapping folds upon the large sofa she claimed as her usual spot for the evening.

There was room for two, maybe three, on that sofa—but no woman would join her there; she was too ancient, too fierce and voluble. Comparisons between her and any of the others—no matter how young, sparkly or well-kept—would be only to their detriment. What could those frillies say that she had not said better—so many times before—and what would she now say that they could never (not in their way of life) ever think of saying?

Her wits, however worn by exile, were still sharp—more penetrating than any in the room would dare to challenge. She put off questions about her past with the lazy wave of a survivor of abasements, lost-fortunes, and small atrocities. She gave a slightly different wave—with wiggling fingers—when asked about the night's performance. Not shocked, not bored—not she. But, goodness, those sweet people need some marinating—tutoring and soaking time in a lexicon of carnal acts—I suggest the Kama-Sutra—before they or I could find their doings really enjoyable.

A few men did join her on her couch—in small shifts as the evening wore on. These were younger, usually gay men who had been invited through their roles as decorators or as understanding friends. The countess (that's what she liked to be called) was kind to them—laid her heavily jeweled hands upon their skinny knees, squeezed their thighs, and whispered secrets which caused gales of laughter—to the consernation of the corporate husbands who were clustered near the windowed doors by the gardens. Secrets, of course, were the real currency of these monied folks, and the countess was feared because she knew so many, and could make up more. (How does one deny the truth of secrets)? Besides, the men knew that she knew—just by looking—how lame they had become in their chosen beds—where thoughts of ledger lists would obscure the pubic curls that once waited for their attention. So they smoked cigars, ate the cavior with the hard-boiled eggs and sour-cream, and continued to plan the logistics of next week's clandestine viewing.

The other woman who insisted on watching was small and tightly formed—a consequence of many hours at the gym and tennis courts, frequent massage, and daily applications of lotions and emollients. She also was European —perhaps Dutch. Her hair and face had been carefully tended, and her speaking voice was cultivated to where an accented phrase could begin as seduction and end as a dismissal. It was a formidable weapon against outsiders. She made abrupt gestures as she talked—often knocking a glass from an admirer's hand who had come too close.

In this sense she was like the Siren of Ulysses: From across the waters, she sings beautifully and looks divine—but how can we get to her, tie her naked to our mast, before she makes us all go dead?

When asked how she liked the night's performance, she laughed that downer laugh, and began to mimic some of the awkward positions that the innocents had taken in their efforts at copulation. Her actions brought us to our knees with laughter. But then—as she always did before her stories ended—she would abruptly straighten up, adjust her small but well-formed breasts, and insist, with multi-lingual intonations, that no cultivated person would ever do such things that way—much too tiring, not at all satisfying, and what if someone innocent were watching? She, herself—as she herself once said—liked being watched, but only by companions of her choice.

Stories are always circulating—in the markets and the coffee houses—about the antics of well-placed folk who are said to like the watching-thing. Such stories make their way into the outer world through servants who lay-out the midnight snacks and wait to remove the leavings—by the electrician who had to push aside the soiled bedding and the sex-toys in order to repair an unresponsive outlet—and through guests who were not privy to the viewings, but made up stories about the noise upstairs, and listened raptly to the chatter after dinner.

Actually, the upstairs crowd rather enjoyed having a downstairs crowd that whispered conjectures about their prurient behaviors. When a certain level of prominence has been reached—as history shows—rumors of displays of what, after all, were once regarded as a Royal right, had now become privileges of the democratic rich. These marks of well-earned affluence and power should be welcome: The competitive powers of equals are civilized by good wine, rich catered food, and lurid spectacles. The jealousies of the juniors in the board-room, when too apparent, can be put down by the level stare of rank—and the denial of promotion.

CLASS STRUGGLES

The stories that are told outside—by the angry and disaffected,
only incidentally criticize kinky behavior in the castle.
Deviance actually doesn't matter much—especially to the poor.
They (despite received wisdom) enjoy sex as much as do their betters.
All it takes is a shower, food and drink, and some time off.
Working-out and dirty-pictures help.

More deeply, though, these stories of deprivation
support the presumption—no longer subscribed to
by the common folk—
that the rich are more entitled than the poor
to the sybaritic comforts
available at exclusive parties.

Tell too many stories and you'll land in jail—
or have your food-stamps cut—together with your balls.
The writings in the tabloids that tell of pecadillos of the famous,
support the claim that there are differences in enjoyment
between the social classes.
It should be so—No? Differences in both kind and quality
of genetic transfer are constants in the history of culture.
And who are we to disagree?
Current fans of lurid lore are fed visions of the Riviera,
and offered partial participation in an upstairs party.
You see, it's become all democratic—the price one pays.
If you can swing it, buy a ticket—if not, just wait
and salivate, and if need be—masturbate.

We now offer new versions of the Roman
"Panem et Circenses"
which means "Bread and Circuses"—
for those of you who have no Latin.
At times, watching Lions eating Christians—
especially the innards of the virgin girls—

is proper fulfillment for late Imagination.
Believe me—all you hungry up-tight boys!

But beware the beasts who have a taste
for complex dissidents—like philosophers and cranks,
flower-children and computer-wonks,
pot-heads and ecstatics.
Lions are straight-forward in their slaughter.
These other beasts are not.
They'll eat you just because they ought'a.

ANNIE WARBUCKS

Sometimes I regret the scattering of my early life while looking for new ways of living. But I do not want to vitiate my recollections of that trying by regrets—particularly not when I have come to enjoy my later efforts at reliving it. Old-ones are usually furious at the betrayals their younger selves have foisted on the coming of ambition's end. But these betrayals—if you look—are all couched in counterfactuals: "Had I done that instead of this, then. . ." Such regret belongs more to gamblers, who never cease blaming the dice for their misfortunes. Still, even this is better than had I joined the rush (I was tempted) to a positive future by painting the whole enterprise, from birth to death, in pretty colors.

I have come to think of life as a struggle with well-meaning conjectures from old and foreign sources that seek to alter one's own attempts to arrive at something plausible for living a life. These intruders do not offer truth—they lack the cosmic sense. But they do offer notions that are more like true-belief (credibility looking for proof) than like the new consumer-friendly fare (seductions of false belief). Yet, given this distinction, the best of our older well-formed notions seem in time to disappear, without much hope for re-assessment or redemption—in spite of dogged recourse to now obscure and unfashionable parts of the historical past.

But even in those opaque waters, there are a few conceits still susceptible to lures, and these can be caught and pulled ashore, to become tasty side-dishes in one's-own post-historical feast. Being caught is indeed better than being ignored—fulmunating quietly and slowly moldering—on the back shelves of a local library. So, friend—if you're not among the lately-hooked, you can go back to a righteous anger (much rehearsed —you've had ample time) which however, when performed, is also seen as a sometime affliction of the obsolete mind—the one that only a short while ago—just the other day it seems—participated in the most recent coming of the latest thing.

The above is such a sad scenario that I should resort to weeping. Instead, in my defence, I offer you a different story—mostly fictional and only sometimes biographical.

The story goes this way: What if I had abandoned east-coast ambition when it was the early wisdom to do so? And what if, before obeying my urge to travel west, I had made one last trip to the Hamptons and there met Annie—the widow Warbucks—and after a short romance (we both were lonely and needy)—I had married her.

Li'l Orphan Annnie (some of you may remember her) was very grateful, when she was a child, that for no reason she could understand, a force would appear—first as the huge and irresistable Punjab —with turban and scimitar—and second as the inscrutable Asp, lean and lithe, whose dagger was quicker than his name-sake's strike. They would rescue Annie—every Sunday—from the serious trouble she always seemed to get into.

The force behind this weekly benevolence was the richest man the comics could devise—"Daddy Warbucks"—whose fortune, as the name implies, was made by financing the wars of his and other nations. There were many breathless episodes and bare escapes for Annie (she was an adventurous child) but the beneficent powers of Daddy and his cohorts always came through in the end. So—orphans and outcasts, don't despair—Daddy is here. Good News in the Great Depression!

Our story continues: After the comic strip was discontinued and Annie grew older, she began to wonder why her rich old daddy—that bald and stick-pinned apparition, who always showed up smiling when the fuss was over—didn't treat her better. When she was a kid, it was OK—although her dog Sandy never liked him. But now Sandy's dead, and she's past twenty-one, and still the old shit (he's still alive—would you believe it?) won't come across with any real money. After reading some books on feminism, Annie decided to confront her daddy in his mansion. Fortunately, Punjab and the Asp had aged, lost their "derring-do"—and didn't think to stop her. They once had been her protectors—but only in extremis—which meant waiting through the week until the danger to Li'l Annie became imminent, then they would strike—otherwise, no use wasting mercenary effort. Perhaps Warbucks thought it was more cost-efficient that way—perhaps he only liked to look on Sunday.

Since then, Annie had grown older, and she began to think he owes her more. For instance, there are all the revenues that came from the comic strips she starred in, and all the adulation that Warbucks received for being an icon of the wealthy and well-born—who also (democratically) had a soft-spot (bless his heart) for an orphan child. That was dynamite publicity—worth gadzillions for Warbucks Inc.

But that was then—she was needy now. When she went to his mansion, unannounced, Punjab and the Asp remembered her from olden times and thought the master would like to see her again—as she had filled out her clothes in ways that he, although he seldom viewed such footage anymore, could still admire.

Old Warbucks was sitting in a leather arm-chair, his spindly legs positioned on a tufted foot-rest. My, she thought, he's smaller than the daddy I remember—the one who sent me cheer and kept the evil ones away. (Why were there so many evil ones when I was little?) But that, as she thought again, was then. So I said to him: "Daddy, I need a better life than what I have been having. I know you're not my father, but you've been fooling around with me for over twenty years. What you gave me in the comics is not enough—I no longer need your bully-boys—but I do need money. The comics are finished, but my rent and groceries are not. So I have two proposals: You can formally adopt me—in which case I will tend to you as befits a loving daughter. Or, you could marry me, in which case I will try to satisfy all the fantasies you still can dream of."

He chose the latter—the old goat. So I married my daddy, and we embarked on re-living the many memories he had of his profligate past. I must say, he was better at remembering such things than I had expected. But he tried too hard—I didn't dissuade him—and then, one night, he died.

I met the widow Warbucks at a party in the Hamptons. Her red hair was now drifting into grey, but it still sat like a big untrimmed bush upon her head. And her eyes were as I remembered them in the comics—green—but a greener green than print can match. The two colors, modulated by freckles and bright white teeth, became a field that held its own against the pink of beach umbrellas, and the tan and blue of sand and ocean. Her body-curves, which as young budding protrusions had so enticed her daddy, were now more ample—enveloped as they were in well-fed cover—but they jiggled nicely as she walked.

My own interests had always been in dewy young things, and I thought that the bedding of willing innocents was preferable to tending to the older, but still-needy matrons of a certain age. Well, I was wrong. I didn't marry Annie—it was a bad career move. I still think of the possibilities: We could have done so well together.

But wait! This is still a story. So let me tell it in another way—after all, we are deep in fiction-land. Let's say I did marry Annie. There are advantages to this scenario: With part of her inheritance, I could have bought-up 1900 acres of river bank in the Ozarks, and built retreats for fellow sensitives in limestone caves already carved by the action of free-flowing rivers. Why, I could now be guru of that whole chigger-ridden region—reciting my poetry at campfires and selling provisions to the passing canoes.

Then, if itching and scratching became a real problem, we could have moved the whole enterprise up north, near the Tetons and past the biting-bugs—to Idaho—where vistas and rivers, pot and meth, are more plentiful than trees. There I could present myself as inscrutable sage of the meaningful demarcation between low scrubs and high plateaus—a latter-day mountain-man of exotic but mysterious origin. Fortunately for this version of the story, there is less curiosity about origins and motives in the high-country than in the Missouri heartlands. It wasn't all that hard to get the locals to believe me.

Annie, despite a lost love (she still wanted "Daddy"—imagine!) and an uncertain new one: (What is he doing—spending all my money on pot and poetry?) would have agreed—if I kept being nice to her—to hand out leaflets and sing Celtic songs at my Sunday gatherings. She would have come to appreciate the mountain folks who cared less about her money than did those weasels in the Hamptons—and she couldn't but have noticed that the locals seemed to like the substantial way she fit into her boots and jeans.

The gatherings—as I scripted them—were not to be religious in nature—but neither would they be non-religious. I would present them as vistas to be marvelled at—storms to be endured—unities to be sought between forces of one's choosing. God is where you want Him to be, I would say—and if, on a winter's night, you suspect that that is where He wants you to want Him to be—why all the better—it takes a load off.

By that time, I had grown a full head of hair, all grey, worn long, still curly in the back. I stood tall, a little stooped, given to peering—even when wearing my reading glasses—into the distance. I spoke mostly to the wind. We did make a handsome couple though, Annie and I. We were, as I said, mysterious—and I thought we fit there better than anywhere so far. We could have (should have) stayed. But as the weeks passed, a declining few came to our gatherings. They, after all, were mountain folks—and had worked out crazy portents on their own—they didn't need me for that.

And then there was the weather: In winter, outside of the twistings of wind and snow, nothing moved. Yes, you could see your tracks—but the mountains, however far you walked, were always in the same cold place.

If you could wait it through, the seasons did change—but that only meant replacing one set of gear with another—in the spring, moccasins instead of boots —in the fall, parkas pulled over sweat-shirts. Living meant changing the methods for coping: Keep enough wood for when the power goes out—watch for signs of frost-bite on your nose when it gets very cold. These rules were self-evident—part of the local lore—found in diaries and ledgers inscribed by those who had the leisure and schooling to write about such things. They were the literature of the Western places—rules of survival like the Bible—to be read, lived, and reread.

But the lack of mobility—especially in the winter months—had become a real problem. Action in that place was largely practical, despite its summer presentation as a walking through the untouched face of nature—it was also brief. In the winter nothing moved, nothing changed—just occasional rumbles announcing avalanches and more snow. That was fine for those competent yet placid folk who lived there—they just wanted to sit by the fire and survive. But I was looking for transcendence—for a place where monotony could be pried open to show a changing face. Such a place, I knew, was not to be entered by chatter with the locals over the need for a good tractor. That would only be to exist by accepting the repetitive passing—with equanimity—of the small warm time between flood and snow, and the large cold time before the flowers showed again.

I wanted to find the other side—to accompany Dante on his journey down to Hell—to understand what living fails to offer—and then return to earth for a passing glimpse of heaven. I began to see that viewing the same mountain at prescribed moments—coping with its seasonal changes—was a way to avoid noticing the changes in myself. It was a low seduction on the high mountain—and its greatest power was in the scenarios that made it seem so innocent—so matter-of-fact—so true to life—so sensible. By then I was sniffing for the ancient spoor: Maybe that's the Devil's disguise for today—masquerading as "just-folks-making-do."

So I told Annie we have to search for another place—a real change from the cold and wet. It wasn't hard to do—we found one right in the travel section of the Times. In a gesture toward ante-bellum history—and after studying accounts of the famous hurricane—we thought that we would travel to Charleston and buy (thanks to "Daddy") an elegant house near the water—battered but still sound—and then restore it to its stately dignity. Annie loved this idea. The mountains had been a suffered obligation—but this could be fun. Once there, and after we became established (restoration is a big social plus in Charleston) we would throw weekend parties, beginning on the lawn each sunset, and continuing indoors through the nights, embracing the full range between formality and abandon. Belles and beaus would come and go. The more mature—those who understand the traditional customs and their modern interpretations—would talk about the potential promise of the waterfront (lifts the whole economy, you know). Then, like in the old days, we would dance and prance and drink till dawn—to achieve the Southern Comfort version of a weekend in the Hamptons.

But after some years (yes, it was nice and warm down there) I found the passage of time too circular—not as in Idaho—well, yes, somewhat like in Idaho—but more chic, more genteel, more decadent, more unbearable. The mild abandon of our gatherings—looked forward to each week—were high-spots for those, such as we, who didn't have to work at living. (I can see "Daddy" nodding approvingly). But eventually, as in Idaho, it became clear to us (to me, at any rate) that these were only more comfortable ways of diminishing the anxious passing of the time of life. (I was smelling the Devil again). Charleston is the eye of the storm—the cyclic turn and return of isolation and community—the post-biblical morality that condones the repetitive rhythm of groundless joy and necessary boredom as part of God's given plan—that we mortals enjoy our fleeting gaieties until comes repentance time.

Certainly, there were other options for us —we had had many experiences of searching out new places. By now, we were seasoned malcontents. Annie actually liked the Southern ways—the swish of long dresses, the courtly repetition of compliments, the period costumes, the sweet-cakes soaked in Bourbon. She would have stayed—but I still had some leverage left—so I demanded (for our own greater good, of course) that we leave. Without a word to the locals, we moved away, early on a weekday morning, away from sweet seduction to have another go at the values of austerity. Upon leaving, I began rehearsing my pensive and penitential look; Annie remained blank and silent.

We moved (it was my decision) to another place of cold-and-wet—to the coast of Maine—to live our lives along its misty islands, and to cohabit (once we learned the customs) with the local fisher-folk. We found a small clap-board house fronting an unnamed inlet—small and poorly insulated—but it had advantages: It gave protection from the winter storms, and proximity to a dock used by lobster fisherman. However, the dirt-road was impassable during a heavy snow, and wine and other staples were some miles away in town. It was again time for patience and reflection.

Oh, it wasn't so bad: We ate a lot of lobster, and waded in the cold-cold water in which one does not swim, and where boats go only carefully. Slickers, clamshells, and rubber boots are not as sexy as the daily dress down-south; indeed, the smells of the ocean and rotting fish are your primal cover through the days and nights. But the natives did fuck like minxes. Fastidiousness has little currency in the eastern north, and, as they say up there—what better is there to do when all liquored up in the winter's dark? Personally, I don't too much mind the smell of wet and cold and the lack of washing. Like the hot and dry, it can be gotten used to—and sometimes works to one's advantage. The appreciation of funky people—as with ugliness in art—can become a special kind of sensory enjoyment. Personally, I seldom mean what I say to others—whether about money matters or body odors.

Annie was never happy in Maine—but she showed her displeasure in ways more subtle than when she had flaunted her attributes in Charleston. The skimpiness of rewards for her acceptance of austerity was met with a corresponding denial of clarity. She stopped showing her daily likes and dislikes—but made them into ancient memories—like her fears of Daddy's motives—that she thought she had left behind.

In truth, I wasn't anymore happy in Maine than was Annie. We both did try, however. I had presented this move as our ultimate moral quest—but neither of us could convincingly go native again. There were the self-righteous chores on fishing boats, the ritual peeling off of oilskins and rotten socks, and the constant smell and slime. Then there was the requisite booze and sex between eight and midnight, and the week-end brawls at the bars. All this seemed like old penitential rites for a failed religion. Why—Annie finally said—did we leave the Hamptons? I was happy there.

And why, given my own illusions, did I want to leave Maine? I confess that I am often too cocooned within myself to recognize the craziness of other places. However much I look for myself in newly minted origins, I find that I accept the local monotonies in mind and soul as my own. But eventually, I come to hate the local customs: The practices of parsimony and the eccentricities of belief. They do not help me stay—however much I dance and pray.

So afflicted, I begin to speak directly to the winds. I say: We have a span of body that we can only celebrate for a short, short time. It is then well that we think on remembering the early sight—and the sound of that first word—of the ones who came and laid down next to us.

In keeping with my fondness for well-tended flesh, I have scurried to avoid the sallow skins that smell of low tide—excused myself from dinners that serve only fish and just-picked vegetables, and ignored the local custom of chanting to the waters with the setting sun. No, none of that—not any more. So again, we left.

Annie hated Maine, for her own reasons. She, being fictional, was more susceptible to ending than was I—a durable mortal, after all. And I suspect that we—not being that similarly real—feared ending in quite different ways. I had my four-score and ten; she had the possibility of renewed interest and historical reprints. In any case, Annie had the advantage of her Daddy's money to spend—she could, before she ended, indulge herself anywhere and in any fashion that fiction permits. I, despite my real-time love of fantasy, could not.

One weekday morning, I found that she was gone. I did try to find her, but the comic-strip in which I first met her, was long out of print. I made some discreet inquiries in Charleston—but no one there had ever heard of her—or me. The folks in Idaho didn't answer my letters. After Maine, what with Annie gone—having returned, as I supposed, to the world of fiction—I went back to Saint Louis.

A time ago, in a mid-age flight from the imperatives of New York, I had come to settle there—in the mid-west by the river. I came to teach the locals crazy art and, later, abstruse philosophy. There, I lost a wife, raised a child, found a love, and earned enough to secure a modest pension. It is a good place, I once thought, to go quietly into that dark night—no pressing ambitions to be cut short, not even by death—no self-given obligations that must at all costs be met.

As a bonus, there would be no legacy to protect, no galleries to entice, no reviews to fish-for, no ladder to climb and leave behind, no style to supercede.

But then I met Annie and, in that fall into inter-acting sub-realms of reality, I lost all sense of the distinction between the actual and the fictional. This is why—if you wonder—we made so many trips and lived in so many places. She was a character in a comic strip that, during the great depression, provided mind-candy to the homeless, and I was a professor looking for a fantasy to make retirement long and real. It must have been my insistence (and her curiosity) that transcended the divide—much like the sculptor who fell so in love with an image he was carving that he willed (asked the Gods) that she come to life. The Gods complied—they, much like Warbucks, like to watch. But after a short infinity of extreme passion, the inexorable divide between fantasy and reality showed up: She (his creation) left him and reverted to the cold-stone indifference of an art-work.

Wasn't he lucky though? (Extreme passion! Imagine!) I, myself (in my heart) would have wanted to play that role with a Titian Venus—but my head instead chose Annie. She was at hand —even if not always real. I became the Pygmalion of a character in the comics.

LIFE AS FICTION

My ways of life have not always been molded by the seductions of geography or vacillations about identity. I have not, in fact, lived any of the lives I describe above. Yet, they are fictions that I have truly lived. You know (if you do) that fiction has a way—when allowed to cohabit with truth (and how can you stop such ancient swains from continuing their affair?) of providing images that encourage the juncture of life and possibility.

Such fictions, as the situation warrants, do many valuable things: They can massage the pointy-nosed versions of "truth in the present tense" (an a-historical strategy) into an acceptance (this is hard for those who fear flying) of the notion of temporal plurality—"truth in process"—which correlates truth-values with changing contexts and methods of determination.

In addition, afficionados of fictions can give their support to the notion of "truth in process," by using the more speculative argument that the world (whatever its future) will certainly change (materially)—and, yet, is bound in the long run to get better. Then truth, in this version, will also get better. But such an argument, when viewed from the perspective of our acrimonious present, is hard to believe. Hegel did not say that the world, in its (spiritual) progress, will get better—only truer.

There is, of course, the popular notion that "truth" is out-moded. Although still not well tolerated, this notion indicates that truth can be both true and useful only if strategically presented. (I accept that an articulated truth need not be useful—I also accept that useless truths, however well articulated, tend to disappear). Fictions provide other ways (which-ever way you want to go) for truth to be useful in other places (contexts) than where we are now. This is not lightly said. Truth, without supporting fictions (and their images)—is in danger of being supplanted by the authority of "self-evident-truth." But this is one of the most absurd (and dangerous) of metaphysical concoctions: Who is the "self" for whom the truth is evident—the truth itself—or the duplicitous politician? Or is this a truth that needs no knowers?

I return to my story: What I tell is as I best remember it—but memory, like fiction and truth, has its own battles—we are inveterate uplifters and sometime downgraders of ourselves—and it requires both fiction and truth to present a coherent self—to our present selves—who don't ever stay put.

What we may need in the future are presentations for our different selves—but our hope is that those selves are as real as is the present one. (You want them to be more real? Don't be greedy).

I now assume (otherwise the story loses shape) that my younger self, despite hostile reports (by people who may still be living) was much as I am now—fluctuating parts of writer, painter, academic, borderline Bohemian, and periodically anxious lover. How then, could my early self have sorted all these out to carve a single identity—with which I could use to woo and capture, say, the Warbucks Annie?

I once practiced consolidating selves by under-taking trips, each with a different cast and separate hopes, seeking out the possibilities for the self that each journey might reveal: For example—as a mere pubescent, I fell in love with the Dragon Lady—that exotic queen of the pirates who once marauded (pillage, sex, and plunder) across the South China seas.

She was slinky and imperious, was this lady—all-powerful—dressed just scantily enough in silks and ornaments to contrast the leather boots and belts from which hung weapons for various uses. But these, were actually not so much weapons as ornaments. They included earrings made of small hand-cuffs, a serrated shark-tooth navel-ring, necklaces festooned with long-dead snake-heads. The other garments she wore were ripped—much like the jeans of our recent times—but the rips provided spaces (just wide enough for a young boy's peering) through which were revealed the incredulities of her lovingly—drawn long-limbs and a bare passing-glimpse into the region of her secrets.

But she frightened me, she did. One never knew back then: On some Sundays, she might rake her stiletto finger-nails across the supine flesh as a first hint of torments she has in mind for Terry, Pat (and me). On other Sundays she dd not appear at all. Nevertheless, I would have gladly gone to her —had she called me then. But by the time I came of age, she was much older—anywhere (I figured) between forty and eighty-four. You couldn't tell, even so—how old she really was—what with all the adornments and perfume. I had been willing all along to come to her—even though she wasn't real. She never did call. But I did experience, thanks to her, the perfection of a sufficient object of pure-belief.

But she wasn't around all that long—my interests were always straying. I remember another comic strip—"L'il Abner"—which was about the Yokums—a hillbilly clan in a place I knew nothing of—the hills of Kentucky (or was it Tennessee?). But the characters there were more approachable than the Dragon Lady: There was DaisyMay—hill-country bare and supple, wearing tattered shorts and a low-cut blouse—innocent enough to remain faithful (at least on Sundays) to that big oaf Li'l Abner. I wanted her like I did a mello-roll.

But I was really more interested in her cousin—Bathless Groggins. Now here was a girl that intruded into my deepest sleep: Kick-ass gorgeous, indifferent to clothes, with a sulky somewhat distant air —and a clear aversion to the practice found in folksy comics to come sit-with-you-on-the-porch. Bathless always sat alone, silent and indifferent to onlookers. Flies swarmed in a continuing circle over her head—attracted to her but never lighting. For reasons not made clear in the strip, Bathless did not wash. I never did get close enough to smell her—but if she had allowed me, I would have done well by both of us. I would fill a pail of warm and soapy water, and carry a bag with soft brushes, body oils and large clean towels. I would walk up the hill to the clearing where she came to sit most aftenoons. She would probably have looked at me with some surprise—it was the first time in the annals of the story that anyone had shown up with washing her in mind. She, fictionally , did smell a mite high—a bit like a stray dog—but it was my first time to think of love as both passionate and compassionate: "Take off those rags you're wearing," I would say in a gruff but kindly voice. "Now lay yourself down on that towel—face down is good for starters. I'm going to soap you a lot and everywhere—even your hair—and you can howl or whimper, curse me out or say anything else that comes to mind—it's all right—no one's around. It will take me some time to clean this side before I turn you—there is so much to get through."

She made no sound except for an occasional grunt when I rubbed too hard. Then I asked her to turn onto her back—which, to my surprise, she did without protesting. Her eyes were more direct now—beading into mine—but Bathless was not willing to let me into the world behind those eyes. This second soaping took longer—as there was much more to attend to. She made more sounds in this position—like mimicking voices on the radio.

The Dragon-lady and her cohorts disappeared with the advent of the Communist revolution in China. Exotica of the five senses gave way to the four horsemen of that apocalypse. There was no future for the new proletariat in the tellings of old piratic pain and pleasure. And I was too young to rescue her—barely a teen when she was gone.

It was much the same with Daisy—May and Bathless. The second war spawned different heroines: Rosie-the-riveter, and USO hostesses. I did try, but I couldn't find Dogpatch on the map—and no-one, even in the hills, knew of any Yokums. Anyway, Daisy, had she encountered facticity, would have borne the standard half-dozen children, and Abner, now fat but still strong, would be rich by transforming Kickapoo Joy-Juice into aged bourbon. Bathless (Ah—Bathless!)—had she survived the trip from the comics to the streets of Brooklyn, she would, in fact, have suited me just fine. But none of them made the trip across.

It is different with Annie—she was a child of the future, one of the many lovely underprivileged who survived their tycoons to grow into a wealthy but lonely middle-age. I was older too. Had I been somewhat different, I could have done what I now write about—live in exotic places, satisfy her every whim and spend her money. But such a story would have shown me as shrewder and more daring than I am, and made Annie into a more predatory and desireable creature than she was. But, in my story, she and I were made (in that reality) to be uniquely fitted to meet each other halfway—she, to greet me at the near edge of actuality, and I, coming closer to being fictional than more circumspect minds would dare.

A few comments on my terminology (not necessary, but it fills unspoke-for time): "Reality" I take to be a broader category than "Actuality." The former designates all-there-is—not only things, but memories, dreams, fantasies, fictions, other worlds—all that we don't know, have forgotten, and all we cannot know. "Actuality," in contrast, is the stuff of here and now, which sometimes includes how far we think we can stretch our here-and-now to keep it and ourselves still around—when later comes.

The boundary between the fictional and the actual became our (Annie's and my) meeting place. This is because we were fitted—historically, sociologically—even tempermentally—to test its porosity together. Of course, Annie could never become completely actual, and I could not disappear, without some physical residue, into the world of fiction. Both the Demiurge and the Immanent God would object.

But we, Annie and I, are survivors, and could both exist as real and fictional—as an expanded series—a sum of partialities—that contains the better part (and sometime art) of each. But as you know, existence—as with other states of affairs—never lasts forever. So we, eventually, would have to —as we did—have gone our separate ways.

You see—the border between fact and fiction depends upon the predictive strength of the future being told. Permeability of borders is a factor in the history of realms and of the languages spoken then, now, and later. Inconceivable existences in unimaginable realities become possibles—sometimes even probables (as close as I want to get to that now) depending on the theoretic (and imagistic) fit between remembered antecedents and suitable successors. The effort is to construct a future (first real, then actual) out of all possibles—a future that is a fit consequence for its antecedents. "Fitness," evidently, is a determination made in the present—but it, too, changes. The unfit possibles retreat into their fictional or speculative places—waiting for the call to become actual (they are already real) if the "fitting thing" changes yet again. Fitness, then, is the hope for a particular kind of future. It is a hope of both people and art.

SELF-KNOWLEDGE

I cannot answer "why" questions for any of my selves at any of my times—why it is that this one appears and not that one. This is because the effort would have to conjure-up a "most-real" self of mine to which the others are historically answerable. My selves can be years apart in emergence, or they can jostle daily with each other like passengers on a crowded train. The answers to their "whys" are dependent on the positionings in their passage. If you are reading this, you yourself might want to look for that one-of-you who will help you understand the why-of-you (right now). If you can't make up your mind, wait a bit and ask another one (like me) who's been around. He'll steer you right (I suppose I would)—but remember that each of your selves has its own journey—to its hard-won boundary—between what it was and what it wants to be. Each such boundary needs some time for crossing.

The terrain to be crossed is always different. People sometimes demand a definitive account: "Who is the real Marilyn Monroe?" That's a fiction too—I doubt the truth will out—there being no such truth that, like the "real Marilyn," will stand and wait for you. It is strange, though, that the clamor that arises for a "true-self" grows louder with notoriety. We want our heroes and heroines to always be what we believe they are. That's dangerous for them.

Better to read this, then, before I become famous and have my array of selves parsed and molded—packaged into one "Real Lucian." As I'm not famous, the uncertainty gives you good excuse for reading further. Afterward, there's a place for sitting on the stump while watching the bugs crawl by until it's time to eat Auntie Em's fried chicken. But look around! Blink your eyes three times! Sitting with you are the old familiar others—friends of yours just being what they are—all together to confirm the fact that you are the one (we all know you) that's always here with us. You might get some comfort out of this—even as you, late sceptic, will doubt—not the food, but the reality of their belief.

But it can be uncomfortable—the nagging notion that you once were something somewhere, and soon you will be something other somewhere else. 'Being-a-thing' is an antidote to this—because, if you are a thing, you have no regrets. it becomes less important (to your thing-ness) that what you were back then is not what you now are—or will be again. If you are not a thing but a person —the danger is that many will encourage you, despite the pain of stasis, to avoid being (becoming?) other than what you are.

But certainly—thinking of the past—if you could go back there to then (being what you are right now) you wouldn't act like the self you were back then. You know better now. So you cannot (should-not) (want to) be your present you —yet be the you that you were before. It would be too hard to cope now.

The other direction—the anticipation of one's future—also has problems: It's hard to find your self in times to come. Your present self—you as of this moment—may, like bad old art, already be out of date. You could-not (wouldn't want to} bring that present self into the future. You wouldn't be appreciated then.

However, it may not be all bad: Your present self may instead, like old good art, be capable of dancing a dance that others were not taught. So it may be better to dispose of shabby baggage —worn beliefs about who you really are—and take on new stuff as you go. Of course, one always needs stuff of some kind to be anyone—the right kind is the question.

Fron the vantage of the philosopher's overlook, there are two main options: One can try to stay with present practices, and win the plaudits of one's peers for being sensible: Wear the pricey stuff you've bought and treasured—but don't be surprised if the younger ones soon find you dull and boring. If you then become afflicted with immortality anxiety, you can make bold predictions that bravely dredge-up some forgotten past for support. But this requires (listen carefully) the sceptical understanding that there is no clear (much less straight) line between back then, now, and later on.

SCHEMATISM OF PAST AND FUTURE

A schematism is (here and now) in order:

REMEMBERING __-____ HOPING
Ruminating / Predicting
Excavating / Projecting

Our past is what we_REMEMBER. We do not remember all our past—just different parts at different times. But to even say that our past has an "all" is to face the question of how we can know—with all the efforts we make—that there is nothing else in the past (like the shot that missed) to not remember. Is it not discomfiting to think that there are times of your life—and of the cosmos—that neither you nor any other will ever remember?

Yet, there are ways of getting at the past; One of the ancient ones is "Rumination"—often given the more formal name of "Contemplation." The first is modelled after "chewing the cud"—reflecting on what you once had eaten before regurgitating it to chew again—in order to extract all you (and yours) previously didn't know was there. Then, continuing to chew, you might discover that taste of some hidden part of the first chew that has—just now—found its place in memory.

The more recent term—"Contemplation"—can be pure as drying bones, or as sprightly as a theatrical act. Sitting on a stump alone at sunset, and looking at the darkening shadows as they evoke memories can be dry. Sometimes, though, others watch and applaud your ancient wisdom and your retreat from action.

Contemplation is also called "omphaloskepsis"—an over-blown term used to describe a custom of Eastern origin for gazing quietly but expectantly at one's navel—so as to achieve wisdom without aggression. In all such cases, the images come unbidden—lighting and lightening the movement of mind away from immediacy into memory. But despite a practiced passivity, such images are quicksilver—they flee at the moment you stand straight again—the very moment you want them to stand fast and tell the truth about how it really was. But that's all right. Let them, says the Guru, have their own ways and times—so that they can get richer, breed and multiply before you summon them again.

But there are the other times when memory is occluded by pain from hostile sources—some outside, others inside. Those efforts to remember require digging deeper—past the surface of the dream into that once awful reality which it configures. I call this "Excavation"—a thrust into the past that is neither ready nor willing to be exposed. Such a past must be nibbled at and the pieces saved—to be later put together. This is Freud's way—and it remains unclear whether such a way can dispel a person's psychic pain (Freud, after all, was concerned with healing) or whether his efforts, more fundamentally, give us a new and radical sense of how to situate ourselves between past and future—birth and death, love and hate, engagement and indifference.

Our future is in the time to come and we address it through our

HOPING. Future time will surely come—however it is measured. But the listing of our hopes is as varied as the peek-a-boo spectrum of our memories. Nothing guarantees that any hoping for our future will become actual —not even the hope that underlies our doing of good deeds. Some disagree: "Good deeds are rewarded." And if they are not, you can always petition God to clarify the fine print. Others who believe there is no God—or that He no longer cares—will disagree—but, as Kierkegaard asked in return: "What else is there?" Further, he would say that the answer "nothing"—does not identify a state of being.

One can have hopes about the future that will—or will not—come true. One can have hopes about the outcome of events which we may predict—but cannot (yet) know. But one does not have hopes about the present where one is: "Hoping" is a future state of "being." To hope entails to be alive. That we are always present somewhere, shows that we have left the reality of our past but have not yet attained the reality of our future. This, our present, is indeed a precarious place—one reason (as proposed by Zeno) is that its "now" —as it is prone to infinite segmentation—can have no "after." In other words: "You can't get to there from here." Yet—time, heedless of this ancient logic, continues to move across from before to after. "You" inevitably follow.

Our methods for ascertaining the future are no more certain than are the ones for retrieving our past. But within our life-parameter of past-present-future, we do have preferences about the direction of knowing: We prefer to know the future more than we do the past. The future, we say, can be altered—while the past can only be reinterpreted, or ignored. But we should not be cavalier. While we cannot know the future as we can the past, we do plot a way to the future through our admiration of (some interpretation of) what has been the past. It is true that the past has often been seen as a hindrance to reaching for the future—a murky and endlessly prolix bag of false beliefs. This criticism of past history is one scenario of Modernism—an increasingly communal search today for the scenario of tomorrow. Our individual pasts, however, are (still) our own. They remain a series of partial revelations (memories, dreams, relics, documents) which contain, through ongoing interpretation, how we came to be what we are. As we have no better way to know ourselves than through these revelations, our anticipations of the future begin with our knowing something (true or useful) about the past.

The future is a way out—out of inadequacy and incompleteness, and towards fulfillment—that is—if we could actually know it before it leaves the present. To know the future in the present is to make a "Prediction." This term can be parsed as "speak—before"—a stated anticipation of what will come—we speak before we know. Such speaking is based on our conditions of present living, and is justified by our desires for optimal completion—how we want to be tomorrow, before our life ends, or, more generously—how we want the world to be after we die.

To "speak before we know" is, in truth, a paradox: Prediction can be a poet's gambit, a card-shark's ploy, a hysteric's plea—as well as a scientist's ambition. We can try (in theory) to reverse uncertainty—by bringing the future into the present. For instance—if we knew the exact position of every grain in a mound of sand—and we could map the size, vector and velocity of the finger with which we poke that mound, then we would know exactly how the new (poked) mound would be constituted. But no poet would presume so much.

"Prediction" is actually too poetic a term for the hard stuff of present-day futurists, so I offer a different locution—one that sidesteps the all too human fallacy of saying before knowing—for we can also believe that our future (if we manage to take it in hand) depends on what we do about it now. Accordingly, I change the language and offer the term "Projection"—which connotes "system"—a controlling of present data in making what were loosely called Predictions. In this way, the "horror vacui" of the future is replaced by schemata devised through applications of specific (present) protocals. The projected schema (the one we choose) contains what we (now) want to know about how we must think—and do—in order to shape the future. Our chosen protocals provide our best ways of preparing now for later. Better than mere hope! Strict protocals also protect against irrelevancies that are enmeshed in hope—bad or faulty memories, unseemly speculations, unbearable dogma. This precision replaces the looseness of hope as a method of bringing the future into the present. Introspection and doubt give way to algorithmic probability—we move from fear and uncertainty to the probity of scientific experimentation. The method of Projection prefers to leave mistakes in the histories of our past—not to find them in our assessments of the future.

ABOVE AND BELOW

The French, when in their arithmetic mode, will have it either way.
Ninety-six or sixty-nine—just as the evening grows.
Spelunkers find that caves are wet —
deep pools occur where hidden waters flow.
They wade into them none-the-less —
some drown, but others swim it through.

Mountaineers are seldom satisfied without the ice and snow.
They climb to where first footprints can be placed, then traced
by others who fear the perils of first attempts—
preferring a well-marked route onto which,
deferentially, they plant their toes.

The Heavenly Host looks down at us below.
The Hordes of Hell look up above.
Their visions meet in the middle ground
where we—poor souls—fret, fulminate,
and then amalgamate the blessed and the damned
into sporadically transgressive folks like us.

But what if we all received a second chance
to live free before our dying resorts to being dead?
With no last-judgment calls to mar
the nothing that (it's somewhere said)
exemplifies the status of eternal rest.

ART FOR THE DEVIL

Once I thought the best of women were in Hell. After considering all the reasons not to think so, I still do. Where else could they be—history's most transgressive, self enamored, and so-doomed beauties? These are the Hell-bent women, who dawdle early in moisty glades and do not think, when the sun begins to set, to heed the gutturals in the forest, and escape to the safety of the castle walls. Some—look at them—are well-muscled and versed in the quick of on-and-off—they'll throw you for a loop—and snap your back in passing. Others, more sedentary, translate baby-fat into the contours of voluptuousness—which is itself a well-formed mix of gluttony and will, overweening when provoked, but the focus of attention even when quiescent. Both kinds find the Devil's interest —either in their sinewy interstices or overlapping sags—to only be their due.

Such creatures are hard to find in this scold of a world—even by lookers and sniffers like me. I sometimes spot one on the edge of things, but she usually moves too fast to be talked to more than twice—the skinny-pretties skip along, the fat and juicy slide away. Damn! Can't lay on the hand like once upon a time.

So I ask you—Lord or Devil: Where are they—my antipodes—when I need them most? Well—the voice replies (it's a recording, of course)—they are in Hell.

This impatience of the damned with the living has been noted in the drawings of Blake for the Divina Commedia. The exposed truth in these images corroborates the notion that fulfilled desire is a target for ideological repression. Free fecundity—casual screwing here on earth —is regarded as an affront to the sacramental view of life. And it continues to offend (after all these millennia) the long-noses (both wet and dry) who shroud their private stirrings with righteousness whenever they appear in public. These stiff-neck sniffers have always been the prime instruments for consigning the sinful into Hell; the Devil usually acts on their advice as a matter of survival. He, after all, needs a constant population to remain a player.

You must understand—the Devil is not angry with his sinner immigrants; they are much like him; after a while, they begin to look like him—all are players in the contest to catch the ring of concupiscence rather than the ring of righteousness.

Here on earth, safety from accusations for sins committed—or considered—is a major industry which provides assurance to the private places where the powerful rest—where neither they nor the objects of their appetites are marred by the stain of public sinning. These places are replete with perfumed satins and down-stuffed pillows, rich damasks and tapestries, bowls of tinted water in which large-eyed creatures patiently swim. All are bounties of the first world of privilege—even the Devil occasionally comes to see the show. These luxuries evoke the memorable times when, on a summer's night on earth, one can hear sounds of pain and pleasure emanating from the suite next door. "Quickly, my dearest, we must also vocalize—if we are to be invited to the party. What a shame that we're still here and not in Hell—to learn first-hand about the genesis of preparatory whimpers and big-time screams!"

Most will never see the show. They are among the many who do not qualify for the festivities of the damned—because—they still attend to the distinction between righteous right and sinful wrong. The men have skinny shanks and bulbous bellies, and wear toupes when the wind is still. The women are, or will soon be, spoken-fors—plump and smug and cheery. But they'll soon widen out—across the thighs and buttocks and then develop bags beneath the chin. And they will take on for their own those matronly faces, well-creased by communal approval, that are suppressants to the dark demands courtship once made on them. Oh, there are the few unseemly thoughts that remained after the rituals of wedding were complete; and they still pine, after all those years of sweat and fumbling, for Trigger and Roy Rogers.

But these lapses in right thinking (the preachers say) can be blamed on the excessive firing of certain glands, or if they recur more than twice, on the continuing interest of the Devil in still-innocent ex-virgins. But no need to worry: The family bosom, when held firm by whale-bones and righteousness, withstands all assaults. Hell is not for you, dear lady.

I have no quarrel with heavenly beauty—although I think that its confirmation ended with the ideologically sequestered artists of the early Renaissance—with, say, Duccio, Cimabue—all those coming by way of Byzantium—skinny bones, gold leaf, geometric gestures. and linear drapery. I admire them, but there are artists of the later Renaissance and the Baroque who are devotees of a more deviant beauty—Titian, Tintoretto, Veronese, Rubens. They still make the requisite gestures to heaven, but they also offer an admiration of the women who have been ill-treated in life—exalting them by offering a later fame. Titian put it squarely in his "Sacred and

Profane Love:" The nude—exposed to all eternity—is the sacred, while the clothed—dressed for the requirements of her time—is profane.

So I must save them—those deliciously damned creatures. I must bring the ones in Hell back into the world, so that the impact of their return upon the uncertainties of living (buffeted as they are between the contumelies of good and evil) will show the world—through the glories accruing from marred flesh and ungodly sentiments—the benefits of desire and appetite.

It is rationally wrong—not right at all—for the most enjoyable sources of human experience to be reduced to ashes upon the white-hot grills of historical scolds. Consider: These most beauteous of God's creations are being punished for having the very properties of life and love that He, the Lord, assigned to them. Ignore the rib-story, that egregious fable of male dominance that only supports wimps and wars. Ask instead: Where is the truth that supports love and license?

I will go to where Charon's ferry crosses the river Styx. It's past time. But if I am to rescue these maidens from the torments foisted on them by their overlords, I must find a way to bring them back to earth. The history of frontal assaults on the Gates of Hell shows that even God-sanctioned strategies can be failures. (Consider the Crusades). So I will not be aggressive. I will slide inside the brimstone barrier through a neutral tunnel, and see what can be worked out, while still in tourist guise, to bring those sin-stained paradigms into my care.

Beelzebub (the most worldly of the Hellish Host) was very nice to me at our first exploratory session. He assured me of a safe return (I believed him) and he listened carefully to the proposal in which I offered the best of my art as a trade for the most beautiful of his sinners. He thought awhile and then said: "Wander down, why don't you, through the various levels of our domain and find the girls you want; later we will come to look at the paintings you offer in exchange. Now don't forget to note the names of your desiderata and their dates of demise—we get so many, you know."

Gradually, I came to understand that he was testing me (as Devils do). Surely there was a more effective strategy for identifying desirables than my clambering about with a sign, some hand-outs, and a supplicating-horn, through the various levels of Hell. First of all, I was not well prepared: Brooklyn (where I was born) is not really Hell, and traversing Hell is not merely a variant on walking the mean streets. It's worse—but only because Hell is anxious to keep up with its media representations. So the Devils have devised, mostly at our worldly urgings, the fire and ice, wails and imprecations, we have been taught to fear.

I had no idea what Hell would look like. The American paintings of the west—Cole, Church, Bierstadt, Moran—have the scale I need, but not the forebodings. Medieval "Last Judgments" have the terror but not the spread of landscape. So there was nothing for it but to review my own visions, as the best way of preparing for my first trip to Hell.

I began with a slow traverse along the rocks that line the edges of the brimstone pits. I resisted both the intentional and pathetic fallacies—of holding back because of logical strictures, or falling in through the gaps of ambivalence. I also succeeded in avoiding the proffered bargains of pre-demonic trinket peddlers, and I studiously ignored the enticements of elderly burnt-out succubi. But then, as happens when passing through the entrance to a national park, the schlock suddenly ceased and I walked into the quiet to find the path that leads to the source of sounds I have been hearing, as it now seems, all my life. This path, while free of worldly distractions, is pure Devil-makery in that it never goes to where the sounds come from.

But after a few wrong turns and minor burns, I found the way (the Devil only wants to discourage sight-seers who lack a point of view) to the clearing where Hell's temple stands—that edifice of autonomy and disbelief the Devil has been building for millennia.

The venerable firm, Hell-Works, is the contractor; but the Devil acts as his own architect, and despite constant changes to the plan, (the Devil is always of two minds) he has almost completed a massive hall, ambitious enough to admit the many manifestations of wrong-belief, mount comprehensive exhibitions of perverse content, and schedule ongoing performances portraying torment of the soul, and its derivative pleasures.

Hell's architectural masterpiece, unlike Heaven's Dome, is all audacious cantilevers and off-center parapets. It teeters on a ledge overlooking the flaming pits in which are engulfed sinners of such grievous faults that they only respond to punishment in babbles and gutterals—so gross that the Devil prefers the noise to be transmitted directly to earth—used, perhaps, as sound-effects in horror movies. Beyond these pits, the cliff falls off sharply; the bottom is not visible because of the constant cloud of steam and smoke. These furthest depths of Hell reach down into the region of fire and ice where the Arch-Devil-Satan (the original) sits without trappings on his frozen slab—intoning his unending list of grievances against the Lord-God-of-all-Creation.

Sitting
naked on a rock that's hot,
is hard.
Fulminating,
with your balls frozen in eternal ice,
is harder.

Situated far above this ravine of cruelty, is the zone of welcome—where, on jutting balconies, initiates sip flaming cocktails and look for their names listed in the various categories on the board of judgment. This tells them of their place in the pattern of descent which takes them to morally calibrated depths—where they are assigned to their specific variation of eternal punishment.

Building an edifice in the style of Demonic duplicity, is part of the Devil's ongoing challenge to the perpetrator of his original undoing. From top to bottom (Hell is fashionably topless but has an infinite base) the renovation must be adequate to the hellish—not the angelic—version of the complexities of eternity.

The hall I first came to (the music hall) is as yet too small to house the Devil's choir. (Both art and music have had a hard go in the history of Hell). The halls in Heaven, in contrast, are more than ample to house the popular cantatas, masses, and sacred chants. But, as my guide pointed out, this disparity is partly because earthly patrons of art and music thought it better to fund sacred music and portraits of saints than risk being themselves accused of impiety. Then too, Heaven enjoys a mild climate, while Hell taxes the resources of the boldest architects to build anything that will withstand the infernal weather. Nevertheless, The design of the Devil's music hall was conceived within an aggressive modern idiom that, on any critical measure, ranks far above its more symmetrical and somewhat conventional Heavenly counterpart.

In actual size, however, the Devil's hall—even after modernization—will be smaller than the one in Heaven—which can house, within its massive columns and beneath a free-floating dome, the full heavenly choir, the celestial philharmonic, along with solo voices of the lustiest saints, all singing and playing variations on the theme of salvation unto eternity—the longest gig in history.

The Devil, since his fall, has had time to develop his own taste in music: contrapuntal, dodecaphonic, aleatoric—nasty stuff—but (some sinners say) better for a shriek-along than those everlasting plain-song hymns that suffuse the domain of the heavenly host. Encouraged, perhaps, by his hall's stylistic daring, the Devil is trying to make it a showplace for advanced aesthetic tastes.

Listed for the next millenium are: Non-stop performances of chants that sound the song of unending pain. Hippety-hopping dances specially choreographed for eternally-tender burning feet. Multi-part fugues counterpointedly protesting overlooked innocence. Solo lieder performances of groveling pleas (sotto-voce) for forgiveness. Deep sighs (Sprach-Stimme) that bemoan the end of hope. Bellowing fulminations of hatred (brasses and bassos) against neo-righteous accusers. Floating wails (wafting over the fiery waters) of primordial despair. And the willow-songs (even in Hell) of indifference to time and pain.

The visual arts, in contrast, have long been co-opted by the Heavenly Host for the celebration of divine events and for portraits of generous supporters of the faith. There is a dearth of the visual arts in Hell—no doubt because of the absence (until lately) of exemplary physicality in the performance of sin, and of a traditional interest in the persuasiveness of music—the sounds of suffering and salvation without having to look too much at bodies.

Commissions that were funded by Heaven's surrogates (popes, kings, and the like) required that the visual arts mirror extant themes of faith and divinity. Successful artists, equipped with a full panoply of techniques, responded accordingly. But there were the times when their given subjects became historically uninteresting and unprofitable—due to a decline in belief— and shifts in interest: from saints to nudes to abstractions to happenings. The accompanying rhetoric also changed—from "art as depiction" to "art as expression" to "art as art," to "art as post-art."

There are different places for all these changes, in both Heaven and in Hell. But even among the prime players, they are not always recognized. The once most-popular theme in art, "the meaning of life," became so conventional (even in Hell) that the Devil ignored its potential—even when some older artists still showed interest in the embattled truths of purity and perversity—and their work was still cheap. How is it that the Devil did not realize that his support of the more controversial art-works would have gained him—if not cosmic parity—at least historical respect? But then, how can we explain his earlier choice of a snake's blandishments to instigate what would have happened anyway?

These lapses in metaphysical acumen and a poor sense of history (the Devil was a drop-out) may explain why Beelzebub—Satan's consigliere—now shows interest in my proposal to swap art for girls.

After our first meeting, Beelzebub encouraged me to explore the less precipitous parts of Hell—for that's where those lovelies are situated who have sinned in body but not in mind. (I trust, he said to me, that these are the ones you are most interested in).

So I clambered up and down these volcanic cliffs, defying smoke, embers, and the cacophonic chorus of new and old entreaties, until I came to a ledge where, through a perilous reaching, I could touch a pale person quivering within its flesh—pained but as yet unmarred by torment. I told her to stop writhing, to listen and believe again in the return of time, while I regaled her with the story (which did in fact concern her) of the bargain I had struck with the Devil. She didn't listen hard—it was all too abstract—until I sang my tribute to her amplitude, and I intoned how much more I love those fulsome mounds and untrimmed meadows than I do the chicken-wings of these-days barely-living, stick-thin women up above. I doubt that she saw me as her savior—but she agreed with my preferences—it was a start. A trip of any kind, she said, is better than the same old embers—and my skin keeps getting redder by the year! But look how it turns white when I press on it! There's still time. What the hell—maybe this time someone (what's your name?) will look after me.

Beelzebub and I agreed, after protracted negotiations, that I give Hell's Museum of Demonic Arts all my paintings in exchange for a reasonable number (remember, I am only mortal) of the most lissome from the Devil's collection of the not-too-grievously flawed. It seemed to me a win-win situaion in that it addresses excess inventory on both sides: I have too many paintings (I did churn them out when I was young) and he has too many sinners (the fall was quite a while ago)—and after some millennia of trying to win the struggle for more territory through protracted conflict with Jehovah and his lawyers, the Devil lost.

But surprisingly, after the fall, sin increased in popularity, and the miscreants kept coming. So the Devil has of late been rethinking his strategy: He would like to concentrate on new forms of sinning that are more intrinsically evil, e.g., genocide and greed, but less readily acknowledged. He could then increase the flow of real baddies, and decrease the number of those applicants for the upper, wind-blown levels—devoted as these are to mere sins of the flesh. We must understand that Hell, although infinite in conceptual scope, is still rental property, subject to the absentee landlord's cutting back the low-rent sections of the demonic realm—which, of late, unprofitably include the growing ghettos of the chemically flawed.

So you see, you sweetest of damned ladies, how the bargain I've struck works for all of us: Hell has walls that need paintings. Most artists, for the sake of that other immortality, have historically portrayed the Devil in an unflattering light, or ignored the poor de-winged soul entirely. My own efforts, of course, are not strong enough to reverse this trend. (Although, I must say: Had I made it my secret program when first in art school—and had I worked it up with well-executed images of perversion and torment—and had I stuck to it through threats of excommunication or bad reviews—I would now be well-known as an early Post-Modern Hell-Painter).

But such conversations—about my regrets and vacillations—were more than even the Devil, for all his love of guilt, and disbelief in repentance, could tolerate. He got bored—but we did agree to further talks.

My more recent paintings contain allusions that might well fit the under-symbolized, over-scarified walls of Hell. The paucity of art adornment on these walls speaks to a certain lack in the Devil's scheme of things—a less than fully formed imagination which, while it does not explain, is yet significant in showing why he was not able, despite early opportunity, to be number one. But whatever are the ancient mist-laden reasons for the Devil's lack of interest in art, his present advisors want him to deal with these issues as they are now: God has had art on His side for too long.

To counter this, Beelzebub, a left-leaning member of Hell's own trinity and an American-schooled MBA, has returned to Hell from Harvard as general administrator for the projection of infernality. Because it is the repository of Hell's collection, the Museum of Abominable Arts naturally falls under his provenance. Understanding the importance of style and presentation, B decided on a strategy that would enliven things by combining symbols with actuality—embellishing the torments of the damned with representations of their sufferings— a display projected through both old and new media. Tormented souls, as B knew well, would complain about being made to act-out their suffering as well as suffer. But their complaints would really be about the inequity between sin and punishment—not about the embarrasment of its representations. Some sinners might actually enjoy the exposure. Imaging the circumstances of their sufferings—showing these images to the still undecided living—would do much, B thought, to adjust the balance between fears of punishment and the joys of Hell. Picturing might just resurrect the waning interest in Hell's ancient task of inflicting eternal pain upon the contingent wicked.

Beelzebub first saw my paintings when I was still too young to spot an infernal ingression. He seemed just a rather fey, well-dressed gentleman who came early to my first opening, briefly looked around and left. But he evidently remained interested—there was, as he said later, the prescient waft of disobedience in my images. So when the matter of the Infernal Museum came up, he thought that my paintings might be suitable (and still cheap enough) for a trial approach to the enhancement of these redone walls of Hell. As recompense for turning over my life's-work to the Devil, he agreed to offer me free choice from among the "damned-pretty-women"—a sub-category of downwardly directed souls. These women would, of course, have to agree (free will—although not free action—continues to exist in Hell) to trade eternal torment for Lucian's contingent ministrations. The price of this swap would be the relinquishing of immortality by those who choose to be brought out of Hell and into my clutches.

This is the conundrum in the offer that the Devil (never one to be kind for its own sake) presented to the women: "Your agreement to return to life entails relinquishing an eternity of the torments of hell in favor of the transient period of ordinary life—which includes—as stipulated—some measure of assuaging Lucian-lust." The Devil made them the offer during their early time of wallowing in fiery brimstone. He put on his cloven hoofs, trotted down the path of cinders, then spoke to the gathering in one of his more social voices—the mellow baritone: "Stop screaming for a moment—and listen. All the good or bad that will happen if you go with Lucian, ends when you get old and die. Nothing follows after that—no Heaven—not even a return to Hell."

This statement of no-return is a theological bomb. It indicates that the doctrine of immortality after death need no longer hold in Hell—also, it disallows any atonement when back on earth that would permit a repeat sinner to instead go to Heaven. Further—it agrees that the durational infinity of the soul after death can be traded-in for a few additional years of life without committing to the Faustian bargain of forty years of youth—then eternity in Hell. That fearful descent is instead replaced by relinquishing any after-life at all. In effect: Living and dying would be all there is.

Did B, with all his duplicities, really mean it? Consider the scenario he presents: If a girl (a pact for boys awaits a different Devil) comes back to life from her fallen place in Hell, she again becomes mortal. But the definition of this mortality, in contrast to her earlier one, is that when the new one ends there is no after-life that follows. The implication, then, is that there is an alternative to both the joys of Heaven and the pains of Hell—that alternative is a longer life after which there is nothing. (Did the Devil check this out with God)?

The conservative majority in Hell, unwilling to support a constitutional revision that would repeal the fundamental principle of an afterlife, lobbied against it. They sent flyers to the girls in question asking for allegience to their community, and offering them a larger say in their slated torments. Of course, these right-wing dissidents might themselves be seeking revenge, after eons of suffering, on the twin perpetrators of their misfortune —both God and the Devil—by denying them theological progress and forcing adherence to a principle of original intent.

The real issue may indeed be political: The Devil, perhaps for reasons of overpopulation, might want to trade the finality of death for repeal of the necessity of an after-life. But the conservative majority in Hell, when faced with a choice between eternality or contingent limits, was unwilling to accept a constitutional revision of that magnitude. It seems that the older

Diabolics do not want to relinquish the fundamental principle of "forever"—even though its end would end their own pain. These old ones, after all, first became sinners because of the blandishments of the original Satan. They lost the war with God but gained their autonomy (such that it is) in Hell—which they are now unwilling to relinquish.

Even if we grant that the cosmos is of divine creation, it need not follow that the world and its inhabitants are completely a divine responsibility. Managing human affairs, assessing praise and blame, and yet allowing the world to change through passing time and the exercise of free will, may be beyond the administrative powers of even a divinity. At different times, God has been absent, hidden, inscrutable, angry, vengeful, compassionate, loving—and often contradictory. The Devil, in like manner, has been narcissistic, demanding, fallen, fearsome, schismatic, wily, theatrical, yet increasingly ignored.

In passing, I must admit that an additional stipulation in this agreement is Lucian's relinquishing his own immortality when it comes his time—however things work out with the women. But this item was buried in the fine print of the contract, and in the turmoil of choosing, I was so busy looking at the girls that I didn't read what I had signed. I don't know how that's all going to work out—I'm still alive. If I die with no prospect of an afterlife—then, of course, I won't know it—I'll just be dead. If I wake up to acrid smoke or the smell of incense—whatever—I can sue for breach of contract. But in either case, it might be that the Devil, as usual, didn't mean what he said—or that God didn't overrule him.

The large black truck came for my paintings in the deepest night, when neither thief nor critic was awake; and I have to say that the art-movers of the nether-realms are very good at their job—not a scratch or stain marred what they were charged to deliver to the dampest, most acrid and corrosively tainted place in all creation. But why, I asked, after seeing my paintings off to be mounted on the sooty walls of Hell, had I, out of all the world's most wanting artists, been so chosen?

Well, being chosen by the Devil is the sign of a specialized approval. Remember: For sophisticates, the nature of Hell is not one of pure evil; it contains all the inversions of above-ground beliefs and tastes, and is thus perfectly compatible with advanced aesthetic sentiment. As you, Lucian, have accepted this trade of girls for art, it will give you a voice in the debate as to whether Hell-advocates should insist on reviving an agreement listed in the original document of the Fall. This issue is contained in a clause, ignored for eons, that does not restrict the distribution of the "Good" to Heaven—but allows some of it to seep into Hell. For the dialectically

minded Diabolics, it has long been a strategy to consider that distribution —however lopsided—to be preferable to the burden of taking on an equal share of Good, which would be threatening to Hell's stability.
But a little bit of Good is better than having no share at all—it provides movement. Too much Good, however, would change Hell's basic mission—to be the distaff side of divine judgment. Additionally, it would let in all sorts of folks whose practices the resident Hellions are not equipped to tolerate.

Take, for example, the torments of the damned. Divine canons contend that such torments are deserved punishments, not merely for being wrongly born (although there is that too) but for self-indulgence or deliberate perversity in the living of one's life. Pain after death, in this view, is a post-material symbol that warns the susceptible and innocent of the ways virtue can slip-slide into vice—and then you're stuck in Hell.

But now that Lucian has found good company among the diabolic dialecticians, he can side with those who, in principal, challenge dogma. I will transform my paintings, he said, through convincing polemics, and exotic performances never before seen in Hell. I will remove aesthetics from its status as mere decoration and transform its issue into tokens of belief (although of what kind I'm not yet sure). But, in general, I will use the forms of art to point to forms of life (straight as well as crooked) that will show the square-heads in both realms how vice is an indispensable component of virtue. I will insist that Hell, to be the repository of evil, must also contain an aspect of the Good.

But there are problems: These days, the punishment of evil is no longer a major preoccupation for God. He has probably jobbed them out—perhaps because of his growing preoccupation with values in other sectors of the universe—those which do not contain the concepts of good and evil.

Then too, there is the political issue of the growing threat of other evangelisms closer to home. God may be puzzled now—given recent changes in the beliefs of His earthly domain—about what God-sanctioned torment is supposed to do: That yowling for all eternity—once said to be a deterrent to committing the standard mortal sins—does not work. Face it—Hell is ineffectual. And no one (let us hope) still views the pains of Hell as appropriate enjoyment for the voyeuristic just!

In respect to torture, we on earth are like the Pagan gods: Torture is theatre, and it mirrors actual transactions between pain and pleasure that continue to be conditions of mortal living. These conditions, in innocent nature, are incompatibles—few organisms experience both without striving for the release from pain, even more so than wanting pleasure—but there is a shifting ratio here between species. Humans enjoy forms of inventiveness that animals lack, and will sometimes bring the two together into what

Nietzsche calls a "witches' brew"—where the ambiguities between pain and pleasure can be experienced within fluctuating grades of sensation (and forms of agreement). Each culture—indeed, each generation—has its own take on how far the extensions of the two may be stretched before the ambiguity disappears. For the Inquisition, this ambiguity was pursued into agonizing certainty by appealing to fixed imperatives of guilt and innocence. In the more recent SM frolics, the levels of unacceptable certainty continue to be tested by consent, and the meliorating presence of make-believe.

Beelzebub, when he was overseeing the transfer of my works from Saint Louis to Hell, remarked on their ambiguity as being the main reason why he was willing to place them on Hell's lonely walls. My paintings contain, so he said, an accommodation of un-likes, disjoints, and other anomalies, that, in addition to being aesthetically questionable, would be regarded in certain quarters as verging on the absurd. B, being a modern sort of Devil, was not so much interested in the aesthetics as in showing that, e.g., in Hell, sinners much prefer the sound of failed fugues that include animal voices, fire-sirens, errant drums, and off-key contraltos, to the saintly alternatives of eternally in-tune cantatas. We here have always produced plenty of noise, said B—you, on earth, have only recently begun to call it music—we have you there. But we're weak on the visual arts. The competition has had altars, cathedral ceilings, palace walls of Carrara marble, to offer as sites to the best talents. We only have these damp, sooty, uneven walls—made up of outworn belief, magma, and dried tears.

When you mortals recently ended art (it was not our fault this time) our committee decided that Hell would be an ideal place to exhibit the incommensurables—drips and drabs, dumb-shows, bombasticules and canny tricks—that you are serving up as post-art art. We once thought, only a hundred years ago, that the "Death of God" had great promise—but the idea faltered. Better luck this time with art. So think of us fiends as cultural commissars who have an admittedly political agenda: To use the marvelous disarray and mis-directed ambition of your aesthetic enterprise as a standard for our view of the future of creation.

B was more ruddy-faced than usual and somewhat out of breath after his declamation. He sat for a while before turning to me: My dear boy, he said, you are certainly not the boldest of the new practitioners; in fact, you want to paint discord within the circumspection of old-master art. My, I do wish you were more talented—someone slipped up when they were mixing your surrogate. Pity. Nevertheless, you are perfect for our transition: Devilish longings constrained by old inhibitions—as perverse as you can make it within an organized pictorial space—no stepping outside the canvas—no throwing things at the audience.

But you must understand: We in Hell don't go in much for openings and publicity—too many saints show up and eat the food. Besides, we've got more time than do earthly galleries to wait for recognition and sales. We may not even print an announcement of your show—don't worry, the news will get out bye and bye. But, dear boy—I am being uncharacteristically honest—you are welcome to come down here and enjoy the mounting of your paintings, have a drink, and afterwards you can stay with us as long as you wish.

I ran from those words like from fire! Cocktails in Hell can wait. The Devil took my art; I want his girls. Oh, I think he'll keep that promise. He doesn't need those demanding souls anymore than I need my lonely paintings. The women I chose are experts in the art of relationships—which, despite my years of study, I know little about. But because they gave up the pain of Hellish immortality to join me in the remaining time of our transient life, I would expect they'd make the most of it. What can happen? They can rob me blind, make fun of my pecker, mess up the house, pee on my paintings. So what! I have been making arty-art for too long. The girls, in their more tranquil moments will, I'm sure, let me trace the elongations, taste the distensions, smell the interstices that first put them on the road to Hell. Maybe I can even translate those qualities into good new art! Why not free one hand to draw them while I wallow in their sooty sweetness with the other?

Women don't age in Hell; they remain voluptuous, although the beauty of their earthly prime—whose defeat can be seen in the looking-glass of timelessness—becomes, with their damnation, a possession of the Devil. What he does with it only God can know. Is the Devil the ultimate voyeur—looking forever at all that he did not make—but now is part of?

Well, whatever the reasons—and however gross their torments (particularly as viewed by those who don't live there)—most of the ones I picked chose to remain in Hell and to continue singing their parts in the chorus of the damned. A few of the girls did agree to come with me—so few I was surprised. I had expected, given the stories about how bad Hell is, that there would be many more. I looked in the mirror and asked: Is unending torment preferable to a few years of me? I had told them I would do my best: Exercise, eat veggies, trim my toenails, and cut down on drinking so as to be with them as long as possible. Maybe that was the problem.

Those few who did come had to choose between an eternity in Hell—and me (priapus-in- finitude). And they chose me! Gloriosky! But, then, their choice does make some sense. Why not fritter away the regained time of mortality in the feverish (but limited albeit gracious) embraces of an old mid-western artist? So cool! So fun!

One advantage to my agreement with the Devil—and this can be a lesson for young itinerant folk who want to be artists—is that inspiration through concupiscence cuts across all of history. My desiderata came from entries in the most-comprehensive category of desirable women. I roamed the reaches of Hell, and like a kid in a candy store, I pointed and pointed and, eventually, the following decided to come:

A Neanderthal teen-ager with the softest fur, prehensile toes, and a fetish for eating ants, whose breasts would fade from indigo to pale violet as they verge toward the nipples; I courted her with raw filets of Sturgeon which I carry around for such occasions.

Behind some molten rocks, there sat a slender slave from Egypt, with whip marks and calloused feet; but with a wonderful rhythm when dancing or kneeling as she once did for the pharaohs. I told her I preferred her dancing to her kneeling—but I would indulge her preferences if she danced with me and taught me how kneeling was properly done.

Standing near a pillar of fire, I found a Greek Aphrodite of ideal proportions, whose body showed the diagonals—the "contraposto" strain—that came from posing the same way all day for a celibate classical sculptor. My own posing regimen, as I told her, is for twenty minute periods in varying attitudes, followed by a luke-warm bubble-bath and some philosophic banter.

At the middle level, I came across a Renaissance lady, once married early to an aging count—whom she later killed and was killed in turn. She once had sat for a famous painter, but was miffed that she couldn't take her clothes off for the sitting—it being a full-portrait, after all—but that painter was preocuppied with drapery and the purity of form. I assured the lady that I had other interests; I would kiss her even as I painted her—and I wasn't concerned that the drawing would be compromised. I could fix it later.

For the modern years, I found a model from the Paris of Lautrec who preferred seductive-hidden poses where she could exhibit her hand-made undergarments—instead of just standing-around stark-naked in cold garrets. She was accustomed to good sex, but often had to do with artists who did not wash and whose prospects for fame were only fair. I showed her my steam-bath schedule and assured her of my meticulous attention to fingernails, underarms, and feet—and I promised her weekly excursions to the finest mid-priced restaurants.

Closer to the present, I chose a flower-child from the early days of the New York tenth-street scene who posed in art schools where students looked but didn't draw, and also for noted painters who drew but barely looked. It didn't matter to her either way—a buck's a buck. She had tattoos of flowers circling each ankle, with a serpent climbing up one shoulder; and she had enough good pot to take her through most anything. My only request when I chose her was that she look, when not too high, at what I paint—and tell me that I'm getting to be as good as maybe deKooning.

My most contemporary addition was a young wife of an old tycoon who held her to her semi-weekly obligation but let her spend as much money as she liked on dinner and servants—as long as she looked her best at corporate parties. She shot him five times. Her skin was tan and somewhat leathery—more from Acapulco than from Hell. Her muscles were well defined, particularly around the calves and deltoids—her breasts were expertly augmented—her mouth was somewhat large because of face-lifts—and she had not yet experienced, what she called a "real come." How did she know? I wondered—but didn't ask. But I did insist that she stay out of the sun, and I promised to massage her hide with the finest emollients, and assured her that, with diligence, coming would surely happen—one way or another.

All these—without exception—had been glad to go to Hell. To get there, they stabbed, poisoned, shot, or disemboweled, their earthly tormentors—fathers, masters, husbands, lovers—and each did so for reason of the gross inattention those shits paid to her reality. The Devil, knowing this—and seeing the opening that male rectitude gives him—assured the condemned that when they reached Hell, he would care for them—although the manifestations of caring would be unusual. When they were put down, delivered into his domain, sitting around the cocktail lounge of entrance into Hell, the Devil offered them warm drinks, and then exhibited —for their choosing—a panoply of fire and feathers, whips, racks and vibrators, hot-hail, boiling oil, and dry-ice—that are among the traditional fixtures provided by Hell for a sinner's future.

This is where I come in: The disembodied-damned eventually found torment boring—they learned that it is but a theatrical addendum to the power plays between low and high belief. Some of these lost souls began to speak in tongues (not permitted in Heaven or Hell)—but over the millenia their sounds became the pervasive whispers just audible above the other sounds of Hell's dark night. Some few did more than whisper; they said (out-loud) that they will revolt rather than go through the unending theatrics of subservience. Too demeaning—even for Hell.

Revolt in Hell? Who would have thought it! Now I know why the Devil wants them out of there. It's not mere over-crowding: These women are trouble-makers, unconvinced by the irrationality of eternity, and unmoved by Hell's incessant game of "proportional deservation."

So the stronger activists began to challenge the conservative factions then ruling in Hell. After many confrontations, however, the parties still could not agree on one crucial point: That those who are willing to give up eternal life in exchange for an earthly period of contingent life, may do so—but only if they give up the right of return.

The Devil, although interested in change, could not budge the conservatives, so he joined with the women, and signed an administrative edict. Thereby, the bonds of Hell were broken and an afterlife was made optional. This decision, while it was legislative anathema for the infinite-eternal crowd, was not all one-sided. It promised its participants only that they would regain a natural course of life to death—and nothing more. Lucian's own mortality became the standard for this agreement. It would give him, as it gave Faust, renewed life—but after (hopefully) forty more years of cavorting—just plain death.

The girls from Hell, already ended in their times, can now
return to earth to watch the winter ice
melt into the rivulets of spring.
They then could swim again in warming waters,
and join with sputters of new growth until that time
when August is again made brown by cold October.

In the chilling afterward, they will find
new reasons for grieving their new finitude.
They must endure November's early frost until
that month's memories of sweet fall
give way to the sleet of February's winter when
the freezing of once-hot flesh will renew
their search for what is fair and just.

Then they can pray
(but now—to whom?)
that we are all still here when spring
expands into the embrace of summer.

Although the time of snow and sleet moves slowly,
it quickens with the sound of water
dripping from beneath the breaking ice.
This marks the true new time for singing —
for urging on the fragile buds of March and April
until they show the coming summer
what again it can and has to do.

My paintings fit well on the Devil's walls—although their formal erratics and aberrant content do not sit easily within the hollows and damps of Hell-style architecture—as when, e.g., I paint a deep space, and a bump in the wall moves out to counter it.

Despite such troubles, the conjunction of crude materials, febrile content—and the constant whisper of destruction—feeds the satanic imagination. B was right! Whose works would be better than mine in pointing the way towards the later arts of desecration, perversion, and sacrilege that the Devil sees as inspiring the Ur-Renaissance to come—signalling the redemption of Hell through art— and art through Hell!

Of course, I was gratified—even though I didn't think the hubbub would last too long— I had seen that kind of stuff before. I was more interested in our agreement— art in exchange for girls. This, I recognized, is the standard description of artists' longings in the Freudian fifties—but no one I knew thought of enlisting Hell to make it happen.

In contrast to my new way, there are the the older traditions of seeking success through muse-artist pairings. I was weaned upon those sad images. Here are a few pairing I remembers: Between the sallow loft-dweller and the unwashed acolyte who offers herself as sustenance for his eventual fame. Between the young earnest with box of slides in hand and the sleek but underpaid receptionist at Gotham Gallery who (maybe) takes a chance on him. Between the art professor and the more promising of his soft and vacant students—both of whom actually prefer low fashion to high art. Between the prominent artist and the rich devotee of his efforts who, during openings, wafts the perfume of success over his accomplishments. Between the old renowned-master and the wrinkled heiress-dealer who assures him that his time (and hers) is not yet over, and that all her friends will come to buy.

So—I asked myself: Why am I still doing this—carrying stacks of canvases—some as yet unwrapped—to places where they were not made—and from where I must move them again? All this is good practice for success, said the wise old daubers: Irrational conviction is good for the aesthetic imagination. What floats the worm-eaten vessel, is not simply a hope that the worms are getting full, but the firm belief that they will, in time, become part of the wood. Using your adversaries to help you float is the lesson that honest art must learn in corrupt times.

I listened and learned: This is a talisman of history, not one invented by the loft-dwellers, nor a slogan circulated by the mid-town bunch; it may indeed be a transcendental truth. If it is such, then one must wait—as long as need be—for die Reine, die Feine. die Eine —I want all three—to come and acknowledge me.

These truths came second-hand from the originary heroes of my time. But such truths, like the guarantees on used cars, are not immune to disenchantment. So after a few bruises from contemporaries, I retreated to the stories of an earlier time, when making art was tied to a romance in which fucking nubiles was considered a mere addendum to the high calling of art—and by extension, to the betterment of the social order. This belief, of course, was based on foreign—mostly European—story-telling. The stories I first responded to were enticing enough for me to consider them as true. When I realized that making art is what I do, the immediate accessories I needed were a place of my own, and money enough to occasionally swing for a pizza for two. In the beginning, I just wanted company, but as I walked the artist's walk, I met the bruised and forlorn women—victims of various indignities perpetrated, as they said to me, by old and ugly nasty smelly stingy famous artists.

The only comforts I could offer—being young, presentable, but not any of the above—were conceits about the historically sturdy alliance between art and love; and its gentle (I am a gentle lover) filtration down to enduring pleasures.

This was good background for my incursion into the commercial realm of Hell. The principals of my pact with the Devil were not the pink ingenues of artistic fame, but scarred veterans of ancient and abominable practices. They spanned millennia in their origins and so offered interesting, sometimes astounding, always unsettling, contrasts in sexual preference and body-style.

Beelzebub said to them in his farewell address: "You are here because you have engaged in mortal sin and monstrous atrocities—often at the same time. And now, because of our new liberal climate, you have been given the opportunity to choose between your secure (if painful) future here, and the uncertainties (however pleasurable) of a finite mortal life. Then he went on to extol the benefits of immortality in Hell as contrasted to life on earth. But this was only to placate the comservative demon faction. Here, B said, you have security forever; you cannot fail and you cannot be dismissed (we see to that). In your earlier life on earth, you careened through other gates of pain and pleasure, thinking that life will last forever. But then, because you overdid it, you found yourselves in Hell.

What I now offer you now is a new product: A second time around on earth. But there is a condition: No matter what you do, your second life will not end as the first one did—in the eternally fulminating but secure bosom of Hell. It will end nowhere. And when there is not a "where" that the no-where is, then you will not be anywhere.

The women's eyes rolled a bit at this, but it led them to wonder why they had not questioned the Devil's judgment about their earlier transgressions—the judgment that led to their damnation. They also wondered why they should believe him now. Well, the Devil always lies—that's what devils do. But he did have a point: Will those who return to earth, especially the most gullible and still-beautiful, look again for pleasure in the kinky ways that damned them when they were first alive?

Lucian—given his central role—was the last to speak: "I don't lie, he cried—I am, at base, a kind and gentle fellow—well yes, I admit, perhaps a bit of a voyeur. But, as you know, I have been instrumental in your return—so when we meet again on earth, I want you to tell me everything about yourself. If you by chance, in your packet of personal belongings, have saved any sketches, paintings, photographs, or video-tapes, that capture you at your finest, bring them along. I am always looking for the old stuff—however faded cracked or wrinkled, however blue what once was pink. This would be additional inspiration for my paintings. The two together, your images and mine (as well as your actual selves, of course) each reaching toward the other through the overlays of underpainting—scumble glaze swerve and splash—would be perfect for delineating my version of the Devil's growing taste in art."

It was once possible (look at Van-Eyck) to bring the worlds of eternal truth and momentary pleasure together within one work. When the expanding theme could no longer fit within a single space—artists would resort to windows. I love windows—to look out of and see another world. But as much as I have tried to distribute unlike contents into internal frames, I could never do it well enough to conjure up a metaphysical sense of the many as one. The "many" is not a problem, but I have (as yet) no sufficient concept of the "one." Actually, this is more a theoretical than artistic issue. To bring the metaphysical, temporal and spatial together is a most vexing challenge.

Yet I can't believe that all this effort—my attempts to resurrect the sophistications of the past for present purposes—has been in vain. Maybe that's why you are here, my lovelies, and why Beelzebub, severe critic that he is, has been so supportive of my vanities. Although vanity is only a venial sin—it is a sin. We agree on that. My ambitions, however, extend further—into the realm of history.

The day came, and the girls arrived in a bus that could have been used for transporting students in a small suburban high-school. It was yellow dented and noisy—maybe B. only rented it for the day. The occupants came dressed in the attire that had adorned their greatest escapades, and they pushed and jostled, laying about with their perfumed stoles and embroidered purses, until they could clamber out and stand again upon a city sidewalk. After breathing the earthly air for a bit, most of them showed a clear disappointment with the amenities their benefactor had provided for their stay.

I had always thought that an artist's loft is irresistible to maidens from the outer boroughs when they come downtown in search of art-world sophistication.

But my charges, before their fall, had been feted and fucked amidst the most luxuriant appointments, their whims anticipated by cadres of experts in the arts of satisfaction.

So why are we here, they asked, in a two-story commercial building situated in a Saint Louis slum; and all he offers is some cheap wine, cheddar cheese and crackers—and then he wants us to look at his latest paintings! Lucian slowly realized, even while tending to the welcoming barbeque of pork-tips and hot peppers (thinking this would effect a bridge to their earlier life) that these women (they all looked older than when highlighted by the flickering flames of Hell) would not honor their part of the agreement he had made with the Devil.

For some nights he tried to be, if not the designated lover, then just a good-friend to the women. Given the enormity of the agreement they had made, a little role-playing seemed perfectly appropriate. But as much as he tried—with dinners, intimate conversations, excursions in the park, tickets for matinee performances of the local symphony—his ménage was rapidly dwindling. Every morning there were fewer at the table, and those still there were sullen, silent, and distant. Shit!

Lily-of-the-Valley will not tarry
even though you take her to the place where lilies grow.
She meets with Hairy-Sally in the alley
just to dally
when, on Monday, all the diners close.

Lucian did not want (he finally told himself) any more of them in his bed. So he made an appointment with the Devil—determined to lodge a complaint about the misrepresentations in their agreement. Beelzebub greeted him with the air of one who has more important things to do, but said he was willing to meet because these days, it is understood that all agreements between the parties of Earth and Hell have to be scrupulously fair. Business, he said, had previously been outsourced to heathens (but they are always corrupt)—so in the current climate, only transparent agreements between our two realms can survive.

Then he turned to the substance of my complaint: The ladies are leaving, you say; fewer and fewer want to share your bed, but they are spending all your money, and trying to convince you to buy property in Las Vegas. Well, they are all sinners, you know. When they left Hell, they became free, and freedom means they can do as they wish. Before the moment when you and I agreed to swap them for your paintings, they belonged to us. Now that we have your paintings, the women belong—not to you—but to the certainty that they will someday die again. It's a short time, really. If you still want to fulfill your dreams of cinematic sex with the most lissome in the Devil's inventory, you had better, now that they're still with you, give them what they want—otherwise, they'll disappear.

He was right; they left—not as a group, but one by one in accelerating numbers for places that I only dimly know about. The last few that left, the more gentle creatures, showed some sadness. After all, I started it all—but would not get what I so much wanted. I convinced them, however—being deep in my cups at our farewell party—that it was a good trade: Art for Life. Their obligation is now the same as mine, I said: It is to live—and anything further is a matter of chance or faith—certainly not of reason. But your stay has given us all—especially me—a new perspective (not yet fully drawn) on life. Actually, I was relieved to see the last ones go. Consider my situation: My paintings now have a home (of sorts) in Hell; and I no longer want to fuck all the girls in the world. But my beauties did not much care about my change of heart—they just went their separate ways: The soft-furred Neanderthal with her velvet breasts disappeared into the Athabasca wilderness; the Ethiopian used her welts as a trademark for a middle-eastern restaurant in Atlanta; the Renaissance Princess had a face-lift and went on an extended trip to Monaco; the Artists' Model found boy and girl-friends and a place to stay in the East Village. The Mogul's Wife still calls from time to time.

I am back to where it started. The story I have told occupies a place of memory. But now my fantasy is ended, and its cinematics have slowed into occasional stills that I look at less and less as my hormones subside.

But some parts remain: The pact with the Devil—my paintings for his sinners—has produced the theological consequence that at least some of us—as in this particular story—will have no after-life existence. That notion may be of greater force than either love or art—or it may just be wrong. Then where am I?

I often wonder about my own status in the shifting play of immortality vs. plain death. When I last spoke to Beelzebub, I did notice that he was sometimes silent, and then he would give me one of these hooded looks —which, I am sure, he has had millenia to perfect. Nevertheless, I would have liked him to describe the future I might have in Hell if I accepted his earlier invitation to relocate: He had once suggested that I could be appointed curator of art and décor, image chronicler of the newly damned before they get too charred. Further, I could give classes on graphic perversity for the recent arrivals and, if they show promise, enlist them in curatorial and other work—performing in films perhaps—for the extant collection (Porn in Hell) that I would oversee.

The Devil knew what I was thinking—this is the principal strength of deviltry—but Beelzebub said nothing. Perhaps he thought, as with his assessment of my debacle with the girls, that I would be more a hindrance than a help in Hell. So it may really be that I will just die.

But yet: Ich hab ein Traum so wunderbar, in Herz und Sinnen immer da.

Perhaps, just maybe, the Lord above would be interested in my more recent work. I have to call. These new paintings are quite different from the Devil-paintings—(consistency, as you know, is not one of my virtues). I am now obsessed with Titian, who didn't have to look for girls in Hell—he found the ones he wanted right there in Venice. (Why didn't I think of that when I lived in Brooklyn?) Some of my recent paintings are labelled—"After Titian." They are neither studies nor copies—I call them "admirations." But all are encounters between his genius and my desire to be better than I am. Lord, you, in fact, might like them; their ineptitude is so confessional. There are artists around (mostly dead) who did more than I with the movement of the figures and the blowing trees. If brought back, they could correct my static drapery, and make the meadows more lush and the skies more various. In that company, I am modest.

But Heaven—no less than the world it takes care of—(I don't have to tell You)—is changing. The ancient strains between the beatific and the beautiful, and the modern collusion between the ugly and the empty, might need rethinking—even in Heaven.

Theology, as with philosophy, can make change plausible—even while its language speaks of eternity and constancy. Art, in its best construal, shows change before it is evident enough to otherwise be noted. Perhaps I can help with that.

So Lord, why don't You send a minor angel (say, a recent PhD in art-history who got hit by a car on Canal Street) to come down, take a look, and talk awhile. Call me. I'm home most days.

BEFORE YOU DIE

It is critical to know what is the case before you die.
Whether you are to be renownedly remembered —
or will be leaving you behind with little trace.

Dying in one's traces is not a disgrace.
Although you may be buried in your harness,
you need not worry that your story—
unlike gossip about the famous dead—
will be told, tut-tuttingly, in the bedrooms
just behind the bar at Harry's place.

I'm so pretty; you're so pretty.
We're both much more pretty than nice.
But pretty can often be shitty—
so it behooves you to take my advice:
Stop searching my cod-piece for lice.

Yet, you will still worry that
the universe may not be at all the way
it should be—especially when I didn't do
what they said I did—the dastardly deed
inflicted upon the entwined bodies
    of good Tom Clancy and the widow Jones.

POST-LUDE

Grudging acknowledgment of the inevitable, with due celebration of the end of effort, is the usual response to dying. To smooth the passage, there are the friendly visits: (My, how good you look!) But affirming real dying can be otherwise: It can be the sharp and fat-smeared knife given to old sled-dogs to lick (an ancient custom) so that their licking, and the blood that trickles down in the unfeeling Arctic cold, will provide a tasty way to slip into the one-time, one-way dark.

It is comforting to think that dying is not fungible—that it parochially goes one way—nothing more need be done. In contrast, living, as here considered, is recurrable whenever someone in another place fishes deep and reels you up from your solitude before you reach the archives of the dead—that is, if you have done enough to be counted with the other deep fish that are still good eating.

But if you have already died, have no illusions—you will not be brought to the surface, at a later time and place, to live some more. Your role (as an end) is only subject to a consideration of what you previously had done. Your friends, those still alive, contribute to this consideration—dead others too—but bear in mind that they all have (had) their end-ambitions. Remember also—if you have too many friends—that your ending will be recounted more than once.

Is ending, then, with all its post-life calumnies and only occasional after-life faint-praise, preferable to simply dying? I think so, yes. But why? Because I don't like anything "simple." Also: I believe that the negative judgments of who you are as an end—laid out by judges however prescient or corrupt—are preferable to the anomy of having just one death, without note of the mentions you deserve. Ending then, especially for those who dislike silence in their absence, is better than dying.

Death has no place—it does show up in places, but then it vanishes into the context of not being anywhere that is a some-where. The old trilogy of Heaven, Hell, and Purgatory—after all this time- no longer does the trick of placing anything you might be interested in—after dying—into a "where." I suggest to you: Avoid mere death—it's no-where.

Ending, on the other hand, is a stronger move. It has a different (better) reason for attracting such as you and me—a reason that demands recollection as a way of continuing to get attention. When you do not—as the poet advised—go quiet into that dark night, your roars (complaints, demands, etc.) will be less a dying than a program for the celebration of your end-game.

Lucian, what a scold you have become!
Yes, I agree—a perk of aging.
But it's not the same for you—you younger folk out there.
I say to you—please listen: Mortality vies with consciousness
as a way to discern the value (formerly—the meaning) of life.
That we must die is a reason for our periodic need
while living
to erect the best construction of our end.

Otherwise, we give up to silence all we've done and want to do
(and by god what the Gods won't do) as our penance for
all those frippety times we've in passing wasted.
Scolds like me now say to lay-a-bouts like you
that having fun and playing games
will surely lead to merely dying.
(And what's the point of that?)

Listen and look, the street-person says: It's what I have—the only thing—but it's more, at my end, than is your simple dying. For I am none other than old Joe Gould—and in this bag (somewhere in there) is my "Oral History of the World." It is, as you know, not finished. How could it be—what with the world still going on?

Also—no one is reading it—perhaps that's because they can't find it, for it has not yet settled into its ending place. Oh yes, there is, yes, one such place—a secret one, which, although obscure, is the place where Seagull-Joe has died but will not end.

A chance to do the shuffle that substitutes an ending for a dying, is worth paying attention to—especially for you pure-potentials who, after all your actualities—are barely alive as yet.

Shuffling is not easy—you must practice. Dying, to the discomfiture of liv-r-upp-rs, occurs in just one place —no practice needed. Ending occurs in many places—wherever the curious and ambitious come to mingle. Each such place expects to prosper in future summers (to the chagrin of other chic-resorts) because of its rich and fertile soil that attracts the most historically prescient of those still living. When you find it—stop your shuffling and bring your ending with you; mix it up with the lovely ladies designed to go to Hell. You can tell them by the texture of their skin, their level stare, and their unwillingness to bargain.

Even with a good place to end, you anyway will die. The aftermath of dying—although you may sprout a bit for art's sake—does not, in-itself, have a place. With Socialism dead, most dying-places cater to the for-themselves. Ending places, however, still prefer the clientele of in-and-for-themselves. But the absence of a place in which to not-be might be preferable, after all, to opting for the fuss—as described in the "Complete Guide To Eternal Things"—that lists the best places for once-alives to go in style towards their hard-won end. Maybe just dying, is better—don't you think? Or can't you answer now?

ENDING

Wheels within wheels,
way up in the middle of the air.
There are many ways to reach them,
but one thing is quite clear.
Even if you climb Rapunzel's hair,
You'll fall to earth in Union Square.

They sing that song down there
when the bottles empty out by noon,
and the twilight light shines
upon a repetitional despair.

But don't stop watching.
It's a direction worth pursuing.
Ride the beam of darkness to where
it's first distilled, then packaged
and distributed—for those who stop
to cheer and then to buy—
before they hurry past
and simply die.

Union Square is not a place.
It is anywhere that solitaries gather
to watch each other disappear.
A collective of self-maligning souls,
stretched from there to
God-knows where.

One way the world will end is when
togetherness is understood to be a myth.
Rather—when recognized as a ploy
by those who stand upon
a stack of others felled in strict order,

while they themselves reach for forbidden
fruits expressly left in looser places.

Watch out—all you cavorting in the square!
The spokes of the wheel from which
strange fruit hangs are sharp.
When they whirl they'll take your head.
An offering, as it's said, to the unsung dead.

Remember when you had a head?
That's the only part you thought you need
to solve the mystery of life with,
and find the deeper secrets of success.

Lucian, I must disagree with your location
as well as your antique locution.
The place to ponder conundra is between
the Pineal Gland and the Gonad Sack—
adjacent to the area where
the Heart has quarrels with the Spleen.

At times we drift into the Mind—
(the Soul is also lurking there).
But certainly, I go right past the brain—
when it claims exclusive residence
In the head.

RETURNING

I came before the time for planting lilies.
Take off that silly coat, she said—
you've always wanted recognition,
but not this way, not yet.

I said:
The black shape in the blue sky needs enlarging—
to face the brown bush with a splash of
darker colors that would separate the green and red—
lacking which, the painting will be not so good.

She said:
You have attention left—so pay it.
Paint the fucking thing more black.
After which you can again
crawl up and rest
in the space
that parts my breasts—
just above
the place between my legs.

www.ingramcontent.com/pod-product-compliance
Lightning Source LLC
LaVergne TN
LVHW050615100826
845148LV00011B/1596

* 9 7 8 1 4 9 8 2 3 0 7 8 0 *